Mother Courage and Her Children

Bertolt Brecht was born in Augsburg on 10 February 1898 and died in Berlin on 14 August 1956. He grew to maturity as a playwright in the frenetic years of the twenties and early thirties, with such plays as *Man Equals Man*, *The Threepenny Opera* and *The Mother*. He left Germany when Hitler came to power in 1933, eventually reaching the United States in 1941, where he remained until 1947. It was during this period of exile that such masterpieces as *Life of Galileo*, *Mother Courage and her Children* and *The Caucasian Chalk Circle* were written. Shortly after his return to Europe in 1947, he founded the Berliner Ensemble, and from then until his death was mainly occupied in producing his own plays.

Other Bertolt Brecht publications by Bloomsbury Methuen Drama

Brecht Collected Plays: One
(Baal, Drums in the Night, In the Jungle of Cities, The Life of Edward II of
England, A Respectable Wedding, The Beggar or the Dead Dog,
Driving Out a Devil, Lux in Tenebris, The Catch)

Brecht Collected Plays: Two
(Man Equals Man, The Elephant Calf, The Threepenny Opera,
The Rise and Fall of the City of Mahagonny, The Seven Deadly Sins)

Brecht Collected Plays: Three
(Lindbergh's Flight, The Baden-Baden Lesson on Consent, He Said
Yes/He Said No, The Decision, The Mother, The Exception and
the Rule, The Horations and the Curiatians, St Joan of the Stockyards)

Brecht Collected Plays: Four
(Round Heads and Pointed Heads, Fear and Misery of the Third Reich,
Señora Carrar's Rifles, Dansen, How Much Is Your Iron?,
The Trial of Lucullus)

Brecht Collected Plays: Five
(Life of Galileo, Mother Courage and Her Children)

Brecht Collected Plays: Six
(The Good Person of Szechwan, The Resistible Rise of Arturo Ui,
Mr Puntila and His Man Matti)

Brecht Collected Plays: Seven
(The Visions of Simone Machard, Schweyk in the Second World War,
The Caucasian Chalk Circle, The Duchess of Malfi)

Brecht Collected Plays: Eight
(The Days of the Commune, The Antigone of Sophocles,
Turandot or the Whitewashers' Congress)

Berliner Ensemble Adaptations
(The Tutor, Coriolanus, The Trial of Joan of Arc at Rouen 1431,
Don Juan, Trumpets and Drums)

Bertolt Brecht Journals, 1934-55
Brecht on Art and Politics
Brecht on Film and Radio
Brecht on Performance
Brecht on Theatre
Brecht in Practice
The Craft of Theatre: Seminars and Discussions in Brechtian Theatre
Brecht, Music and Culture
Brecht in Context
The Theatre of Bertolt Brecht
Brecht: A Choice of Evils
Bertolt Brecht: A Literary Life
A Guide to the Plays of Bertolt Brecht

BERTOLT BRECHT

Mother Courage and Her Children

Translated and with a preface by
TONY KUSHNER

Introduction and notes by
CHARLOTTE RYLAND

Original work entitled
Mutter Courage und ihre Kinder

Bloomsbury Methuen Drama
An imprint of Bloomsbury Publishing Plc

B L O O M S B U R Y
LONDON • OXFORD • NEW YORK • NEW DELHI • SYDNEY

Bloomsbury Methuen Drama

An imprint of Bloomsbury Publishing Plc

50 Bedford Square	1385 Broadway
London	New York
WC1B 3DP	NY 10018
UK	USA

www.bloomsbury.com

Bloomsbury is a registered trade mark of Bloomsbury Publishing Plc

This translation first published in Great Britain in 2009 by Methuen Drama
Original work entitled *Mutter Courage und ihre Kinder*, published by
Suhrkamp Verlag Frankfurt am Main 1949
Reprinted by Bloomsbury Methuen Drama 2016 (three times), 2017

Translation copyright © Bertolt-Brecht-Erben und Suhrkamp Verlag Berlin

Introduction and notes copyright © 2010 Charlotte Ryland
Preface copyright © 2010 Tony Kushner
Methuen Drama series editor for Bertolt Brecht: Tom Kuhn

The authors have asserted their rights under the Copyrights, Designs and
Patents Act 1988 to be identified as the authors of this work.

British Library Cataloguing-in-Publication Data
A catalogue record for this book is available from the British Library.

ISBN: 978-1-408-11151-2

Library of Congress Cataloging-in-Publication Data
A catalog record for this book is available from the Library of Congress.

Series: Modern Classics

Typeset by Mark Heslington Limited, Scarborough, North Yorkshire
Printed and bound in Great Britain

Contents

Preface

Although I neither read nor speak German, I've translated *Mother Courage and Her Children*, and I feel I ought to explain how.

In my head there's a random but not insubstantial accumulation of German vocabulary, a vague sense of syntax and an even vaguer sense of German case and tense. I have a Langenscheidt's dictionary, German-language textbooks, and I've formed intense relationships with several online translation engines. While I worked on *Courage*, I placed many phone calls and sent many emails to German-fluent friends, and to my brother, who lives in Vienna. I worked very, very slowly on the translation, spending many, many more hours, days, weeks, months than I'd imagined the task would require, as a consequence of which I missed many, many, many deadlines and kept my star, Meryl Streep, my director, George C. Wolfe, and my producer, Oskar Eustis, and the Public Theater waiting and worrying. Finally the chutzpah (Yiddish, it turns out, helps!) or hubris (if you prefer) necessary to attempt this, insufficiently equipped and credentialed as I am, was made possible by thirty-four years of reading and thinking about Brecht generally, and this play in particular.

Finally, I felt not only that I might be able to translate *Courage*, but, if for no reason other than my great love for the play, I felt I needed to translate it.

Devoting an entire day to a single page of a text you love, teasing it apart, learning something about how it's constructed, line by line, word by word – translation is an act of delicious, irresistible intimacy. When you're horny and available and the opportunity to get into bed with someone you find hot presents itself, knowledge of your amorous ineptitude may make you hesitate, but if your desire insists, you'll summon your derring-do, close your eyes, say a prayer and plunge.

I'm too puritanical, however, to plunge without requiring a self-justifying pretext. I justified translating *Courage* by telling myself I'd be providing a public service. I'm an American playwright, and it seemed to me a new version of Brecht's masterpiece was needed, rendered in an idiom at home in the mouths of American actors and the ears of American audiences.

(It was with considerable surprise, given my avowed patriotic intentions, to get a call from Deborah Warner, asking to use my version for her production with Fiona Shaw at the National Theater in London. After surprise came great joy.)

There are several terrific English-language *Courages*. I first read the play in Eric Bentley's powerful translation. Bentley occupies a place of enormous significance in Brecht's life and work; among other things, Bentley's request for a consolidation and clarification of his aesthetic theory led Brecht to write 'The Short Organum for the Theater', arguably after Aristotle's *Poetics* the most important essay on dramatic art ever written. John Willett, a central figure in Brecht's reception and vast influence in the British theater, wrote a tough, politically astute translation, while Ralph Mannheim remains most successful, in my opinion, at finding an English-language equivalent to the Bavarian-scented hybrid of modernist-medieval German that Brecht invented to give the half-modern, half-feudal men and women in *Courage* a simultaneous contemporaneity and antiquity, befitting the characters in an old chronicle written by a mid-twentieth-century refugee.

I invoke these translations in order to shift from my shoulders some of my anxiety at the prospect of this present, bilingual edition, and also of course to acknowledge my indebtedness. But Willett's and Mannheim's versions are unmistakably British, Willet's being especially regionally specific. A kind of secondary translation is required for use in American theatrical production. Fifty-five years have passed since Bentley translated the play, thirty-eight since Mannheim's translation and thirty since Willett's. The political and theatrical landscapes have changed radically. A new rendition might provide opportunities for alternative readings and insights.

I felt that the play's lyrics hadn't been entirely successfully translated. *Mother Courage* is a musical, with nine songs, one of them, Courage's signature salespitch song, reprised three times. The translated lyrics often honor Brecht's imagery and give reasonable accounts of his meaning, but there's a forced quality that's clearly the cost of preserving the original rhyme structures and scansion. Others have approximated Brecht's elegant ease as a lyricist, but only by opting for free-verse. None of the lyrics in translation appeared to me to be especially singable.

For the Berliner Ensemble's landmark production, directed by Brecht and starring his wife, Helene Weigel, the songs were set by Paul Dessau. Whether Brecht shaped the lyrics to fit Dessau's

music, or vice versa, the score offers a wealth of information to the
translator. Since Brecht was a poet as well as a playwright, and since
poetry's meaning is to be found as much in its structural details as
in its overtly expressed content, fitting the English lyrics precisely
to Dessau's score seemed to me vital in attempting to salvage the
poetry in the translated poems.

I wanted to do a stageworthy translation, which meant lyrics that
would meet the requirements of musical performance. After
shaping them to the Dessau score, I was able to develop them
further in production, working with actors and musicians, during
rehearsals for the premiere performances of this translation at the
New York Shakespeare Festival's Delacorte Theater in Central Park.

For that production, however, Dessau's music was replaced with
a new score by Jeanine Tesori. The rhymes and scansion fitted to
the Dessau were unaltered, so the lyrics work with both scores.

Dessau's settings, martial and melodic, are played by a trio on
trumpet, drum and prepared piano, an upright piano onto the felt
hammers of which thumbtacks have been driven, producing tinny,
chilly, nerve-grating, bone-rattling notes. When I've watched *Mother
Courage*, and when, in 1988, I directed it at the University of New
Hampshire, I've noticed that Dessau's *Courage* songs, unlike the
songs in any other musical play with which I'm familiar (including
several by Brecht), are experienced by the audience as harder, less
pleasing, more stressful to hear than the spoken dialogue. While
this is not at all an uninteresting phenomenon, it seemed to me
that the discomfort the music provoked had little to do with the
sort of rich, complexifying distantiation Brecht sought to achieve,
which has nothing to do with precluding intellectual and
emotional engagement (quite the opposite, in fact); Dessau's
music, wonderful as it is, sounds trapped between the familiar
Weimar-era sound of the Brecht-Weill collaborations, and the
Second Viennese School as exemplified by Brecht's other great
composer–collaborator, Hanns Eisler. In other words, Dessau's
music sounds specific to its historical moment, while the play, like
all truly great plays, manages to seem a product not only of the
time in which it was written, but of the time it depicts, and also as if
written yesterday.

Jeanine Tesori wrote new settings for the Delacorte production.
Her ensemble of twelve musicians played a score employing variety
of idioms, including medieval plainchant, Lutheran chorales, high
modernist dissonance, and rhythm and blues and vaudeville, deftly
locating and strengthening threads that unify these into a distinct,

singular voice, repeating in music Brecht's reverberant historiography, in which echoes of the past play dissonantly and consonantly against present crises.

I've tried to translate rather than adapt *Mother Courage*. I think Brecht's play is unimprovable, at least I'm certain it is by me. This doesn't mean, however, that there are no points at which my text varies from the German. Most of the variances arose from the task of making a play in one language work onstage in another.

For instance: humour, in its way, is as exacting and unforgiving as poetry, and nearly as elusive in translation. This is a serious problem for plays, because laughter in the theatre is crucial. With the first good laugh, the audience noisily recognises itself, organises its collective force and announces that force to the actors. The volume and quality of its laughter contain vital information about an audience's coherence, intelligence, aggression or passivity.

Brecht's plays are funny, even one as bleak, dark and heartbreaking as *Courage*. It's easy enough to spot the jokes in the play, less easy to render them effective, to get the audience to respond with more than mild amusement to something it realises was probably funny in German being said, unfunnily, in English. I took as many liberties as I deemed necessary in the hope of provoking out-loud laughter.

There are obscenities in my version not to be found in the original, or for that matter in any of the versions mentioned above. I believe these epithets are consonant with the play's hard-bitten, often scabrous spirit. Furthermore, profanity is necessary if a contemporary audience is to credit the play's presentation of people in wartime, under extreme conditions of duress.

There's room for discussion and contention regarding whether and to what extent Brecht meant for his audiences to 'credit' what they're watching. In my opinion, there's much more realism (as opposed to naturalism) in Brecht's plays, at least in the narrative dramas I call the Big Brechts (*Mother Courage, Caucasian Chalk Circle, The Life of Galileo, The Good Person of Szechwan*), than is presumed in the catastrophic production practices which have accreted around his work. These practices are predicated on a calamitous, widespread misunderstanding of Brecht's theoretical writings, according to which misunderstanding the audience shouldn't feel empathy for the characters. I'm reasonably certain that the man who wrote this devastatingly sad play wasn't indifferent to empathy. It's the dialectic of feeling and thinking, empathy and clinical detachment, belief and disbelief that Brecht valued, explored and privileged in theatre. Theatrical realism is realism of an inherently dialectical nature, real and unreal simultaneously. The real requires those theatre tricks that assist an audience's ability to credit what they're watching.

I'm completely confident that whatever the playwright intended, dialogue that sounds academic, curated or polite, which effect the absence of profanity in dire circumstances produces, must have been the last thing he wanted. I petitioned Barbara Brecht-Schall to permit my use of expletives; she consented, cautioning 'only perhaps not too much.'

My fidelity to Brecht's original text was most sorely tested, occasionally to its breaking point, in a few passages I found so exciting, moving or important that I elaborated, adding text, extending the pleasure these moments gave me, attempting to draw out what I believe Brecht might be up to.

An example of this can be found in Scene Six. Mother Courage responds to the Chaplain's compliment about her indomitability by speaking about the lives of the poor. In the original, this is how the speech goes:

Die armen Leut brauchen Courage. Warum, sie sind verloren. Schon dass sie aufstehen in der Früh, dazu gehört was in ihrer Lag. Oder dass sie einen Acker umpflügen, und im Krieg! Schon dass sie Kinder in die Welt setzen, zeigt, dass sie Courage haben, denn sie haben keine Aussicht. Sie müssen einander den Henker machen und sich gegenseitig abschlachten, wenn sie einander da ins Geschicht schaun wolln, das braucht wohl Courage. Dass sie einen Kaiser und einen Papst dulden, das beweist eine unheimliche Courage, denn die kosten ihnen das Leben.

My translation:

I'm not courageous. Only poor people need courage. Why, because they're hopeless. To get out of bed each morning, or plow a potato field in wartime, or bring kids with no prospects into the world – to live poor, that takes courage. Consider how easily and often they murder each other, they need courage just to look one another in the face. They trudge along, uncomplainingly carrying the emperor and his heavy throne and the pope and his stone cathedral, they stagger, starving, bearing the whole thundering weight of the great wealth of the wealthy on their broad stupid backs, and is that courage? Must be, but it's perverted courage, because what they carry on their backs will cost them their lives.

The speech, accurately translated, begins with a simple 'Poor people need courage.' I added a new first sentence, 'I'm not courageous,' and then an 'only' to the German first sentence. The next sentences are essentially the same in German and English, but then I substantially elongated and elaborated Brecht's final sentence, an accurate translation of which might be 'To carry a Kaiser and a Pope displays a strange (weird? uncanny?) courage, because it'll cost them their lives.' The version I arrived at begins with 'They trudge along' and goes on quite a bit longer, adding verbs, nouns, objects and adjectives, with a rhetorical build and a question and answer that aren't in the original. I chose to turn 'unheimliche' – literally 'not home-like' – into 'perverted.'

I made these alterations to emphasise what I understand to be a decisive turning point in Courage's transmogrification over the course of the play. After the death of her simple son, Swiss Cheese, we watch her grief and the bitter awareness of her utter powerlessness lead her to an deepening disidentification with her own class, and, in Scene Six, to a pathetic attempt to identify herself with her rulers and oppressors, with the men who are ultimately responsible for the war, hence the murder of Swiss Cheese. She's ditched her former cynicism, which, making her immune to patriotic, militaristic cant, made her clear-eyed about the dangers of the army from which she derives a meagre subsistence. She now makes profits, has a fixed establishment (even if it's just a tent), and has learned to speak respectfully of, perhaps even to feel respect for fallen field marshals and their bloody plans. Her former contempt for the military leadership has been replaced by contempt for the foot soldiers she forces to stand drinking in the rain. Hoping to facilitate switching classes by pushing her daughter into the company of an officer, the Regimental Secretary, she brings ruin upon Kattrin, and finally upon herself.

I altered Courage's speech about the poor in order to emphasise what I hear in the original. She's distancing herself from the powerless poor, her scorn and derision regarding their bestial lives existing alongside some remnant of her sympathy for their suffering, manifest as anger towards them. So I have her begin by making sharp distinction between herself and poor people, and I followed an impulse to let her expand upon her subject, the expansion probably fuelled by divided loyalties and unresolved conflict within.

License to alter for the purpose of emphasising is inexcusable in a translator, and I can't make a defence of it, except to postulate that Brecht might not object to a translator making evident the fact of his imposition between German playwright and American audience. All difficulties, including difficulties of translation, conceal or reveal uneasy relationships, obscure or delineate contradictions and add to our experience a dynamic instability that resists closure.

Having created an interpolative role for myself, I'll proceed to confess that in this and other elaborations, I was anxious to steer readers and stage interpreters away from a sentimental misinterpretation, namely, in this instance, that Courage is merely expressing her admiration for poor people. If one anticipates nothing from the characters in *Courage* than that they will adhere to cartoony type, that they're embodied, costumed political positions rather than fully realised representations of contradictory, changeable human beings; if one approaches the play as if it were the sloganeering, illustrational, heavy-handed propaganda its detractors and, alas, some of its fans imagine it to be, it's fatally easy to miss many of *Courage*'s turning points, for the play is subtle, complex, vast, even mysterious. These are not qualities we're told to anticipate in Brecht.

I find Courage hateful in Scene Six, as indeed she is in the previous scene, when she refuses to allow her shirts to be shredded for bandages to aid a severely injured farmer and his wife. And I find it impossible to hate her. The selfishness, snobbery and blind stupidity we see growing in her are born directly from her son's murder. The *unheimliche* world of the war perverts every attempt at self-preservation, while leading to a tragic conclusion, namely Kattrin's death in Scene 11. It's tragic but transformational (as true tragedy is); it interrupts the downward spiral of futile attempts at self-preservation (Courage's self includes her children, which is itself fascinatingly, dramatically complicated) with Kattrin's stunning act of self-sacrifice.

Other than *Threepenny Opera*, Brecht's most famous plays – *Mother Courage, Caucasian Chalk Circle, The Life of Galileo, The Good Person of Szechwan* – were written in the first six years of his thirteen-years-long exile. Separated by force from the energies of Germany's radicalised working class, Brecht abandoned the experimentation of his *Lehrstücke*, and after 1933, while circumnavigating the globe, wrote the 'Big Brechts', modelled on classic drama, on the enduring texts of Schiller, Goethe and

Shakespeare, with powerful narratives, stunning emotional force, and protagonists at the centre of the story.

From the beginning of his life as a theatre artist, Brecht insistently strove for a theatre conscious of its ideology, or rather theatre that struggles to become conscious, and makes theatre of that struggle. He insisted that ideological analysis, political and historical thinking were salutary for theatre practice, but much more importantly, this kind of thinking – the refusal of received wisdom and eternal, eternally unexamined verities, the revelation of how politics, history, economics, aesthetics, psychology, ethics, taste and common-sense evolve through contradiction and conflict, and are historically and politically grounded, if not determined – this labour of critical thinking Brecht identifies as not only salutary but in an important sense the true subject of all theatrical art. He assigned to that quality we call 'theatrical' a profound value: in *what* it tells the theatre *may*, and in *how* it tells the theatre absolutely unavoidably *will* instruct the eye to see double, the mind to become capable of paradox, the heart to break free of sentiment and the soul to escape its fetishisms, contributing to the struggle to become capable of human connection, and through connection to the liberating power of meaning, the discovery of human-ness, of pleasure and love.

His plays are composed of magnificent, dense, electrifyingly dramatic scenes peopled by characters whose motives and inner lives reward prolonged scrutiny and investigation as splendidly as any ever written.

This translation of *Mother Courage and her Children* owes its existence to my love affair with this play. I suppose that would be the case even if a powerful personal nostalgia wasn't attached to the play, even if my first reading of *Courage*, while I was an undergraduate, hadn't coincided with a time when I needed a common ground on which newly received ideas and experiences, rioting in my head, could meet and negotiate cooperative existences. I'd had my first tastes of political activism, been introduced to dialectics, to Marxism and to other philosophies of history, re-learned the act of reading by being introduced to critical analyses of literature, most formatively, most earth-shakingly of Shakespeare's plays; and an ardent, but secret and entirely unrealised desire to write plays was emerging into consciousness, fuelled by my insatiable gobbling up, since arriving in New York from Louisiana, of cheap tickets to all manner of plays and operas.

I needed a common ground, a meeting place for assimilating

and reconciling this overwhelm into a functional synthesis. *Mother Courage* provided the key. *Courage* led to Brecht's plays, poems, stories, letters, journals and essays, to a model, problematic, contradictory, controversial and admirable, of an engaged artist. I read *Courage* in my Columbia dormitory room during a late-night thunderstorm, and I got so excited and upset that I overturned an open bottle of black ink, which covered and rendered unreadable my just-purchased copy of *A Long Day's Journey Into Night*. Several years would pass before I bought a new copy and discovered for myself not only a great play but the power and glory of American dramatic literature. On that stormy night in my dorm room, my heart belonged to Bertolt Brecht. Even now, thirty-five years later, a part of it still does.

Courage moved me deeply the first time I read it, and it continues to break my heart and to challenge my understanding, and to provide me with pleasure, albeit painful pleasure, each time I read it, watch it or work on it. All its complex, anguished contemplation of the dreadful question of whether we make history or are made by history, all of its great tragic/progressive vision is carried in the relentlessly simple story it tells.

> The Story of Mother Courage
> Oh, once there was a mother;
> Selling was her game.
> In the Thirty Years' War she made money,
> And Courage was her name.
> She couldn't afford to be frightened:
> The war kept her family fed.
> It fed and clothed her three kids until
> It took their lives instead.
> Her brave son's daring destroyed him.
> Her honest son perished too.
> Her poor daughter's heart was a little too good
> And a bullet pierced it through.
> From *Five Childrens' Songs*

Bertolt Brecht, 1950
Tony Kushner
August 2010

Introduction

A play such as Brecht's *Mother Courage*, which owes so much to its
historical content and context, to theatrical theory and political
ideology, and to linguistic play and nuance, risks losing much in
translation. Yet Tony Kushner has transposed the play into English
without compromising any of the rawness and verve of the original.
Far from the pseudo-naturalism that plagues much contemporary
translation for the theatre, Kushner's English reproduces the
rough edges and idiosyncratic language and rhythms of Brecht's
German. The irreverent humour of the original, often originating
in wordplay, is re-invented in English through equivalent linguistic
gags or added jokes. Kushner's version steps up the pace of the
action and wit, turning longer speeches into dialogues and taking
advantage of the many opportunities for visual comedy; and his
treatment of Brecht's rich idiomatic language results in a text that
is as complex and vibrant as the original.

Language and idiom

Throughout the play, Kushner's English faithfully reproduces the
raw and colloquial tone of the German dialogue. Mother
Courage's character is defined largely by her rough and
uncompromising approach to all aspects of war, commerce and
emotional relations, which shines through in the idiom that Brecht
lends her. It is her vitality and brash outspokenness that brings
much of the colour and humour to the play, and it is consequently
imperative that a successful translation reflect this tone. Indeed,
almost all the exchanges in the play are defined by an earthy and
often bawdy register, and a rich idiomatic language in which
images never depart from the historical, cultural and geographical
location of Brecht's setting in the Thirty Years' War.

There are moments when English does not seem to offer an
appropriate idiom for the German, and where there is consequently
not absolute equivalence in the translation. In the second scene, for
example, the starvation of the poor is effectively evoked by the
saying 'am Hungertuch nagen' [gnawing at the hunger-cloth], an
archaic phrase originating in the medieval Christian practice of

hanging a cloth before the altar during periods of fasting. Kushner renders this simply 'starving', thus at this point losing the echoes of medieval religion that are so central to the play (pp. 30–1). However, far more frequent in the English version are moments where equivalence or compensation mean that the full semantic and cultural connotations of the original phrase are reproduced in the English. The third scene, for example, sees 'The One with the Eyepatch', a thoroughly unsavoury fellow, greet Kattrin with the religiously-inspired colloquial 'Gott zum Gruß, liebes Fräulein' (roughly, 'God greets you, dear miss'). Kushner's rendering of this as 'Nominy dominy, pretty girlie' (p. 75) is a perfectly pitched alternative, reflecting the character's faux-friendly, conversational tone as well as the medieval religious connotations.

At other moments, Kushner adds or elaborates images and idioms, which represent departures from the German text but remain in tune with the rich figurative language of the play and with the cultural and political context of the Thirty Years' War. So, for example, Mother Courage's jibing of the Young Soldier in the fourth scene, dissuading him from complaining to the General, is intensified by her description of what the ensuing torture will be like ('after the whip's blistered all the skin off you and you're raw and bleeding', p. 101). Similarly, in the sixth scene, the Chaplain's claims that normal life simply carries on during war is given added flavour by his description of the people 'breeding like maggots in raw meat', where the original merely mentions their 'reproduction' (p. 121).

In addition to these injections of figurative language, Kushner occasionally takes advantage of a wordplay that is possible in English but not in the original German. The name of Yvette's Colonel, Poldi, offers a handy rhyme in English with 'mouldy', reflecting Mother Courage's derision of the old fool and her lack of respect for status: 'What's his name? Mouldy?' (p. 85). Later, Kushner makes use of a double meaning in the English phrase 'touch and go' (p. 153), unavailable in German, to express Yvette's flighty behaviour, dropping one rich lover as soon as a richer one comes along: not so much 'touch and go' as 'I touch them for their money and then I go'. The inherent differences in idiom and structure between German and English mean, then, that deviations from the original text are inevitable; but Kushner uses these differences to his advantage to produce a text that pulses with the same levels of linguistic wordplay and irreverent, caustic wit as Brecht's original.

Indeed, the coarseness of Brecht's language is updated to a degree by Kushner with his tendency to intensify the vulgar speech of the less salubrious characters – usually soldiers – by lending them streams of curses. Kushner's Young Soldier, for example, expresses his anger at his general as follows: 'I'm not letting myself get fucked like this. You come outside now and let me cut your fucking head off!' (p. 99), where there is no equivalent expression in the original German text. This particular point in the play further exemplifies Kushner's intensification of the aggression and agitation on stage, as his stage directions show the Older Soldier restraining the Young Soldier, where Brecht made no such direction.

Speech patterns

The rich idiomatic language of Brecht's German is one of the defining features of the play, as is a tendency towards non-naturalistic forms of speech. Kushner does not iron out these odd stylisations, but finds an equivalent oddness in his English. Perhaps the most striking of these moments is in the final lines of the first scene, when Brecht's Sergeant suddenly utters a dark warning in awkward German: 'Will vom Krieg leben. Wird ihm wohl müssen auch was geben.' The string of three verbs in the second part of this phrase (wird, müssen, geben) is grammatically possible in German, though it sounds odd and stilted. Since English functions differently in this case, Kushner cannot reproduce the string of verbs, yet his couplet succeeds both in reproducing the end-rhyme and in creating a syntactical oddness that contributes to the ominous content of the words themselves: 'If off the war you hope to live, / Take what you can. You'll also give' (pp. 26–7).

In the following scene, Brecht's neologistic compound 'Kochbestie' (p. 33), reflecting the General's irritation at the Cook, is rendered 'beast-who-barely-learned-to-cook'. As the General goes on addressing Eilif, his words become a paratactic stream of clauses ('Trink noch einen, mein Sohn ...', pp. 34–5). This syntactical strangeness reflects the extremes of the General's emotions at this stage – his exuberant praise of Eilif and his virulent censure of the Chaplain. Kushner reproduces this zeal less through the syntax (which is not as flexible in English) than through the lexical features. So the General's 'favourite Falernian' becomes a 'lip-smacking Falernian', and the 'soul-shepherd' becomes 'this watery-eyed old simp of a soul-shepherd'. Subsequently, the

General's shift from his rush of emotive language to the more officious tone of the end of his speech ('Und jetzt, mein Sohn Eilif, …') sees a further lexical change in Kushner's version. The vibrant colloquial language of the first half of the speech gives way to ridiculously bureaucratic phrasing: 'you showed an initiative which eventuated in the requisitioning of twenty head of cattle.' Thus the change in tone, effected largely through the syntax in the original, is reproduced here by way of a lexical shift.

Humour

Much of the humour of Brecht's play derives from the language, and a translation must consequently seek to reproduce the linguistic humour as much as possible. Some is inevitably lost in translation, such as the pun on the words 'Hoffart' and 'hoffärtig' (p. 72) in Scene Three. In modern usage, this German term refers to vanity and arrogance, but originates in notions of courtliness and nobility. The exchange between Mother Courage and the Chaplain in the original thus evokes this double meaning and produces comedy, although Kushner does not find an equivalent in English and so the humour is lost. However, in the majority of cases, Kushner finds effective equivalents for the linguistic wit, and where this is impossible, he compensates for the loss by inserting jokes of his own making. An example of equivalence occurs in Eilif's description of the soldiers' extreme hunger, such that their mouths water when they hear a word that begins with the same letters as 'meat'. In German, the word is 'Fleisch', and Eilif compares it to the word 'Fluß' (river). It is essential, then, for Kushner to make a change here, or the joke becomes nonsensical. He does so as follows: 'they'd drool if they just heard the word "meat", if they even heard a word beginning with "M", like… um… "meat"!' (p. 35). Though the content of the joke has changed slightly, the sense of the soldiers' starvation is reproduced, and the new version adds further to the impression of Eilif's brutish lack of imagination.

Throughout the play, Kushner makes the most of the comic potential of Brecht's characters, such that any humour that is lost in translation is more than compensated for in his own jokes. A key example of this practice occurs in the third scene, with Yvette's panic about the effect of her 'disease' on her profession as a prostitute (p. 49). In the original, Yvette moans that everyone is avoiding her 'like a rotten fish' because of the 'lies' about her

disease. In English, Kushner replaces the rotten fish image with a
yet more fitting one, 'customers avoid me like the plague', and
then adds the following humorous remark: 'it's like I hung a sign
over my cootch saying "Remember you must die"'. In this way, the
potential for comedy in Yvette's predicament is exploited by
Kushner to great effect.

Indeed, the sexual innuendo that is latent in much of Brecht's
play is brought to the fore on more than one occasion by Kushner.
In Scene Three, the apparent sexual tension between Yvette and
the 'young blond lieutenant', which she uses to emotionally
blackmail her Colonel into lending her money, is intensified by
Kushner's free rendering of Yvette's words. The lieutenant is not
simply 'nuts' about her, saying that she 'reminds him of
somebody', but he is 'that young blond lieutenant with the
enormous feet. Know who I mean, Poldi? He's always waving it at
me!' (p. 83). Sexual innuendo is similarly increased in Scene Eight,
when the Cook tells Courage that she 'still has hair on her teeth',
but that he treasures her all the more for it. This idiom refers to
Courage's brusque and acid-tongued character, but Courage's
retort lends it a sexual undertone – 'Don't tell me you were
dreaming about my hairy teeth!' (p. 150). Kushner brings this
undertone into the Cook's words, too, with the rakish comment: 'I
like a woman who knows how to handle a harmonica' (referring to
the harmonica that Courage has just mentioned). Courage's
response then introduces a new sexual pun, on the word 'snatch'
(slang for vagina): 'Maybe later, if the mood strikes me, I might
play a snatch' (p. 143).

The humour in Brecht's play is often at the expense of religion.
The characters' religious allegiances are shown to be contingent
not on matters of faith but on whichever side appears to be
winning the war, and the piety and restraint associated with men of
the cloth is replaced with hypocrisy and profligate behaviour.
Kushner reproduces this element of humour and, with relative
frequency, adds jokes at the expense of religion. This is perhaps
most notable in Scene Three, when 'the Catholics' (the enemy of
the army that Mother Courage is currently serving) attack. Yvette
panics, suddenly intent on making herself look presentable for the
Catholics. Although, in the original, this implies that she considers
them to be potential customers, her interest in them is made much
more patent in Kushner's version, with jokes at the Catholics'
expense. 'Oh please God let it be the Catholics!', cries Yvette,
implying that she hopes for their trade, followed by a side-swipe at

their sartorial obsessions: 'I can't run around in that, not if it's Catholics, they're finnicky about costumes' (p. 65). Later in this scene, the Chaplain mutters – in a new addition by Kushner – 'I don't know any Latin hymns', which seems to be his only cause for concern about the necessity to appear to be Catholic (p. 69). And finally, in the same exchange, Brecht's Mother Courage describes the Chaplain as having 'religious belief' (which, it is suggested, is useless in war), yet according to Kushner he has rather 'an ecclesiastical sense of humour'. Thus the frivolity associated with religion in the play is brought to the fore in Kushner's version.

It is also a religious joke that ushers in the episode of the play that Kushner has altered most radically. The exchange between the Chaplain, Mother Courage and the Cook, which in the original is dominated by the Cook's long speech, is redeployed around a more vibrant and confrontational debate, bringing the issues discussed into sharper focus. When the Chaplain expresses an interest in Kattrin, Mother Courage retorts that she is not 'comely' but 'stay-at-homely', and Kushner then adds: 'and I don't want clergy sniffing up my daughter' (p. 57). This is followed by the Cook's exclamation about the Chaplain's 'revolting' jokes, which Kushner has moved from earlier in the scene, so building up a stronger impression of the Chaplain's salacious appetites. As this episode continues, Kushner's alterations develop a more acute criticism of both religious and political leaders. 'He rolled here, he rolled there, he's ready to roll back to Sweden', Mother Courage says of the Swedish king, belittling the monarch's supposed grandeur. The Chaplain protests, arguing that the King just wanted freedom from the Kaiser – but in Kushner's version this becomes freedom from the tyranny of both Kaiser and *Pope*. Finally, when the Cook weighs in, Kushner has him complain about attempts to 'export' liberty to other countries, and about the rich getting tax exemptions. These additions by Kushner give the debate a contemporary twist.

This episode, where long speeches become swifter interchanges, and where some parts of the dialogue are invented by Kushner, represents a more general principle of Kushner's translation practice in this play. Some longer speeches are shortened, and others – as here – are transformed into dialogues, increasing the dynamism of the onstage action. The dialogue on p. 59 ('You shouldn't mock liberty' until 'I'm sure you do') is entirely new material by Kushner, and is a moment of pure comic jousting, with undertones of religious hypocrisy. Later, the Chaplain's anecdote about finding a spy in the latrine (p. 71) is turned into a dialogue with Swiss Cheese, allowing for increased comedy to come from Swiss Cheese's incredulity and the threefold repetition of 'in the latrine?'.

Songs

It is most significantly in the songs, however, that Kushner turns monologue into dialogue. Invariably, a piece sung by one character in the original play will be shared out among others. This is the case in the very first song, which is sung in the original by Mother Courage alone (pp. 6–8), but which Kushner alternates between Mother Courage solo and singing with her sons. This tendency continues throughout the play (see for example p. 165) until the song that closes the action, which in Kushner's version is sung by soldiers. Here, Kushner breaks the song half-way through by delaying Mother Courage's final cry, 'Take me with you', so that she shouts it over the singing.

In the songs, Kushner has made the most alterations to the wording of the original play, which is inevitable given his success in reproducing their metre and rhyme. Apart from the songs in Scene Seven and in the final scene, which are lengthened by Kushner and commented on here in the end notes, his songs reproduce the sense of the originals and reflect closely their form and rhythm.

The songs, then, provide a fitting example of Kushner's capacity to meld his mother tongue to fit Brecht's rhythms, without compromising the quality of the writing. Brecht's rhythms and phrasing are retained as much in the dialogue as in the songs; and if there is a strangeness in Kushner's version, it results not from the infelicities that often arise when English meets German, but from the translator keeping faith with the oddities that Brecht wove into his original piece. The play in English is thus still unmistakably Brecht's creation, but with a wit, pace and verve that makes it Kushner's own, too.

Mother Courage and
her Children
A Chronicle of the Thirty Years' War

Mutter Courage und ihre Kinder
Eine Chronik aus dem Dreißigjährigen Kreig

Translated by Tony Kushner

Personan

Mutter Courage
Kattrin, *ihre stumme Tochter*
Eilif, *der ältere Sohn*
Schweizerkas, *der jüngere Sohn*
Der Werber
Der Feldwebel
Der Koch
Der Feldhauptmann
Der Feldprediger
Der Zeugmeister
Yvette Pottier
Der mit der Binde
Ein anderer Feldwebel
Der alte Obrist
Ein Schreiber
Ein junger Soldat
Ein älterer Soldat
Ein Bauer
Die Bauersfrau
Der junge Mann
Die alte Frau
Ein anderer Bauer
Die Bäuerin
Der Fähnrich
Soldaten
Eine Stimme

Characters

Mother Courage
Kattrin, *her mute daughter*
Eilif, *her oldest son*
Swiss Cheese, *her youngest son*
The Sergeant *in Scene One*
The Army Recruiter
The Cook
The General
The Chaplain
The Quartermaster
Yvette Pottier
The One with the Eyepatch
The Colonel
The Sergeant *in Scene Three*
The Clerk
The Young Soldier
The Older Soldier
The Farmer *in Scene Five*
The Farmer's Wife *in Scene Five*
The Regimental Secretary
The Old Woman
The Young Man
The Voice Inside
The Lieutenant
The Farmer *in Scene Eleven*
The Farmer's Wife *in Scene Eleven*
The Farmer's Son
Soldiers

One

Frühjahr 1624. Der Feldhauptmann Oxenstjerna wirbt in Dalarne Truppen für den Feldzug in Polen. Der Marketenderin Anna Fierling, bekannt unter dem Namen **Mutter Courage**, *kommt ein Sohn abhanden.*

Landstraße in Stadtnähe. Ein **Feldwebel** *und ein* **Werber** *stehen frierend.*

Der Werber   Wie soll man sich hier eine Mannschaft zusammenlesen? Feldwebel, ich denk schon mitunter an Selbstmord. Bis zum zwölften soll ich dem Feldhauptmann vier Fähnlein hinstelln, und die Leut hier herum sind so voll Bosheit, daß ich keine Nacht mehr schlaf. Hab ich endlich einen aufgetrieben, und schon durch die Finger gesehn und mich nix wissen gemacht, daß er eine Hühnerbrust hat und Krampfadern, ich hab ihn glücklich besoffen, er hat schon unterschrieben, ich zahl nur noch den Schnaps, er tritt aus, ich hinterher zur Tür, weil mir was schwant: Richtig, weg ist er, wie die Laus unterm Kratzen. Da gibts kein Manneswort, kein Treu und Glauben, kein Ehrgefühl. Ich hab hier mein Vertrauen in die Menschheit verloren, Feldwebel.

Der Feldwebel   Man merkts, hier ist zu lang kein Krieg gewesen. Wo soll da Moral herkommen, frag ich? Frieden, das ist nur Schlamperei, erst der Krieg schafft Ordnung. Die Menschheit schießt ins Kraut im Frieden. Mit Mensch und Vieh wird herumgesaut, als wärs gar nix. Jeder frißt, was er will, einen Ranken Käs aufs Weißbrot und dann noch eine Scheibe Speck auf den Käs. Wie viele junge Leut und gute Gäul diese Stadt da vorn hat, weiß kein Mensch, es ist niemals gezählt worden. Ich bin in Gegenden gekommen, wo kein Krieg war vielleicht siebzig Jahr, da hatten die Leut überhaupt noch keine Namen, die kannten sich selber nicht. Nur wo Krieg ist, gibts ordentliche Listen und Registraturen, kommt das Schuhzeug in Ballen und das Korn in Säck, wird Mensch und Vieh sauber gezählt und weggebracht, weil man eben weiß: Ohne Ordnung kein Krieg!

One

Spring 1624. The Protestant King of Sweden invades Catholic Poland. Recruiters for the Swedish General Oxenstjerna search in Dalarna for soldiers. The merchant, Anna Fierling, who goes by the name **Mother Courage**, *loses a son.*

A road outside of town.

A **Sergeant** *and an* **Army Recruiter** *stand waiting, shivering.*

The Army Recruiter   How's a recruiter going to find recruits in a place like this? Orders from the General Staff, *four fresh companies* in two weeks' time! I contemplate suicide, Sergeant. And the people here are so lacking in fundamental decency they've given me insomnia! Imagine if you will some jerk, concave chest, veiny legs, a total zero. I buy him beers till he's shitfaced, he signs up, and then: I'm paying the tab, he's off to take a leak, he says, I try to keep an eye on him because I've learned the smell of rat, and sure enough, zzzzzzzip! Jumped up and fled like a louse flees louse-powder. A handshake's meaningless, honour and duty are empty words. A place like this, you lose your conviction in the Inner Goodness of Man, Sergeant.

The Sergeant   The problem with these people is they haven't had enough war. Where else do morals come from? War! Everything rots in peacetime. People turn into carefree rutting animals and nobody fucking cares. Everyone overeats, whatever they want, 'Oh I'll just sit down now and eat a big cheese and fatback sandwich on fluffy white bread.' Think these people know how many young men and horses they've got? Why count? It's peacetime! I've been in some towns that've gone seventy years without any war whatsoever, people hadn't even bothered naming their children, no one knew whose was whose. You need a bit of butchery to get them counting and listing and naming: big piles of empty boots, corn bagged for portage, man and cow alike stamped and mobilised. War makes order, order makes war.

Der Werber   Wie richtig das ist!

Der Feldwebel   Wie alles Gute ist auch der Krieg am
Anfang halt schwer zu machen. Wenn er dann erst
floriert, ist er auch zäh; dann schrecken die Leut zurück
vorm Frieden, wie die Würfler vorm Aufhören, weil
dann müssens zählen, was sie verloren haben. Aber
zuerst schreckens zurück vorm Krieg. Er ist ihnen was
Neues.

Der Werber   Du, da kommt ein Planwagen. Zwei Weiber
und zwei junge Burschen. Halt die Alte auf, Feldwebel.
Wenn das wieder nix ist, stell ich mich nicht weiter in den
Aprilwind hin, das sag ich dir.

*Man hört eine Maultrommel. Von zwei jungen Burschen
gezogen, rollt ein Planwagen heran. Auf ihm sitzen* **Mutter
Courage** *und ihre stumme Tochter* **Kattrin**.

Mutter Courage   Guten Morgen, Herr Feldwebel!

Der Feldwebel *sich in den Weg stellend*

Der Feldwebel   Guten Morgen, ihr Leut! Wer seid ihr?

Mutter Courage   Geschäftsleut.

Singt.
Ihr Hauptleut, laßt die Trommel ruhen
Und laßt eur Fußvolk halten an:
Mutter Courage, die kommt mit Schuhen
In denen es besser laufen kann.
Mit seinen Läusen und Getieren
Bagage, Kanone und Gespann –
Soll es euch in die Schlacht marschieren
So will es gute Schuhe han.
    Das Frühjahr kommt. Wach auf, du Christ!
    Der Schnee schmilzt weg. Die Toten ruhn.
    Und was noch nicht gestorben ist
    Das macht sich auf die Socken nun.

The Army Recruiter   Amen.

The Sergeant   It isn't easy, starting a war, but nothing worthwhile is easy. And once you're in, you're hooked like a gambler, you can't afford to walk away from the crapshoot once you're deep into it. You become as afraid of peace as you ever were of war, no one really wants the fighting to end. You just have to get people used to the idea. Everyone's scared of anything changing.

The Army Recruiter   Heads up, a wagon. Two boys appropriate age. Tell 'em to pull over. If this goes bust I'm packing it in, I'm kissing the April wind goodbye.

A Jew's harp offstage. A canteen wagon comes down the road. It's pulled by two young men, **Eilif** *and* **Swiss Cheese**. *In the wagon, driving it,* **Mother Courage***; seated besides her, playing the Jew's harp, her mute daughter* **Kattrin**.

Mother Courage   Morning, Sergeant.

The **Sergeant** *blocks the wagon.*

The Sergeant   Morning, people. Declare yourselves!

Mother Courage   Retail!

She sings:
> To feed a war you have to pillage,
> But let your soldiers rest a bit:
> For what they need, here's Mother Courage,
> With woollen coats and boots that fit!
> Their heads ablaze with lice and liquor,
> The boys are marching to the beat!
> I guarantee they'll step it quicker
> With boots upon their blistered feet!

Mother Courage and her Sons (*singing*)*
> Now spring has come, and winter's dead.
> The snow has gone, so draw a breath!
> Let Christian souls crawl out of bed,
> Pull on their socks and conquer death!

Ihr Hauptleut, eure Leut marschieren
Euch ohne Wurst nicht in den Tod.
Laßt die Courage sie erst kurieren
Mit Wein von Leibs- und Geistesnot.
Kanonen auf die leeren Mägen
Ihr Hauptleut, das ist nicht gesund.
Doch sind sie satt, habt meinen Segen
Und führt sie in den Höllenschlund.
    Das Frühjahr kommt. Wach auf, du Christ!
    Der Schnee schmilzt weg. Die Toten ruhn.
    Und was noch nicht gestorben ist
    Das macht sich auf die Socken nun.

Der Feldwebel   Halt, wohin gehört ihr, Bagage?

Der Ätere Sohn   Zweites Finnisches Regiment.

Der Feldwebel   Wo sind eure Papiere?

Mutter Courage   Papiere?

Jüngerer Sohn   Das ist doch die Mutter Courage!

Der Feldwebel   Nie von gehört. Warum heißt sie Courage?

Mutter Courage   Courage heiß ich, weil ich den Ruin gefürchtet hab, Feldwebel, und bin durch das Geschützfeuer von Riga gefahrn mit fünfzig Brotlaib im Wagen. Sie waren schon angeschimmelt, es war höchste Zeit, ich hab keine Wahl gehabt.

Der Feldwebel   Keine Witze, du. Wo sind die Papiere!

Mutter Courage (*aus einer Zinnbüchse einen Haufen Papiere kramend und herunterkletternd*)   Das sind alle meine Papiere, Feldwebel. Da ist ein ganzes Meßbuch dabei, aus Altötting, zum Einschlagen von Gurken,

Mother Courage (*singing*)
   Unless his belly's full of porridge,
   A soldier's sure to turn and run.
   Buy him some grub from Mother Courage –
   So he'll know where to point his gun.
   They fight for God and legal tender,
   I'll see them clothed, and feed them well,
   And bless the boys, in all their splendour,
   As they march down the road to hell.

Mother Courage and her Sons (*singing*)
   Now spring has come, and winter's dead.
   The snow has gone, so draw a breath!
   Let Christian souls crawl out of bed,
   Pull on their socks and conquer death!

The wagon starts to roll again. Again the **Sergeant** *blocks it.*

The Sergeant   Hang on a minute, garbage. What's your regiment?

Eilif   Second Finnish.

The Sergeant   Paperwork!

Mother Courage   Paperwork?

Swiss Cheese   She's Mother Courage.

The Sergeant   I never heard of her. Why's she called 'Courage'?

Mother Courage   They called me Courage because I was scared of financial ruin, Sergeant, so I drove my wagon straight through the cannon fire at Riga, with fifty loaves of bread turning mouldy – I didn't see that I had a choice.

The Sergeant   Fascinating, now I know your life's story,* gimme your paperwork.

Mother Courage *reaches behind her, finds a battered tin box, removes a big stack of tattered paper. She climbs down off the wagon.*

Mother Courage   Here's paper, all I possess. A prayer book I bought in Alt-Ötting, I use the pages to wrap pickles,

und eine Landkarte von Mähren, weiß Gott, ob ich da je
hinkomm, sonst ist sie für die Katz, und hier stehts
besiegelt, daß mein Schimmel nicht die Maul- und
Klauenseuch hat, leider ist er uns umgestanden, er hat
fünfzehn Gulden gekostet, aber nicht mich, Gott sei
Dank. Ist das genug Papier?

Der Feldwebel Willst du mich auf den Arm nehmen?
Ich werd dir deine Frechheit austreiben. Du weißt, daß
du eine Lizenz haben mußt.

Mutter Courage Reden Sie anständig mit mir und
erzählen Sie nicht meinen halbwüchsigen Kindern, daß
ich Sie auf den Arm nehmen will, das gehört sich nicht,
ich hab nix mit Ihnen. Meine Lizenz beim Zweiten
Regiment ist mein anständiges Gesicht, und wenn Sie es
nicht lesen können, kann ich nicht helfen. Einen
Stempel laß ich mir nicht draufsetzen.

Der Werber Feldwebel, ich spür einen unbotmäßigen
Geist heraus bei der Person. Im Lager da brauchen wir
Zucht.

Mutter Courage Ich dacht Würst.

Der Feldwebel Name.

Mutter Courage Anna Fierling.

Der Feldwebel Also dann heißts ihr alle Fierling?

Mutter Courage Wieso? Ich heiß Fierling. Die nicht.

Der Feldwebel Ich denk, das sind alles Kinder von dir?

Mutter Courage Sind auch, aber heißen sie deshalb alle
gleich? (*Auf den älteren Sohn deutend.*) Der zum Beispiel
heißt Eilif Nojocki, warum, sein Vater hat immer
behauptet, er heißt Kojocki oder Mojocki. Der Junge hat
ihn noch gut im Gedächtnis, nur, das war ein anderer,
den er im Gedächtnis hat, ein Franzos mit einem
Spitzbart. Aber sonst hat er vom Vater die Intelligenz
geerbt; der konnt einem Bauern die Hos vom Hintern
wegziehn, ohne daß der was gemerkt hat. Und so hat
eben jedes von uns seinen Namen.

Der Feldwebel Was, jedes einen anderen?

Mutter Courage Sie tun grad, als ob Sie das nicht kennten.

and a map of Moravia, will I ever get to Moravia? God
knows. If I don't the map's for the cat to shit on. And
here, official proof my horse doesn't have hoof-and-
mouth disease, which is swell except the horse is dead,
poor thing, fifteen guilders she cost, although praise
Jesus, not *my* fifteen guilders. I have more paper if you
want it.

The Sergeant What I want is, I want your licence to sell.
You want my boot up your ass?*

Mother Courage Excuse me but you may not discuss my
ass in front of my children, that's disgusting. And my ass
is not for you. The Second Finnish Regiment never
required any licence besides my patent honesty which, if
you had a better character, you could read off my face.

The Army Recruiter Sergeant, I think this woman's
insubordinate. The King's army needs discipline.

Mother Courage And sausages!

The Sergeant Name.

Mother Courage Anna Fierling.

The Sergeant And these others are Fierlings?

Mother Courage Who? I'm Fierling. Not them.

The Sergeant They're your children.

Mother Courage They are. What's your problem?
(*Pointing to her elder son.*) Take him for example, he's
Finnish, he's Eilif Nojocki, why? His father was Kojocki or
Mojocki so I split the difference. The boy's got fond
memories of his father, only it's not actually his father he
remembers but a French guy with a goatee. Regardless,
he inherited the Kojocki or Mojocki brains; that man
could steal a farmer's socks without removing the boots
first. None of us has the same name.

The Sergeant None of you?

Mother Courage Four points on the compass and I've
been pricked in every direction.*

Der Feldwebel   Dann ist der wohl ein Chineser? (*Auf den Jüngeren deutend.*)

Mutter Courage   Falsch geraten. Ein Schweizer.

Der Feldwebel   Nach dem Franzosen?

Mutter Courage   Nach was für einem Franzosen? Ich weiß von keinem Franzosen. Bringen Sies nicht durcheinander, sonst stehn wir am Abend noch da. Ein Schweizer, heißt aber Fejos, ein Name, der nix mit seinem Vater zu tun hat. Der hieß ganz anders und war Festungsbaumeister, nur versoffen.

Schweizerkas *nickt strahlend, und auch die stumme* **Kattrin** *amüsiert sich.*

Der Feldwebel   Wie kann er da Fejos heißen?

Mutter Courage   Ich will Sie nicht beleidigen, aber Phantasie haben Sie nicht viel. Er heißt natürlich Fejos, weil, als er kam, war ich mit einem Ungarn, dem wars gleich, er hatte schon den Nierenschwund, obwohl er nie einen Tropfen angerührt hat, ein sehr redlicher Mensch. Der Junge ist nach ihm geraten.

Der Feldwebel   Aber er war doch gar nicht der Vater?

Mutter Courage   Aber nach ihm ist er geraten. Ich heiß ihn Schweizerkas, warum, er ist gut im Wagenziehen. (*Auf ihre Tochter deutend.*) Die heißt Kattrin Haupt, eine halbe Deutsche.

Der Feldwebel   Eine nette Familie, muß ich sagen.

Mutter Courage   Ja, ich bin durch die ganze Welt gekommen mit meinem Planwagen.

Der Feldwebel   Das wird alles aufgeschrieben. (*Er schreibt auf.*)

Der Werber   Ihr solltet lieber Jakob Ochs und Esau Ochs heißen, weil ihr doch den Wagen zieht. Aus dem Gespann kommt ihr wohl nie heraus?

Eilif   Mutter, darf ich ihm aufs Maul hauen? Ich möcht gern.

The Sergeant (*pointing at the youngest son*)   I bet. Was his father Chinese?

Mother Courage   Bad guess. Swiss.

The Sergeant   He came along after the French guy?

Mother Courage   French guy? I never knew any French guys, try to follow or we'll be here till night falls. His father was Swiss, as in Switzerland, but *his* name's Fejos because he's not named after his father, who built fortresses, drunk.

Swiss Cheese *smiles proudly, nodding.* **Kattrin** *hides a laugh.*

The Sergeant   Then who was Fejos?

Mother Courage   I don't mean to be rude, but you're entirely devoid of imagination, aren't you? I more or less had to call him Fejos because when he came out I was with a Hungarian. He couldn't care less, the Hungarian, he was dying, his kidneys shrivelled up even though he was abstemious. A nice man, the boy looks just like him.

The Sergeant   But he wasn't the father.

Mother Courage   Nevertheless. His big talent is pulling the wagon, so I call him Swiss Cheese. (*Pointing to her daughter.*) She's Kattrin Haupt. Half-German.

The Sergeant   Jesus. A nice wholesome family.

Mother Courage   We are. I've crossed the wide world in this wagon.

The Sergeant   You're Bavarian. I'm guessing Bamberg.* What're you doing in Sweden?

Mother Courage   There's no war in Bamberg, is there? Was I supposed to wait?

The Army Recruiter   So, Jacob and Esau Ox. Does she ever unstrap the rig and turn you loose to graze?

Eilif   Mama, can I punch this asshole in the mouth? Please?

Mutter Courage   Und ich untersags dir, du bleibst stehn. Und jetzt, meine Herren Offizier, brauchens nicht eine gute Pistolen, oder eine Schnall, die Ihre ist schon abgewetzt, Herr Feldwebel.

Der Feldwebel   Ich brauch was andres. Ich seh, die Burschen sind wie die Birken gewachsen, runde Brustkästen, stämmige Haxen: warum drückt sich das vom Heeresdienst, möcht ich wissen?

Mutter Courage (*schnell*)   Nicht zu machen, Feldwebel. Meine Kinder sind nicht für das Kriegshandwerk.

Der Werber   Aber warum nicht? Das bringt Gewinn und bringt Ruhm. Stiefelverramschen ist Weibersache. (*Zu* **Eilif**.) Tritt einmal vor, laß dich anfühlen, ob du Muskeln hast oder ein Hühnchen bist.

Mutter Courage   Ein Hühnchen ist er. Wenn einer ihn streng anschaut, möcht er umfallen.

Der Werber   Und ein Kalb dabei erschlagen, wenn eins neben ihm stünd. (*Er will ihn wegführen.*)

Mutter Courage   Willst du ihn wohl in Ruhe lassen? Der ist nix für euch.

Der Werber   Er hat mich grob beleidigt, und von meinem Mund als einem Maul geredet. Wir zwei gehen dort ins Feld und tragen die Sach aus unter uns Männern.

Eilif   Sei ruhig. Ich besorgs ihm, Mutter.

Mutter Courage   Stehen bleibst du. Du Haderlump! Ich kenn dich, nix wie raufen. Ein Messer hat er im Stiefel, stechen tut er.

Der Werber   Ich ziehs ihm aus wie einen Milchzahn, komm, Bürschchen.

Mutter Courage   Herr Feldwebel, ich sags dem Obristen. Der steckt euch ins Loch. Der Leutnant ist ein Freier meiner Tochter.

Der Feldwebel   Keine Gewalt, Bruder. (*Zu* **Mutter Courage**.) Was hast du gegen den Heeresdienst? War sein Vater nicht Soldat? Und ist anständig gefallen? Das hast du selber gesagt.

Mother Courage   Can you stay where you are and keep quiet, please? Now, Officers, how's about a good pistol, or a belt buckle? Sergeant, your buckle's all bent.

The Sergeant   How's about you tell me instead why these two boys who are solid as birch trees with chests and legs like Arabian chargers aren't in the army.

Mother Courage (*quick*)   Drop it, Sergeant, my kids aren't suited for war work.

The Army Recruiter   They look suitable to me. Make a little money, get famous. Selling shoes, that's for women. (*To* **Eilif**.) Come here. You talk big. But maybe you're a chicken.

Mother Courage   He is. He's a chicken. Look at him cross-eyed, he'll faint.

The Army Recruiter   I'm crossing my eyes, he still looks good to me!*

The **Army Recruiter** *gestures to* **Eilif** *to follow him.*

Mother Courage   He's mine, not yours.

The Army Recruiter   He called me an asshole. I invite him to accompany me to the field over there so I can clobber him.

Eilif   Glad to. Don't fret, Mama, I'll be right back.

Mother Courage   Don't you move, you brawling lump! (*To the* **Army Recruiter**, *pointing at* **Eilif**.) Watch out, he's got a knife sheathed in his boot!

The Army Recruiter   A knife, huh? I'll extract it easy as a baby tooth. This way, baby boy.

Mother Courage (*to the* **Sergeant**)   You listen to me, your Captain has been ogling my daughter, and I'm going to tell him you're making her unhappy and he'll clap you in the stocks.

The Sergeant (*to the* **Army Recruiter**)   No fighting, OK? (*To* **Mother Courage**.) What's so terrible about a job in the army? Bet his daddy was a soldier! Died a hero or something?

Mutter Courage   Er ist ein ganzes Kind. Ihr wollt ihn mir zur Schlachtbank führen, ich kenn euch. Ihr kriegt fünf Gulden für ihn.

Der Werber   Zunächst kriegt er eine schöne Kappe und Stulpenstiefel, nicht?

Eilif   Nicht von dir.

Mutter Courage   Komm, geh mit angeln, sagte der Fischer zum Wurm. (*Zum* **Schweizerkas**.) Lauf weg und schrei, die wollen deinen Bruder stehlen. (*Sie zieht ein Messer.*) Probierts nur und stehlt ihn. Ich stech euch nieder, Lumpen. Ich werds euch geben, Krieg mit ihm führen! Wir verkaufen ehrlich Leinen und Schinken und sind friedliche Leut.

Der Feldwebel   Das sieht man an deinem Messer, wie friedlich ihr seid. Überhaupt sollst du dich schämen, gib das Messer weg, Vettel! Vorher hast du eingestanden, du lebst vom Krieg, denn wie willst du sonst leben, von was? Aber wie soll Krieg sein, wenn es keine Soldaten gibt?

Mutter Courage   Das müssen nicht meine sein.

Der Feldwebel   So, den Butzen soll dein Krieg fressen, und die Birne soll er ausspucken! Deine Brut soll dir fett werden vom Krieg, und ihm gezinst wird nicht. Er kann schauen, wie er zu seine Sach kommt, wie? Heißt dich Courage, he? Und fürchtest den Krieg, deinen Brotgeber? Deine Söhn fürchten ihn nicht, das weiß ich von ihnen.

Eilif   Ich fürcht kein Krieg.

Der Feldwebel   Und warum auch? Schaut mich an: ist mir das Soldatenlos schlecht bekommen? Ich war mit siebzehn dabei.

Mutter Courage   Du bist noch nicht siebzig.

Der Feldwebel   Ich kanns erwarten.

Mutter Courage   Ja, unterm Boden vielleicht.

Der Feldwebel   Willst du mich beleidigen, und sagst, ich sterb?

Mother Courage Or something, dead at any rate, and (*pointing at* **Eilif**) he's just a child! I know your kind, you'll get a five-guilder fee and he'll get slaughtered!

The Army Recruiter We'll give him a soldier's snazzy hat and brand new regulation boots when he signs.

Eilif I don't want you to give me shit.

Mother Courage Hey hey hey, I got a fun idea, let's you and me go fishing said the fisherman to the worm. (*To* **Swiss Cheese**.) Run tell the Captain they're stealing your brother!

She pulls a knife.

He's mine! He's not going to war! I'll poke your eyes out first, you cannibals. We're merchants, we sell ham and shirts and we're friendly people.*

The Sergeant Yeah, you look friendly. Put up the knife, you old cunt. If there's a war, there have to be soldiers, right?

Mother Courage Somebody else's kids, not mine.

The Sergeant And there it is, your brood gets fat off the war* but you think it's a one-way transaction. Maybe your sons have courage even if you don't.

Eilif The war doesn't scare me.

The Sergeant Why would it? See any bruises on me? I joined at seventeen!

Mother Courage Let's see how close you get to seventy.

The Sergeant What're you insinuating? I'm gonna get killed?

Mutter Courage   Und wenns die Wahrheit ist? Wenn ich
seh, daß du gezeichnet bist? Wenn du dreinschaust wie
eine Leich auf Urlaub, he?

Schweizerkas   Sie hat das Zweite Gesicht, das sagen alle.
Sie sagt die Zukunft voraus.

Der Werber   Dann sag doch mal dem Herrn Feldwebel
die Zukunft voraus, es möcht ihn amüsieren.

Der Feldwebel   Ich halt nix davon.

Mutter Courage   Gib den Helm.

Er gibt ihn ihr.

Der Feldwebel   Das bedeutet nicht so viel wie ins Gras
scheißen. Nur daß ich was zum Lachen hab.

Mutter Courage (*nimmt einen Pergamentbogen und zerreißt
ihn*)   Eilif, Schweizerkas und Kattrin, so möchten wir alle
zerrissen werden, wenn wir uns in'n Krieg zu tief
einlassen täten. (*Zum* **Feldwebel**.) Ich werds Ihnen
ausnahmsweis gratis machen. Ich mal ein schwarzes
Kreuz auf den Zettel. Schwarz ist der Tod.

Schweizerkas   Und den anderen läßt sie leer, siehst du?

Mutter Courage Da falt ich sie zusammen, und jetzt
schüttel ich sie durcheinander. Wie wir alle gemischt
sind, von Mutterleib an, und jetzt ziehst du und weißt
Bescheid.

Der Feldwebel *zögert.*

Der Werber (*zu* **Eilif**)   Ich nehm nicht jeden, ich bin
bekannt für wählerisch, aber du hast ein Feuer, das mich
angenehm berührt.

Der Feldwebel (*im Helm fischend*)   Blödheit! Nix als ein
Augenauswischen.

Schweizerkas   Ein schwarzes Kreuz hat er gezogen. Hin
geht er.

Der Werber   Laß du dich nicht ins Bockshorn jagen, für
jeden ist keine Kugel gegossen.

Mother Courage   You look marked to me. What if you're just a cadaver who hasn't heard the bad news, hmm?

Swiss Cheese   She can see things, everyone knows that, she sees into the future.

The Army Recruiter   Tell the Sergeant his future then. He likes a good laugh.

The Sergeant   That's crap. Seeing things.

Mother Courage   Give me your helmet.

He does.

The Sergeant   Whatever you're doing, it means as much as dried turds in dead grass.

Mother Courage *looks at him, asking if she should continue.*

The Sergeant   Go ahead, it'll make a good story

She tears a piece of paper in two.

Mother Courage   Eilif, Swiss Cheese, Kattrin, we'll all be torn to scraps like this, if we let the war pull us in too deeply. (*To the* **Sergeant**.) For a friend I do it for free. I make a black cross on the paper. Black is death.

Swiss Cheese   And see the other piece of paper's empty.

Mother Courage   I fold them, I tumble 'em together, topsy turvy as we all tumble together, the marked and unremarkable, from mother love onward, and now draw and now you'll know.

The **Sergeant** *hesitates.*

The Army Recruiter (to **Eilif**)   I'm the pickiest recruiter in the Swedish Army, most don't come close to making the cut but maybe you've got the grit, the beans, that special fire.

The **Sergeant** *reaches in the helmet.*

The Sergeant   It's all gobbledegook, oooh, the scales are falling from my eyes!

He draws a piece of paper, unfolds it.

Swiss Cheese   Uh-oh! The black cross! He's going away!

The Army Recruiter   There are more soldiers than bullets. Don't let them scare you.

Der Feldwebel (*heiser*)   Du hast mich beschissen.

Mutter Courage   Das hast du dich selber an dem Tag, wo du Soldat geworden bist. Und jetzt fahrn wir weiter, es ist nicht alle Tag Krieg, ich muß mich tummeln.

Der Feldwebel   Hölle und Teufel, ich laß mich von dir nicht anschmieren. Deinen Bankert nehmen wir mit, der wird uns Soldat.

Eilif   Ich möchts schon werden, Mutter.

Mutter Courage   Das Maul hältst du, du finnischer Teufel.

Eilif   Der Schweizerkas will jetzt auch Soldat werden.

Mutter Courage   Das ist mir was Neues. Ich werd euch auch das Los ziehen lassen müssen, euch alle drei.

Sie läuft nach hinten, auf Zettel Kreuze zu malen.

Der Werber (*zu* **Eilif**)   Es ist gegen uns gesagt worden, daß es fromm zugeht im schwedischen Lager, aber das ist üble Nachred, damit man uns schadet. Gesungen wird nur am Sonntag, eine Stroph! und nur, wenn einer eine Stimm hat.

Mutter Courage (*kommt zurück mit den Zetteln im Helm des Feldwebels*)   Möchten ihrer Mutter weglaufen, die Teufel, und in den Krieg wie die Kälber zum Salz. Aber ich werd die Zettel befragen, und da werden sie schon sehen, daß die Welt kein Freudental ist, mit »Komm mit, Sohn, wir brauchen noch Feldhauptleut«. Feldwebel, ich hab wegen ihnen die größten Befürchtungen, sie möchten mir nicht durch den Krieg kommen. Sie haben schreckliche Eigenschaften, alle drei. (*Sie streckt* **Eilif** *den Helm hin.*) Da, fisch dir dein Los raus. (*Er fischt, faltet auf. Sie entreißt es ihm.*) Da hast dus, ein Kreuz! Oh, ich unglückliche Mutter, ich schmerzensreiche Gebärerin. Er stirbt? Im Lenz des Lebens muß er dahin. Wenn er ein Soldat wird, muß er ins Gras beißen, das ist klar. Er ist zu kühn, nach seinem Vater. Und wenn er nicht klug ist,

The Sergeant (*hoarse*)   You cheated me.

Mother Courage   You did that to yourself the day you enlisted. Now we'll get going, it isn't every day there's a war on, we don't want to miss out on the fun.

The Sergeant   Hell and the Devil, you cheated me, bitch, but you'll be sorry you did! Your bastard's a soldier now!

Eilif   I wanna go with them, Mama.

Mother Courage   Shut your mouth, nasty!

Eilif   Swiss Cheese too, he wants to be a soldier too!

Mother Courage   You think so? Says who? Draw your own papers from the helmet, all three of you, then we'll see what's what.

She goes behind the wagon, where she tears paper and marks slips with crosses.

The Army Recruiter (*to* **Eilif**)   And I've heard the enemy propaganda, in the Swedish Army it's Bible study and hymn singing night and day, but between us, the army's the army and once you're in you're washed clean of sin,* and you can sing any song you like.

Mother Courage *returns with the helmet.*

Mother Courage   Time to abandon mother, huh, my two terrors? War is irresistible to young knuckleheads like you. Draw, draw and see what a welcome the world has in store. You bet I'm terrified, Sergeant, you would be too if you'd given birth to 'em, each one has a horrible personality defect. (*To* **Eilif**.) Here. Fish out your ticket.

Eilif *picks a slip of paper. She snatches it from him and unfolds it.*

Mother Courage   Oh I'm an unlucky mother! My womb only ever gave me grief after grief after grief! So young, into the army and then rotting in the ground, grass waving over him, it's hideously clear. You see, you see! A cross! Marked! Your father was a brazen idiot, like you,

geht er den Weg des Fleisches, der Zettel beweist es. (*Sie
herrscht ihn an.*) Wirst du klug sein?

Eilif   Warum nicht?

Mutter Courage   Klug ist, wenn du bei deiner Mutter
bleibst, und wenn sie dich verhöhnen und ein Hühnchen
schimpfen, lachst du nur.

Der Werber   Wenn du dir in die Hosen machst, werd ich
mich an deinen Bruder halten.

Mutter Courage   Ich hab dir geheißen, du sollst lachen.
Lach! Und jetzt fisch du, Schweizerkas. Bei dir fürcht ich
weniger, du bist redlich. (*Er fischt im Helm.*) Oh, warum
schaust du so sonderbar auf den Zettel? Bestimmt ist er
leer. Es kann nicht sein, daß da ein Kreuz drauf steht.
Dich soll ich doch nicht verlieren. (*Sie nimmt den Zettel.*)
Ein Kreuz? Auch er! Sollte das etwa sein, weil er so
einfältig ist? Oh, Schweizerkas, du sinkst auch dahin,
wenn du nicht ganz und gar redlich bist allezeit, wie ichs
dir gelehrt hab von Kindesbeinen an, und mir das
Wechselgeld zurückbringst vom Brotkaufen. Nur dann
kannst du dich retten. Schau her, Feldwebel, obs nicht
ein schwarzes Kreuz ist?

Der Feldwebel   Ein Kreuz ists. Ich versteh nicht, daß ich
eins gezogen hab. Ich halt mich immer hinten. (*Zum
Werber.*) Sie treibt keinen Schwindel. Es trifft ihre
eigenen auch.

Schweizerkas   Mich triffts auch. Aber ich laß mirs gesagt
sein.

Mutter Courage (*zu* **Kattrin**)   Und jetzt bleibst mir nur
noch du sicher, du bist selber ein Kreuz: du hast ein gutes
Herz. (*Sie hält ihr den Helm zum Wagen hoch, nimmt aber
selber den Zettel heraus.*) Ich möcht schier verzweifeln. Das
kann nicht stimmen, vielleicht hab ich einen Fehler
gemacht beim Mischen. Sei nicht zu gutmütig, Kattrin,
seis nie mehr, ein Kreuz steht auch über deinem Weg.
Halt dich immer recht still, das kann nicht schwer sein,
wo du doch stumm geboren bist. So, jetzt wißt ihr. Seid

but you learned from me: think or die. Just like the paper shows.

She flattens **Eilif**.

Mother Courage   ARE YOU GOING TO THINK???!!!

Eilif   Sure, why not?

Mother Courage   And if they laugh and call you a chicken just cluck at them, who cares?

The Army Recruiter   If you've crapped your pants we can take your brother instead.

Mother Courage   Cluck! Cluck! Laugh right back! (*To* **Swiss Cheese**.) Now you, Swiss Cheese, fish for it. I'm not much worried about you, honest as you are.

Swiss Cheese *draws a slip from the helmet. He stares at it.*

Mother Courage   It's empty, isn't it? It can't be you pulled a black cross, that I'm losing you too, can't be.

She takes the slip from him.

Mother Courage   A cross! I guess because he's the simple son? Swiss Cheese, you're also going down unless you're always honest, like I taught you when you were a tiny kid – always bring back exact change from the baker. Otherwise you're lost. See, Sergeant, a black cross, yeah?

The Sergeant   Yeah. But I don't get it. I stay back, I never go near the fighting, why'd I get one? (*To the* **Army Recruiter**.) She's not a swindler, even her own kids get marked.

Swiss Cheese   Even I'm marked. But I get it, I'm obedient.

Mother Courage (*to* **Kattrin**)   You're safe, I know it, you won't draw a cross because you are the cross I bear: your good heart.

She holds the helmet up to **Kattrin**, *but she snatches the slip out herself before* **Kattrin** *has a chance.*

Mother Courage   I'm completely desperate. Something's wrong, maybe the way I stirred them. You can't be so kind, Kattrin, not any more, a cross stands athwart the road for you too. Stay quiet always, that should be easy for

alle vorsichtig, ihr habts nötig. Und jetzt steigen wir auf und fahren weiter.

Sie gibt dem **Feldwebel** *seinen Helm zurück und besteigt den Wagen.*

Der Werber (*zum* **Feldwebel**)   Mach was!

Der Feldwebel   Ich fühl mich gar nicht wohl.

Der Werber   Vielleicht hast du dich schon verkühlt, wie du den Helm weggegeben hast im Wind. Verwickel sie in einen Handel. (*Laut.*) Du kannst dir die Schnalle ja wenigstens anschauen, Feldwebel. Die guten Leut leben vom Geschäft, nicht? He, ihr, der Feldwebel will die Schnalle kaufen!

Mutter Courage   Einen halben Gulden. Wert ist so eine Schnall zwei Gulden. (*Sie klettert wieder vom Wagen.*)

Der Feldwebel   Sie ist nicht neu. Da ist so ein Wind, ich muß sie in Ruh studieren. (*Er geht mit der Schnalle hinter den Wagen.*)

Mutter Courage   Ich finds nicht zugig.

Der Feldwebel   Vielleicht ist sie einen halben Gulden wert, es ist Silber.

Mutter Courage (*geht zu ihm hinter den Wagen*)   Es sind solide sechs Unzen.

Der Werber (*zu* **Eilif**)   Und dann heben wir einen unter Männern. Ich hab Handgeld bei mir, komm.

Eilif *steht unschlüssig.*

Mutter Courage   Dann ein halber Gulden.

Der Feldwebel   Ich verstehs nicht. Immer halt ich mich dahint. Einen sichereren Platz, als wenn du Feldwebel bist, gibts nicht. Da kannst du die andern vorschicken, daß sie sich Ruhm erwerben. Mein ganzes Mittag ist mir versaut. Ich weiß genau, nix werd ich hinunterbringen.

Mutter Courage   So sollst du dirs nicht zu Herzen nehmen, daß du nicht mehr essen kannst. Halt dich nur dahint. Da, nimm einen Schluck Schnaps, Mann. (*Sie gibt ihm zu trinken.*)

a mute. So now you all know, safety first, all of you. Back to the wagon and let's get far away from here.

Mother Courage *hands the* **Sergeant** *his helmet and climbs back up on the wagon.*

The Army Recruiter (*to the* **Sergeant**)   Do something!

The Sergeant   I feel funny.

The Army Recruiter   You have to wear your hat in wind like this, now you're getting sick. Catch her up in some haggling. (*Loud.*) At least take a look at the merchandise, Sergeant, these nice people have to make a living, right? Wait a minute, lady, the Sergeant here wants a buckle.

Mother Courage   A half-guilder. Though buckles like mine are worth two guilders easy.

She climbs down from the wagon, pulls out a box of belt buckles.

The Sergeant   It looks like it was chewed on. I'm shivering with this wind, let me look it over back here.

He goes behind the wagon.

Mother Courage   Doesn't seem windy to me.

The Sergeant   A half-guilder, maybe, it's silver.

Mother Courage (*going behind the wagon*)   Solid six ounces.

The Army Recruiter (*to* **Eilif**)   And now let's go get drunk, you and me, man to man, I have a pocket full of change.

Eilif *hesitates, undecided.*

Mother Courage   OK, a half-guilder, done deal.

The Sergeant   I just don't get it. I stay in the rear, I find a safe place, a sergeant's prerogative, I let the others go for the glory. Now I won't manage to keep my lunch down, I can tell, I'm queasy all of a sudden.

Mother Courage   Don't let it ruin your appetite. Here, take a slug of schnapps, man, and stick to the rear.

She gives him a drink. The **Army Recruiter** *has taken* **Eilif**'*s arm and is leading him away.*

Der Werber (*hat* **Eilif** *untern Arm genommen und zieht ihn nach hinten mit sich fort*)   Zehn Gulden auf die Hand, und ein mutiger Mensch bist du und kämpfst für den König, und die Weiber reißen sich um dich. Und mich darfst du in die Fresse hauen, weil ich dich beleidigt hab. (*Beide ab.*)

Die stumme **Kattrin** *springt vom Wagen und stößt rauhe Laute aus.*

Mutter Courage   Gleich, Kattrin, gleich. Der Herr Feldwebel zahlt noch. (*Beißt in den halben Gulden.*) Ich bin mißtrauisch gegen jedes Geld. Ich bin ein gebranntes Kind, Feldwebel. Aber die Münz ist gut. Und jetzt fahrn wir weiter. Wo ist der Eilif?

Schweizerkas   Der ist mitm Werber weg.

Mutter Courage (*steht ganz still, dann*)   Du einfältiger Mensch. (*Zu* **Kattrin**.) Ich weiß, du kannst nicht reden, du bist unschuldig.

Der Feldwebel   Kannst selber einen Schluck nehmen, Mutter. So geht es eben. Soldat ist nicht das Schlechteste. Du willst vom Krieg leben, aber dich und die Deinen willst du draußen halten, wie?

Mutter Courage   Jetzt mußt du mit deinem Bruder ziehn, Kattrin.

Die beiden, Bruder und Schwester, spannen sich vor den Wagen und ziehen an. Mutter Courage geht nebenher. Der Wagen rollt weiter.

Der Feldwebel (*nachblickend*)   Will vom Krieg leben. Wird ihm wohl müssen auch was geben.

The Army Recruiter   Ten guilders up front, and you're a brave warrior for the King, and all the women go for you. And you can punch me in the mouth for insulting you.

They go out. Dumb **Kattrin** *jumps down from the wagon and starts making wild loud noises.*

Mother Courage   Wait Kattrin, wait a minute. The Sergeant's paying.

She bites the half-guilder the **Sergeant***'s given her.*

I've been burned, Sergeant, never learned to trust money. And now – where's Eilif?

Swiss Cheese   With the recruiter. Gone.

Mother Courage (*stands frozen, then*)   You're simplicity itself, you are. (*To* **Kattrin**.) I know, I know, you can't speak, it isn't your fault.

The Sergeant   Give yourself a little schnapps, Mama. So goes the world. It's not so terrible, a soldier's life.*

Mother Courage   You have to help your brother pull, Kattrin.

Side by side, brother and sister harness themselves to the wagon and pull it away. **Mother Courage** *walks alongside. They exit.*

The Sergeant (*watching them leave*)
   If off the war you hope to live,
   Take what you can. You'll also give.*

Two

In den Jahren 1625 und 26 zieht **Mutter Courage** *im Troß der schwedischen Heere durch Polen. Vor der Festung Wallhof trifft sie ihren Sohn wieder. – Glücklicher Verkauf eines Kapauns und große Tage des kühnen Sohnes.*

Das Zelt des **Feldhauptmanns**. *Daneben die Küche. Kanonendonner. Der* **Koch** *streitet sich mit* **Mutter Courage**, *die einen Kapaun verkaufen will.*

Der Koch   Sechzig Heller für einen so jämmerlichen Vogel?

Mutter Courage   Jämmerlicher Vogel? Dieses fette Vieh? Dafür soll ein Feldhauptmann, wo verfressen ist bis dorthinaus, weh Ihnen, wenn Sie nix zum Mittag haben, nicht sechzig Hellerchen zahlen können?

Der Koch   Solche krieg ich ein Dutzend für zehn Heller gleich ums Eck.

Mutter Courage   Was, so einen Kapaun wollen Sie gleich ums Eck kriegen? Wo Belagerung ist und also ein Hunger, daß die Schwarten krachen. Eine Feldratt kriegen Sie vielleicht, vielleicht sag ich, weil die aufgefressen sind, fünf Mann hoch sind sie einen halben Tag hinter einer hungrigen Feldratt her. Fünfzig Heller für einen riesigen Kapaun bei Belagerung!

Der Koch   Wir werden doch nicht belagert, sondern die andern. Wir sind die Belagerer, das muß in Ihren Kopf endlich hinein.

Mutter Courage   Aber zu fressen haben wir auch nix, ja weniger als die in der Stadt drin. Die haben doch alles hineingeschleppt. Die leben in Saus und Braus, hör ich. Aber wir! Ich war bei die Bauern, sie haben nix.

Der Koch   Sie haben. Sie versteckens.

Two

From 1625 to 1626 **Mother Courage** *follows the Swedish army as it crosses Poland. Near the fort at Wallhof she sees her son again. The lucky sale of a chicken and a great day for the brave son.*

The **General**'s *tent.*

Beside the tent, the kitchen. Cannon fire in the distance. The **Cook** *argues with* **Mother Courage** *who hopes to sell him a chicken.*

The Cook   Sixty hellers for that scraggly hen?

Mother Courage   Scraggly? This fat beast? What, your General, who can outeat anyone from Sweden to Poland and back again, and woe unto the cook who serves him up a skimpy table, he can't cough up sixty little hellers?

The Cook   For ten hellers on any street corner I can fetch a dozen birds better looking than that.

Mother Courage   Sure, sure you can get a fat chicken like this on a street corner with everyone from miles about all withered and skeletal. You'll fetch a rat from the fields, maybe, *maybe*, if you can find one, they've all been eaten, I saw five men chase one rat for hours. Fifty hellers for this, this, what would you call it, well it's practically a turkey,* it's so big. And in the middle of a siege.

The Cook   We're not in the middle of a siege, it's them up in the fort that are in the middle of the siege, we're the besiegers. Try to keep it straight.

Mother Courage   Why bother, the besiegers have less food than the besieged. They hauled all the crops and cattle up to the fort before they locked themselves in. I hear they're swimming in sauce and beer up there. Down here, well, I've been to the farms. Grim. Zilch.

The Cook   They've got it, the farmers. They hide it.

Mutter Courage (*triumphierend*)   Sie haben nicht. Sie sind ruiniert, das ist, was sie sind. Sie nagen am Hungertuch. Ich hab welche gesehn, die graben die Wurzeln aus vor Hunger, die schlecken sich die Finger nach einem gekochten Lederriemen. So steht es. Und ich hab einen Kapaun und soll ihn für vierzig Heller ablassen.

Der Koch   Für dreißig, nicht für vierzig. Ich hab gesagt für dreißig.

Mutter Courage   Sie, das ist kein gewöhnlicher Kapaun. Das war ein so talentiertes Vieh, hör ich, daß es nur gefressen hat, wenn sie ihm Musik aufgespielt haben, und es hat einen Leibmarsch gehabt. Es hat rechnen können, so intelligent war es. Und da solln vierzig Heller zu viel sein? Der Feldhauptmann wird Ihnen den Kopf abreißen, wenn nix aufm Tisch steht.

Der Koch   Sehen Sie, was ich mach? (*Er nimmt ein Stück Rindfleisch und setzt das Messer dran.*) Da hab ich ein Stück Rindfleisch, das brat ich. Ich geb Ihnen eine letzte Bedenkzeit.

Mutter Courage   Braten Sies nur. Das ist vom vorigen Jahr.

Der Koch   Das ist von gestern abend, da ist der Ochs noch herumgelaufen, ich hab ihn persönlich gesehn.

Mutter Courage   Dann muß er schon bei Lebzeiten gestunken haben.

Der Koch   Ich kochs fünf Stunden lang, wenns sein muß, ich will sehn, obs da noch hart ist. (*Er schneidet hinein.*)

Mutter Courage   Nehmens viel Pfeffer, daß der Herr Feldhauptmann den Gestank nicht riecht.

Ins Zelt treten der **Feldhauptmann**, *ein* **Feldprediger** *und* **Eilif**.

Der Feldhauptmann (**Eilif** *auf die Schulter schlagend*) Nun, mein Sohn, herein mit dir zu deinem Feldhauptmann und setz dich zu meiner Rechten. Denn

Mother Courage (*playing her trump*)   They've got
nothing, starving, I've seen them, digging roots up out of
the ground and sucking their fingers after a meal of
boiled leather. And I'm supposed to sell a gourmet capon
for forty hellers.

The Cook   I offered thirty, not forty.

Mother Courage   This isn't any workaday chicken. He
was musically gifted, he'd eat only to the tune of his
favourite marches, and he could do arithmetic. All that
for forty hellers? If you don't have something to serve
him, your General's liable to eat your head.

The Cook   Know why I'm not worried?

He spears a piece of beef with his knife and lifts it up.

A roast for roasting. I've tendered you my final offer.

Mother Courage   Roast it, but hurry, it's been dead
three weeks and it stinks.*

The Cook   I saw it running across the fields yesterday.

Mother Courage   Praise Jesus, a dead dog, running
around. It's a miracle.

The Cook   It was a cow, not a dog, and after two hours
in a stewpot, it'll be tender as a tit.

Mother Courage   After five hours, it'll be glue, but say a
prayer if the general comes hungry, and keep the pepper
handy, I'm telling you, it stinks.

*The **General**, a **Chaplain** and **Eilif** enter the **General**'s tent.*
*The **General** claps **Eilif**'s shoulder.*

The General   Come on, son, sit at the right hand of your
General. You're a hero and a real Christian and this is a
war for God and what's done is done because God wants
it done and you did it and I feel fantastic! When we take
the goddamned fort I'm going to give you a gold
bracelet. We come to set their souls free, and what do
they do, these farmers who've happily let centuries of
their beefsteak disappear down the gullets of fat Polish

du hast eine Heldentat vollbracht, als frommer Reiter,
und für Gott getan, was du getan hast, in einem
Glaubenskrieg, das rechne ich dir besonders hoch an,
mit einer goldenen Armspang, sobald ich die Stadt hab.
Wir sind gekommen, ihnen ihre Seelen zu retten, und
was tun sie, als unverschämte und verdreckte Saubauern?
Uns ihr Vieh wegtreiben! Aber ihren Pfaffen schieben
sies vorn und hinten rein, aber du hast ihnen Mores
gelehrt. Da schenk ich dir eine Kanne Roten ein, das
trinken wir beide aus auf einen Hupp! (*Sie tun es.*) Der
Feldprediger kriegt einen Dreck, der ist fromm. Und was
willst du zu Mittag, mein Herz?

Eilif   Einen Fetzen Fleisch, warum nicht?

Der Feldhauptmann   Koch, Fleisch!

Der Koch   Und dann bringt er sich noch Gäst mit, wo
nix da is.

Mutter Courage *bringt ihn zum Schweigen, da sie lauschen will.*

Eilif   Bauernschinden macht hungrig.

Mutter Courage   Jesus, das ist mein Eilif.

Der Koch   Wer?

Mutter Courage   Mein Ältester. Zwei Jahr hab ich ihn
aus den Augen verloren, ist mir gestohlen worden auf der
Straß und muß in hoher Gunst stehen, wenn ihn der
Feldhauptmann zum Essen einlädt, und was hast du zum
Essen? Nix! Hast du gehört, was er als Gast gern speisen
will: Fleisch! Laß dir gut raten, nimm jetzt auf der Stell
den Kapaun, er kost einen Gulden.

Der Feldhauptmann (*hat sich mit* **Eilif** *und dem* **Feldprediger**
gesetzt und brüllt)   Zu essen, Lamb, du Kochbestie, sonst
erschlag ich dich.

Der Koch   Gib her, zum Teufel, du Erpresserin.

Mutter Courage   Ich dacht, es ist ein jämmerlicher Vogel.

Der Koch   Jämmerlich, her gib ihn, es ist ein
Sündenpreis, fünfzig Heller.

priests? They decide to turn their livestock loose so we
can't eat. Savages. Ingrates. Stinky little shitpeople. But
they'll remember what they learned from you, boy!*

He pours wine into two tin cups, then offers one to **Eilif**.

The General   Here's a can of my best red, we'll bolt it
down together.

Eilif *and* **General** *gulp down the wine.*

The General   Chaplain can lap up the dregs, like the
suffering Christ he is.* Now what's for lunch, heart of my
hearts?

Eilif   Umm . . . steak!

The General (*screaming to the kitchen*)   Cook! Meat!

The Cook   He knows we're out of everything so he
brings guests.

Mother Courage *gestures to him to be silent, so she can hear
what's happening in the tent.*

Eilif   You really work up an appetite, butchering
peasants.

Mother Courage   Jesus, it's my Eilif.

The Cook   Who?

Mother Courage   My eldest. Haven't laid eyes on him for
two years, stolen from me on the open road, and he must
be in great good favour with the General, his special
lunch guest, and what're you going to feed them,
nothing! You heard the General: meat! My advice: buy
the chicken. Price: one hundred hellers.

The General   Lunch, Lamb, you beast-who-barely-
learned-to-cook,* or I'll hook and gut you!

The Cook   Oh hell, give it, it's blackmail.

Mother Courage   This shabby bird?

The Cook   Just give it to me, it's a sin, fifty hellers for
scraggle like that.

Mutter Courage   Ich sag einen Gulden. Für meinen Ältesten, den lieben Gast vom Herrn Feldhauptmann, ist mir nix zu teuer.

Der Koch   Dann aber rupf ihn wenigstens, bis ich ein Feuer mach.

Mutter Courage (*setzt sich, den Kapaun zu rupfen*)   Was mag der für ein Gesicht machen, wenn er mich sieht. Er ist mein kühner und kluger Sohn. Ich hab noch einen dummen, der aber redlich ist. Die Tochter ist nix. Wenigstens red sie nicht, das ist schon etwas.

Der Feldhauptmann   Trink noch einen, mein Sohn, das ist mein Lieblingsfalerner, ich hab nur noch ein Faß davon oder zwei, höchstens, aber das ists mir wert, daß ich seh, es gibt noch einen echten Glauben in meinem Heerhaufen. Und der Seelenhirt schaut wieder zu, weil er predigt nur, und wies gemacht werden soll, weiß er nicht. Und jetzt, mein Sohn Eilif, bericht uns genauer, wie fein du die Bauern geschlenkt und die zwanzig Rinder gefangen hast. Hoffentlich sind sie bald da.

Eilif   In einem Tag oder zwei höchstens.

Mutter Courage   Das ist rücksichtsvoll von meinem Eilif, daß er die Ochsen erst morgen eintreibt, sonst hättet ihr meinen Kapaun überhaupt nicht mehr gegrüßt.

Eilif   Also, das war so: ich hab erfahren, daß die Bauern unter der Hand, in der Nacht hauptsächlich, ihre versteckten Ochsen aus den Wäldern in ein bestimmtes Holz getrieben haben. Da wollten die von der Stadt sie abholen. Ich hab sie ruhig ihre Ochsen eintreiben lassen, die, dacht ich, finden sie leichter als ich. Meine Leut habe ich lustig auf das Fleisch gemacht, hab ihnen zwei Tag lang die schmale Ration noch gekürzt, daß ihnen das Wasser im Maul zusammengelaufen ist, wenn sie bloß ein Wort gehört haben, das mit Fl angeht, wie Fluß.

Mother Courage   I said a hundred, one whole guilder. Nothing's too nice for my eldest, the General's special guest.

The **Cook** *gives her the money.*

The Cook   Plucking included. While I get the fire up.

Mother Courage (*sitting down, plucking*)   The look on his face when he sees it's me! He's my brave, clever boy. I've got another one, stupid but honest. The girl's nothing. At least she's quiet, at least there's that.

The **General** *pours another drink. They keep drinking, getting drunker.*

The General   Have another, son, a lip-smacking Falernian, only one or maybe two kegs left, but I don't begrudge my best for my true believers. Who act! Not like this watery-eyed old simp of a soul-shepherd, he preaches sunup to sundown till the whole church is out cold and snoring but we still haven't taken the goddamned fort and don't ask him how to do it, or how to do anything. You, Eilif, my son, on the other hand, you showed an initiative which eventuated in the requisitioning of twenty head of cattle from some farmers. Which will arrive soon I hope.*

Eilif   By morning.

Mother Courage   That's thoughtful of my Eilif, delivering the oxen tomorrow, otherwise I doubt my chicken would've had such an enthusiastic reception.

The General   Regale us!

Eilif   Yep, well, this is the way it went: I heard the farmers were sneaking out at night all hush-hush to round up these cows they were hiding in a wood. They'd arranged a sale of the cows with the people up in the fort. I held back, let the farmers do all the work rounding up the cows – they're good at herding, saved me the work. Meanwhile I got my men good and ready, for two days I fed them only bread and water, so they got crazy for meat, they'd drool if they just heard the word 'meat', if they even heard a word beginning with 'M', like … um … 'meat'!*

Der Feldhauptmann   Das war klug von dir.

Eilif   Vielleicht. Alles andere war eine Kleinigkeit. Nur
daß die Bauern Knüppel gehabt haben und dreimal so
viele waren wie wir und einen mörderischen Überfall auf
uns gemacht haben. Vier haben mich in ein Gestrüpp
gedrängt und mir mein Eisen aus der Hand gehaun und
gerufen: Ergib dich! Was tun, denk ich, die machen aus
mir Hackfleisch.

Der Feldhauptmann   Was hast getan?

Eilif   Ich hab gelacht.

Der Feldhauptmann   Was hast?

Eilif   Gelacht. So ist ein Gespräch draus geworden. Ich
verleg mich gleich aufs Handeln und sag: zwanzig
Gulden für den Ochsen ist mir zu viel. Ich biet fünfzehn.
Als wollt ich zahlen. Sie sind verdutzt und kratzen sich
die Köpf. Sofort bück ich mich nach meinem Eisen und
hau sie zusammen. Not kennt kein Gebot, nicht?

Der Feldhauptmann   Was sagst du dazu, Seelenhirt?

Der Feldprediger   Streng genommen, in der Bibel steht
der Satz nicht, aber unser Herr hat aus fünf Broten
fünfhundert herzaubern können, da war eben keine Not,
und da konnt er auch verlangen, daß man seinen
Nächsten liebt, denn man war satt. Heutzutage ist das
anders.

Der Feldhauptmann (*lacht*)   Ganz anders. Jetzt kriegst
du doch einen Schluck, du Pharisäer. (*Zu* **Eilif**.)
Zusammengehauen hast du sie, so ists recht, damit meine
braven Leut ein gutes Stückl zwischen die Zähn kriegen.
Heißts nicht in der Schrift: Was du dem geringsten von
meinen Brüdern getan hast, hast du mir getan? Und was
hast du ihnen getan? Eine gute Mahlzeit von
Ochsenfleisch hast du ihnen verschafft, denn
schimmliges Brot sind sie nicht gewöhnt, sondern früher
haben sie sich in der Sturmhaub ihre kalten Schalen von
Semmel und Wein hergericht, vor sie für Gott gestritten
haben.

The General   You're smart.

Eilif   I dunno. After that it was basically one-two-three. Except the farmers had huge clubs and they outnumbered us three to one and when they saw we wanted their cows they came after us like murder. Four of them got me backed up against a thornbush and one of them clouted the sword from out of my hand and they were hollering 'give up' and I thought right, I give up and you pound me to paste.

The General   What'd you do?

Eilif   I started laughing.

The General   What?

Eilif   I laughed. So then they wanted to discuss that. So I start bargaining: 'You're fucking kidding, twenty guilders for that ox? More like fifteen tops!' Like we're doing business. Which confuses them, they're scratching their heads. And that's when I picked up my cutlass and I cut their heads off, HUH! HUH! HUH! HUH!* All four of them. Necessity trumps the commandments. Right?

The General   Want to rule on that, you pious pedant?

The Chaplain   There's no such exemption in the Bible, in the literal sense, but back then Our Lord could take five loaves of bread and make five hundred, so there was no necessity per se. You can command people to love their neighbours and if they're full of bread they may comply. That was then and this is now.

The General (*laughing*)   You can say that again. Here, you need to whet your whistle after that, Pharisee.

He pours the **Chaplain** *a glass of wine.*

The General (*to* **Eilif**)   You massacred the farmers* and now my brave boys'll bite down on a bit of real red meat, and how could God gripe about that? Doesn't His Holy Writ say 'Whateversoever thou dost for the least of My brethren is done for Me'? It'll be like in the old days again, a bit of beef, a gulp of wine and then fight for God.

Eilif   Ja, sofort bück ich mich nach meinem Eisen und hau sie zusammen.

Der Feldhauptmann   In dir steckt ein junger Cäsar. Du solltest den König sehn.

Eilif   Ich hab von weitem. Er hat was Lichtes. Ihn möcht ich mir zum Vorbild nehmen.

Der Feldhauptmann   Du hast schon was von ihm. Ich schätz mir einen solchen Soldaten wie dich, Eilif, einen mutigen. So einen behandel ich wie meinen eigenen Sohn. (*Er führt ihn zur Landkarte.*) Schau dir die Lage an, Eilif; da brauchts noch viel.

Mutter Courage (*die zugehört hat und jetzt zornig ihren Kapaun rupft*)   Das muß ein sehr schlechter Feldhauptmann sein.

Der Koch   Ein verfressener, aber warum ein schlechter?

Mutter Courage   Weil er mutige Soldaten braucht, darum. Wenn er einen guten Feldzugsplan machen könnt, wozu bräucht er da so mutige Soldaten? Gewöhnliche täten ausreichen. Überhaupt, wenn es wo so große Tugenden gibt, das beweist, daß da etwas faul ist.

Der Koch   Ich dacht, es beweist, daß etwas gut ist.

Mutter Courage   Nein, daß etwas faul ist. Warum, wenn ein Feldhauptmann oder König recht dumm ist und er führt seine Leut in die Scheißgass, dann brauchts Todesmut bei den Leuten, auch eine Tugend. Wenn er zu geizig ist und zu wenig Soldaten anwirbt, dann müssen sie lauter Herkulesse sein. Und wenn er ein Schlamper ist und kümmert sich um nix, dann müssen sie klug wie die Schlangen sein, sonst sind sie hin. So brauchts auch die ganz besondere Treue, wenn er ihnen immer zuviel zumutet. Lauter Tugenden, die ein ordentliches Land und ein guter König und Feldhauptmann nicht brauchen. In einem guten Land brauchts keine Tugenden, alle können ganz gewöhnlich sein, mittelgescheit und meinetwegen Feiglinge.

Der Feldhauptmann Ich wett, dein Vater war ein Soldat.

Eilif   I snatched up my sword and I split their skulls in two!

The General   You're a Caesar in the making. You ought to meet His Majesty.

Eilif   I saw him once, distantly. He kind of gives off light. I want to be just like him.

The General   You already are. I treasure you, Eilif, brave soldier boy, you're my own son, that's how I'll handle you.

He leads **Eilif** *to a big map.*

The General   Here's the picture, Eilif, the whole campaign. So much to do.

In the kitchen, **Courage** *stops eavesdropping and resumes plucking the chicken, furious.*

Mother Courage   That's one lousy General.

The Cook   No he's not, he eats to excess but he's good at what he does.

Mother Courage   If he knew what he was doing he wouldn't need brave soldiers, he could make do with ordinary soldiers. It's when the General's a moron the soldiers have to be brave. It's when the King's pinching his pennies and doesn't hire enough soldiers, every soldier has to be hard-working. You only need brave hard-working patriot soldiers when the country's coming unglued. In a decent country that's properly managed* with decent kings and generals, people can be just what people are, common and of middling intelligence and for all I care every one of them a shivering coward. In a decent country that's properly managed.

The General   A man like you was born a soldier.*

Eilif   Ein großer, hör ich. Meine Mutter hat mich gewarnt deshalb. Da kann ich ein Lied.

Der Feldhauptmann   Sings uns! (*Brüllend.*) Wirds bald mit dem Essen!

Eilif   Es heißt: Das Lied vom Weib und dem Soldaten. (*Er singt es, einen Kriegstanz mit dem Säbel tanzend.*)

Das Schießgewehr schießt, und das Spießmesser spießt
Und das Wasser frißt auf, die drin waten.
Was könnt ihr gegen Eis? Bleib weg, 's ist nicht weis!
Sagte das Weib zum Soldaten.
Doch der Soldat mit der Kugel im Lauf
Hörte die Trommel und lachte darauf:
Marschieren kann nimmermehr schaden!
Hinab nach dem Süden, nach dem Norden hinauf
Und das Messer fängt er mit Händen auf!
Sagten zum Weib die Soldaten.

Ach, bitter bereut, wer des Weisen Rat scheut
Und vom Alter sich nicht läßt beraten.
Ach, zu hoch nicht hinaus! Es geht übel aus!
Sagte das Weib zum Soldaten.
Doch der Soldat mit dem Messer im Gurt
Lacht ihr kalt ins Gesicht und ging über die Furt
Was konnte das Wasser ihm schaden?
Wenn weiß der Mond überm Schindeldach steht
Kommen wir wieder, nimms auf ins Gebet!
Sagten zum Weib die Soldaten.

Mutter Courage *in der Küche singt weiter, mit dem Löffel einen Topf schlagend.*

Eilif   My daddy was. A soldier. My mother taught me a song* about it.

The General   Sing it for me! (*Hollering.*) Where's my goddam food?!

Eilif   It's called 'The Song about the Soldier and His Wife'.

He sings, doing a sabre dance:

'Your gun is precise, and your bayonet's nice –
But the ice on the river won't hold you.
You'll drown in a trice if you march on the ice.
And lonely cold death shall enfold you!'

Thus spoke his wife, as he whetted his knife;
Hoisting his pack he said, 'Marching's my life!
When you're marching no woman can scold you.
When you're marching no woman can scold you.
We're marching into Poland,
Then we're marching off to Spain!
With your bayonet sharpened –
With your sharp bayonet you've no need to explain!
No woman ever controlled you!'

Oh bitter her tears, she was younger in years,
But wiser than he, so she told him.
March off if he must, it will all come to dust –
For only a coffin shall hold him.
Off goes her man, he will write when he can,
And women have wept since the world first began,
And her weeping has often consoled him.
The sound of her sorrow consoled him.

With the moon on the shingles,
Icy white on the snow,
Wave goodbye to your husband!
So long to your husband and then back home you go,
Where you'll wait for the fate you foretold him!

Mother Courage, *in the kitchen, takes up his song, beating time on a pot with spoon.*

Mutter Courage

Ihr vergeht wie der Rauch! Und die Wärme geht auch
Denn uns wärmen nicht eure Taten! Ach, wie schnell
geht der Rauch! Gott behüte ihn auch! Sagte das Weib
vom Soldaten.

Eilif   Was ist das?

Mutter Courage (*singt weiter*)   Und der Soldat mit dem
Messer am Gurt Sank hin mit dem Spieß, und mit riß ihn
die Furt Und das Wasser fraß auf, die drin waten. Kühl
stand der Mond überm Schindeldach weiß Doch der
Soldat trieb hinab mit dem Eis Und was sagten dem Weib
die Soldaten? Er verging wie der Rauch, und die Wärme
ging auch Denn es wärmten sie nicht seine Taten. Ach,
bitter bereut, wer des Weisen Rat scheut Sagte das Weib
zum Soldaten.

Der Feldhauptmann   Die erlauben sich heut allerhand
in meiner Küch.

Eilif (*ist in die Küche gegangen. Er umarmt seine Mutter*)
Daß ich dich wiederseh! Wo sind die andern?

Mutter Courage (*in seinen Armen*)   Wohlauf wie die Fisch
im Wasser. Der Schweizerkas ist Zahlmeister beim
Zweiten geworden; da kommt er mir wenigstens nicht ins
Gefecht, ganz konnt ich ihn nicht heraushalten.

Eilif   Und was macht dein Fußwerk?

Mutter Courage   Am Morgen komm ich halt schwer in
die Schuh.

Der Feldhauptmann (*ist dazugetreten*)   So, du bist die
Mutter. Ich hoff, du hast noch mehr Söhn für mich wie
den da.

Eilif   Wenn das nicht mein Glück ist: sitzt du da in der
Küch und hörst, wie dein Sohn ausgezeichnet wird!

Mutter Courage   Ja, ich habs gehört. (*Sie gibt ihm eine
Ohrfeige.*)

Eilif *sich die Backe haltend.*

Mother Courage (*singing*)
   It isn't a joke. Your life is like smoke.
   And someday you'll wish you had tarried.
   Oh, how quickly you'll fall. Oh God. Help us all.
   Soldiers should never get married.

Eilif   Who's that?

Mother Courage (*singing*)
   He tumbled the dice and he soon paid the price:
   They gave him his orders to march on the ice.
   And the water rose up all around him.
   And the water rose up and it drowned him.
   Through Poland, through Spain, his poor wife searched
      in vain.
   But he'd vanished, and she never found him.
   He was gone and his wife never found him.

The General   Who told them they could sing in my
kitchen?

Eilif *goes into the kitchen. He sees his mother. He embraces her.*

Eilif   I missed you! Where's everybody else?

Mother Courage *stays in his embrace.*

Mother Courage   Everyone's fine, stout as trout in a
brook. Swiss Cheese is paymaster for the Second
Regiment; that keeps him away from fighting, even if I
couldn't keep him out of the army.

Eilif   How are your feet?

Mother Courage   Too swollen for shoes in the morning.

The **General** *has joined them.*

The General   So you're his mother! Got any more sons
like this one?

Eilif   That's what my luck's like. You happen to be sitting
in the kitchen so you can hear your son called a hero.

Mother Courage   You're goddamned right I heard.

She slaps **Eilif**.

Eilif   Weil ich die Ochsen gefangen hab?

Mutter Courage   Nein. Weil du dich nicht ergeben hast, wie die vier auf dich losgegangen sind und haben aus dir Hackfleisch machen wollen! Hab ich dir nicht gelernt, daß du auf dich achtgeben sollst? Du finnischer Teufel!

Der **Feldhauptmann** *und der* **Feldprediger** *stehen lachend in der Tür.*

Three

Weitere drei Jahre später gerät **Mutter Courage** *mit Teilen eines finnischen Regiments in die Gefangenschaft. Ihre Tochter ist zu retten, ebenso ihr Planwagen, aber ihr redlicher Sohn stirbt.*

Feldlager. Nachmittag. An einer Stange die Regimentsfahne. **Mutter Courage** *hat von ihrem Planwagen, der reich mit allerhand Waren behangen ist, zu einer großen Kanone eine Wäscheleine gespannt und faltet mit* **Kattrin** *auf der Kanone Wäsche. Dabei handelt sie mit einem Zeugmeister um einen Sack Kugeln.* **Schweizerkas**, *nunmehr in der Montur eines Zahlmeisters, schaut zu.*

Eine hübsche Person, **Yvette Pottier**, *näht, ein Glas Branntwein vor sich, an einem bunten Hut. Sie ist in Strümpfen, ihre roten Stöckelschuhe stehen neben ihr.*

Der Zeugmeister   Ich geb Ihnen die Kugeln für zwei Gulden. Das ist billig, ich brauch das Geld, weil der Obrist seit zwei Tag mit die Offizier sauft und der Likör ausgegangen ist.

Mutter Courage   Das ist Mannschaftsmunition. Wenn die gefunden wird bei mir, komm ich vors Feldgericht. Ihr verkaufts die Kugeln, ihr Lumpen, und die Mannschaft hat nix zum Schießen vorm Feind.

Eilif (*holding his cheek*)   For taking the oxen?

Mother Courage   For not surrendering! Four peasants!?
Are you nuts?! I taught you always to watch out for
yourself! You brazen sticky-fingered fork-tongued son of a
Finn!*

The **General** *and the* **Chaplain** *laugh.*

Three

Three years later, **Mother Courage** *and the remnants of the second
Finnish regiment, still in Poland, are made prisoners of war. Her
daughter is saved, and also her wagon, but her honest son dies.*

The army camp.

*Afternoon. The regimental flag hangs from a flagpole. A clothes-
line stretches from* **Mother Courage**'*s wagon to the pole, and a
variety of merchandise is hanging from it. Near the wagon is a
large cannon, on which laundry has been draped for drying.*
Mother Courage *is simultaneously folding clothes that have
dried with* **Kattrin** *and negotiating the purchase of a sack of
bullets with a* **Quartermaster**. **Swiss Cheese**, *in his
paymaster's uniform, is watching all this.*

Yvette Pottier, *a pretty woman, sits nearby drinking brandy
and sewing vivid things to her hat. She's in her stockinged feet,
her red high-heeled shoes lying nearby.*

The Quartermaster   Two guilders. That's cheap for
bullets, but I need money now, the Colonel's been on a two-
day bender, celebrating with his staff, they drank us dry and
where am I supposed to get money for more liquor?

Mother Courage   Not from me. That's official
ammunition, they catch me holding a bag of that, I'll be
court-martialled and shot. You crooks sell the soldiers'
ammo out from under them, in the thick of battle
what're they supposed to do?* Throw rocks?

Der Zeugmeister   Sinds nicht hartherzig, eine Hand
wäscht die andre.

Mutter Courage   Heeresgut nehm ich nicht. Nicht für
den Preis.

Der Zeugmeister   Sie könnens für fünf Gulden, sogar
für acht noch heut abend diskret an den Zeugmeister
vom Vierten verkaufen, wenns ihm eine Quittung auf
zwölf Gulden ausstellen. Der hat überhaupt keine
Munition mehr.

Mutter Courage   Warum machens das nicht selber?

Der Zeugmeister   Weil ich ihm nicht trau, wir sind
befreundet.

Mutter Courage (*nimmt den Sack*)   Gib her. (*Zu* **Kattrin**.)
Trag hinter und zahl ihm eineinhalb Gulden aus. (*Auf des
Zeugmeisters Protest.*) Ich sag, eineinhalb Gulden. (**Kattrin**
schleppt den Sack hinter, der Zeugmeister folgt ihr. **Mutter
Courage** *zum Schweizerkas.*) Da hast du deine Unterhos
zurück, heb sie gut auf, es ist jetzt Oktober, und da kanns
leicht Herbst werden, ich sag ausdrücklich nicht muß,
denn ich hab gelernt, nix muß kommen, wie man denkt,
nicht einmal die Jahreszeiten. Aber deine Regimentskass
muß stimmen, wies auch kommt. Stimmt deine Kass?

Schweizerkas   Ja, Mutter.

Mutter Courage   Vergiß nicht, daß sie dich zum
Zahlmeister gemacht haben, weil du redlich bist und
nicht etwa kühn wie dein Bruder, und vor allem, weil du
so einfältig bist, daß du sicher nicht auf den Gedanken
kommst, damit wegzurennen, du nicht. Das beruhigt
mich recht. Und die Hos verleg nicht.

The Quartermaster   What am I supposed to do when he wants his wine, serve rainwater?

Mother Courage   It's immoral.* I don't want army ammunition. Not for two guilders.

The Quartermaster   Two little guilders, come on, buy them from me then sell them to the Fourth Regiment's quartermaster, the Fourth's clean out of bullets, he'll give you five guilders for them, eight guilders if you make him out a receipt says he paid twelve guilders, and one hand washes the other and who isn't happy?

Mother Courage   Go to the Fourth's quartermaster on your own, why do you need me?

The Quartermaster   I don't trust him and he doesn't trust me, we've been friends for years.

Mother Courage   Give.

She takes the sack and gives it to **Kattrin**.

Mother Courage (*to* **Kattrin**)   Stow this in the back and give the man one and a half guilders.

The **Quartermaster** *starts to complain; she stops him.*

Mother Courage   No more discussion.

Kattrin *drags the sack behind the wagon. The* **Quartermaster** *follows her.*

Mother Courage (*to* **Swiss Cheese**)   Here's your woollens, look after them, it's October and frosty soon, at any rate it should be, who knows, you can't expect anything with any certainty, not even fall following summer. Only one thing must be as must be: and that's your regimental cash box, whatever else is awry, you keep their cash pin-tidy. Is it pin-tidy?

Swiss Cheese   Yes, Mama.

Mother Courage   They made you paymaster because you're honest, you're not brave like your brother, they like it that you're too feeble-minded to get your mind around the idea of stealing it. Which puts my mind at ease. Cash in the cash box and where do the woollies go?

Schweizerkas   Nein, Mutter, ich geb sie unter die Matratz. (*Will gehen.*)

Der Zeugmeister   Ich geh mit dir, Zahlmeister.

Mutter Courage   Und lernens ihm nicht Ihre Kniffe!

*Der **Zeugmeister** ohne Gruß mit dem Schweizerkas ab.*

Yvette (*winkt ihm nach*)   Könntest auch grüßen, Zeugmeister!

Mutter Courage (*zu* **Yvette**)   Die seh ich nicht gern zusammen. Der ist keine Gesellschaft für meinen Schweizerkas. Aber der Krieg läßt sich nicht schlecht an. Bis alle Länder drin sind, kann er vier, fünf Jahr dauern wie nix. Ein bissel Weitblick und keine Unvorsichtigkeit, und ich mach gute Geschäft. Weißt du nicht, daß du nicht trinken sollst am Vormittag mit deiner Krankheit?

Yvette   Wer sagt, daß ich krank bin, das ist eine Verleumdung!

Mutter Courage   Alle sagens.

Yvette   Weil alle lügen. Mutter Courage, ich bin ganz verzweifelt, weil alle gehen um mich herum wie um einen faulen Fisch wegen dieser Lügen, wozu richt ich noch meinen Hut her? (*Sie wirft ihn weg.*) Drum trink ich am Vormittag, das hab ich nie gemacht, es gibt Krähenfüß, aber jetzt ist alles gleich. Beim Zweiten Finnischen kennen mich alle. Ich hätt zu Haus bleiben sollen, wie mein Erster mich verraten hat. Stolz ist nix für unsereinen, Dreck muß man schlucken können, sonst gehts abwärts.

Mutter Courage   Nur fang jetzt nicht wieder mit deinem Pieter an und wie alles gekommen ist, vor meiner unschuldigen Tochter.

Yvette   Grad soll sies hören, damit sie abgehärtet wird gegen die Liebe.

Swiss Cheese   Under my mattress, Mama, except when I'm wearing 'em.*

He starts to go.

The Quartermaster   Wait for me, paymaster, I'll go with you.

Mother Courage   Don't teach him your tricks.

The **Quartermaster** *walks off with* **Swiss Cheese**. **Yvette** *waves to the* **Quartermaster** *as he leaves. He doesn't wave back.*

Yvette   Whatever happened to 'So long, nice to meet you'?

Mother Courage (*to* **Yvette**)   I don't want my Swiss Cheese consorting with people like him, I don't even like to see them walking together, it makes me worry, though in general everything's OK, the war's going well, every other day fresh countries are joining in, it'll last four or five years easily. Thinking ahead and no impulsive moves, I can build a good business. And you, with your disease, don't you know you should lay off the booze?

Yvette   What disease, it's a lie, who says so?

Mother Courage   Everybody does.

Yvette   Everybody lies.* I'm panicked, Mother Courage, customers avoid me like the plague, it's like I hung a sign over my cootch saying 'Remember you must die.' Why the hell am I stitching new crap to this fucking hat?

She throws it to the ground.

I never used to drink in the morning, it gives you crow's feet, but so what? Pride isn't for people like us. If you can't learn to eat shit and like it, down you go.

Mother Courage   Here it comes, the why-oh-why and woe-is-me, your Piping Pieter and how he done you dirt. Just don't start your filthy yowling where my innocent daughter can hear you.

Yvette   Let her listen, she should learn what it's like to lose a man* and spend ten bad years looking everywhere for him, never finding him, she should learn what love is.

Mutter Courage   Da wird keine abgehärtet.

Yvette   Dann erzähl ichs, weil mir davon leichter wird.
Es fangt damit an, daß ich in dem schönen Flandern
aufgewachsen bin, ohne das hätt ich ihn nicht zu Gesicht
bekommen und säß nicht hier jetzt in Polen, denn er war
ein Soldatenkoch, blond, ein Holländer, aber mager.
Kattrin, hüt dich vor den Mageren, aber das wußt ich
damals noch nicht, auch nicht, daß er schon damals noch
eine andere gehabt hat und sie ihn überhaupt schon
Pfeifenpieter genannt haben, weil er die Pfeif nicht aus
dem Maul genommen hat dabei, so beiläufig wars bei
ihm. (*Sie singt das Lied vom Fraternisieren.*)

Ich war erst siebzehn Jahre
Da kam der Feind ins Land.
Er legte beiseit den Säbel
Und gab mir freundlich seine Hand.
　　Und nach der Maiandacht
　　Da kam die Maiennacht
　　Das Regiment stand im Geviert
　　Dann wurd getrommelt, wies der Brauch
　　Dann nahm der Feind uns hintern Strauch
　　Und hat fraternisiert.

Da waren viele Feinde
Und mein Feind war ein Koch
Ich haßte ihn bei Tage
Und nachts, da liebte ich ihn doch.
　　Denn nach der Maiandacht
　　Da kommt die Maiennacht
　　Das Regiment steht im Geviert
　　Dann wird getrommelt, wies der Brauch
　　Dann nimmt der Feind uns hintern Strauch
　　Und's wird fraternisiert.

Die Liebe, die ich spürte
War eine Himmelsmacht.
Meine Leut habens nicht begriffen
Daß ich ihn lieb und nicht veracht.
　　In einer trüben Früh
　　Begann mein Qual und Müh

Mother Courage   That's something they never learn.

Yvette   Then I'll talk just for the relief of talking, I need
some relief. It started in Flanders because I was a girl
there, if I'd been a girl someplace else I wouldn't have
seen him that day, Dutch, blond and thin, and now I'm in
Poland just because he cooked for the army, a thin cook.
What I didn't know then, Kattrin, is stay away from the
thin boys, and also I didn't know he had another
girlfriend or that they called him Piping Pieter because
even when he did it, he kept his pipe in his mouth, with
him doing it was just a casual thing.

Yvette *sings 'The Song of Fraternisation'.*

Yvette (*singing*)
 We hated the soldiers,
 Their army took our town.
 I was sixteen. The foreign occupier
 Grinned as he loosened my nightgown.
   May mornings are so bright.
   But comes the dark May night . . .
   The Captain shouts 'You're all dismissed!'
   Then boys with mischief in their eyes
   Will find the girls who fraternise.
   How could I hate him when we kissed?

 The foreign occupation
 Brought sorrows – and a cook!
 By day I would despise him, then when night fell,
 I loved the liberties that he took!

   May mornings are so bright.
   But comes the dark May night . . .
   The Captain shouts 'Boys, hit the hay!'
   But one with something on his mind
   Knows just the kind of girl to find.
   We fraternised till day.

 My oppressor and my lover
 For me were one and the same.
 Everyone said, 'Her love's just convenient.'
 What we agreed on was my shame.

Das Regiment stand im Geviert
Dann wurd getrommelt, wies der Brauch
Dann ist der Feind, mein Liebster auch
Aus unsrer Stadt marschiert.

Ich bin ihm leider nachgefahren, hab ihn aber nie
getroffen, es ist fünf Jahr her. (*Sie geht schwankend hinter
den Planwagen.*)

Mutter Courage Du hast deinen Hut liegenlassen.

Yvette Den kann haben, wer will.

Mutter Courage Laß dirs also zur Lehre dienen, Kattrin.
Nie fang mir was mit Soldatenvolk an. Die Liebe ist eine
Himmelsmacht, ich warn dich. Sogar mit die, wo nicht
beim Heer sind, ists kein Honigschlecken. Er sagt, er
möcht den Boden küssen, über den deine Füß gehn, hast
du sie gewaschen gestern, weil ich grad dabei bin, und
dann bist du sein Dienstbot. Sei froh, daß du stumm bist,
da widersprichst du dir nie oder willst dir nie die Zung
abbeißen, weil du die Wahrheit gesagt hast, das ist ein
Gottesgeschenk, Stummsein. Und da kommt der Koch
vom Feldhauptmann, was mag der wollen?

Der **Koch** *und der* **Feldprediger** *kommen.*

Der Feldprediger Ich bring Ihnen eine Botschaft von
Ihrem Sohn, dem Eilif, und der Koch ist gleich
mitgekommen, auf den haben Sie Eindruck gemacht.

Der Koch Ich bin nur mitgekommen, ein bissel Luft
schnappen.

Mutter Courage Das können Sie immer hier, wenn Sie
sich anständig aufführen, und auch sonst, ich werd fertig
mit euch. Was will er denn, ich hab kein Geld übrig.

Der Feldprediger Eigentlich sollt ich dem Bruder was
ausrichten, dem Herrn Zahlmeister.

Mutter Courage Der ist nicht mehr hier und woanders
auch nicht. Der ist nicht seinem Bruder sein Zahlmeister.
Er soll ihn nicht in Versuchung führen und gegen ihn
klug sein. (*Gibt ihm Geld aus der umgehängten Tasche.*)

A cloud that hid the sun
Announced my joy was done.
You have your fun but troops move on.
You wait all night. Where can he be?
Your lover and your enemy?
His army's marching, and he's . . . gone.

She stumbles back behind the wagon. As she goes:

Mother Courage   Your hat.

Yvette   Anyone wants it, be my guest.

She goes behind the wagon.

Mother Courage   You heard, Kattrin? Don't start up with soldiers.* He tells you he wants to kiss the ground over which your delicate feet have trod – and did you wash your delicate feet yesterday, as long as we're talking about feet – and bang, you're his goat cow mule and whatever else he's itching after. Be happy you're a mute, when you've finally got a husband you'll never contradict yourself or bite your tongue because you told the truth, it's a blessing from God, being dumb. And here comes the General's cook, what brought him?

The **Cook** *and the* **Chaplain** *enter.*

The Chaplain   I bring a message from your son, Eilif, and the cook wanted to accompany me, you've made an impression.

The Cook   I accompanied you for the exercise and air.

Mother Courage   Air's free so breathe all you want, just mind your manners, and if you forget, I'm ready for you. (*To the* **Chaplain**.) So what's Eilif want? I have no extra money.

The Chaplain   Truth to be told the message is for his brother, Mr Paymaster.

Mother Courage   He isn't his brother's paymaster. And he's gone, so he can't get led into temptation by bright ideas.

She takes money from her money belt and hands it to the **Chaplain**.

Geben Sie ihm das, es ist eine Sünde, er spekuliert auf die Mutterliebe und soll sich schämen.

Der Koch   Nicht mehr lang, dann muß er aufbrechen mit dem Regiment, wer weiß, vielleicht in den Tod. Sie sollten noch was zulegen, hinterher bereuen Sies. Ihr Weiber seid hart, aber hinterher bereut ihr. Ein Gläschen Branntwein hätt seinerzeit nix ausgemacht, ist aber nicht gegeben worden, und wer weiß, dann liegt einer unterm grünen Rasen, und ihr könnt ihn euch nicht mehr ausscharren.

Der Feldprediger   Werden Sie nicht gerührt, Koch. In dem Krieg fallen ist eine Gnad und keine Ungelegenheit, warum? Es ist ein Glaubenskrieg. Kein gewöhnlicher, sondern ein besonderer, wo für den Glauben geführt wird, und also Gott wohlgefällig.

Der Koch   Das ist richtig. In einer Weis ist es ein Krieg, indem daß gebrandschatzt, gestochen und geplündert wird, bissel schänden nicht zu vergessen, aber unterschieden von alle andern Kriege dadurch, daß es ein Glaubenskrieg ist, das ist klar. Aber er macht auch Durst, das müssen Sie zugeben.

Der Feldprediger (*zu* **Mutter Courage**, *auf den* **Koch** *zeigend*)   Ich hab ihn abzuhalten versucht, aber er hat gesagt, Sie habens ihm angetan, er träumt von Ihnen.

Der Koch (*zündet sich eine Stummelpfeife an*)   Bloß daß ich ein Glas Branntwein krieg von schöner Hand, nix Schlimmeres. Aber ich bin schon geschlagen genug, weil der Feldprediger den ganzen Weg her solche Witze gemacht hat, daß ich noch jetzt rot sein muß.

Mutter Courage   Und im geistlichen Gewand! Ich werd euch was zu trinken geben müssen, sonst macht ihr mir noch einen unsittlichen Antrag vor Langeweil.

Der Feldprediger   Das ist eine Versuchung, sagte der Hofprediger und erlag ihr. (*Im Gehen sich nach* **Kattrin** *umwendend.*) Und wer ist diese einnehmende Person?

Mother Courage Give this to him, it's a sin, calculating on maternal instinct and he should be ashamed of himself.

The Cook His regiment's marching out, who knows, maybe off to die. Add a little to that pittance, lady, or later on you'll regret. You women come on hard, but later on, you regret. A guy pleads for a glass of brandy, but you're not feeling generous, so the brandy isn't flowing, and he goes off dry, next thing he's dead under the green green ground in some place far away and, oh, you wish you could serve him that brandy now, but forget it, he's gone where you'll never claw him up.

The Chaplain Any soldier who falls in a religious war will go straight to heaven, where he can have all the brandy he wants.*

The Cook Point taken,* though still the woman who turns him away without a little brandy to burn his belly should burn with shame, and not because he's a holy kind of soldier – she shouldn't turn him away unrefreshed even if he was just your normal undistinguished infidel infantryman off to meet St Peter with all his venality, shooting and looting, and don't forget a rape here and there, completely unexculpated by virtue of his having done all those things but in the service of his Protestant faith. Thirsty's thirsty is my point.

The Chaplain (*to* **Mother Courage**, *indicating the* **Cook**) I didn't want him to come with me but he says he's dreaming about you.

The Cook (*lighting his pipe*) Brandy poured by a slender hand, nothing contemptible on my mind.*

Mother Courage Who'd say no to a drink?

The Chaplain Temptation! shrieked the Bishop, and fell. (*Looking at* **Kattrin**.) And who is this comely young lady?

Mutter Courage   Das ist keine einnehmende, sondern eine anständige Person.

Der **Feldprediger** *und der* **Koch** *gehen mit* **Mutter Courage** *hinter den Wagen.* **Kattrin** *schaut ihnen nach und geht dann von der Wäsche weg, auf den Hut zu. Sie hebt ihn auf und setzt sich, die roten Schuhe anziehend. Man hört von hinten* **Mutter Courage** *mit dem* **Feldprediger** *und dem* **Koch** *politisieren.*

Mutter Courage   Die Polen hier in Polen hätten sich nicht einmischen sollen. Es ist richtig, unser König ist bei ihnen eingerückt mit Roß und Mann und Wagen, aber anstatt daß die Polen den Frieden aufrechterhalten haben, haben sie sich eingemischt in ihre eigenen Angelegenheiten und den König angegriffen, wie er gerad in aller Ruh dahergezogen ist. So haben sie sich eines Friedensbruchs schuldig gemacht, und alles Blut kommt auf ihr Haupt.

Der Feldprediger   Unser König hat nur die Freiheit im Aug gehabt. Der Kaiser hat alle unterjocht, die Polen so gut wie die Deutschen, und der König hat sie befreien müssen.

Der Koch   So seh ichs, Ihr Branntwein ist vorzüglich, ich hab mich nicht getäuscht in Ihrem Gesicht, aber weil wir

Mother Courage She isn't comely, she's stay-at-homely, and I don't want clergy sniffing up my daughter.*

The Cook Keep a gimlet eye on this dirty dog, you oughta hear his jokes! Revolting!

The **Chaplain** *and the* **Cook** *go behind the wagon with* **Mother Courage**. **Kattrin** *watches them leave, then she leaves her washing and goes to* **Yvette**'s *hat. She puts it on, then sits and puts on the red shoes. From behind the wagon* **Mother Courage** *is heard talking politics with the* **Chaplain** *and the* **Cook**.

Mother Courage What's the news from the front?*

The Cook Nobody knows where that is.

Mother Courage It's a mess. It was a nice peaceful invasion, the Swedish king rolled in with his troops and horses and wagons, waving the Protestant flag, he rolled here, he rolled there, he's ready to roll back to Sweden and now, now the Poles break the peace and look, blood's poured down on their heads.

The Cook The way I see it is, I knew you'd serve exquisite brandy, I never misread a face.

The Chaplain All our King ever wanted was to set Poland free from the tyranny of the Pope and his crony the Kaiser.

In front of the wagon, **Kattrin**, *checking to make sure she's not being seen, wearing the hat and shoes, begins imitating* **Yvette**'s *provocative walk. As she continues she abandons the imitation; she becomes more confident, more mature, a pretty young woman. She even dances a little. The talk behind the wagon is continuous.*

The Cook Absolutely. Liberty! Everybody craves liberty, the human body needs it like it needs water or bread or salt. Who knows why we need liberty? What humans need is a mystery. Who knows why we need salt? We need what we need.

The Chaplain Amen.

The Cook But it's expensive, liberty, especially when you start exporting it to other countries, so the King has

vom König sprechen, die Freiheit, wo er hat einführen
wollen in Deutschland, hat sich der König genug kosten
lassen, indem er die Salzsteuer eingeführt hat in
Schweden, was die armen Leut, wie gesagt, was gekostet
hat, und dann hat er die Deutschen noch einsperren und
vierteilen lassen müssen, weil sie an ihrer Knechtschaft
gegenüber dem Kaiser festgehalten haben. Freilich, wenn
einer nicht hat frei werden wolln, hat der König keinen
Spaß gekannt. Zuerst hat er nur Polen schützen wolln vor
böse Menschen, besonders dem Kaiser, aber dann ist
mitn Essen der Appetit gekommen, und er hat ganz
Deutschland geschützt. Es hat sich nicht schlecht
widersetzt. So hat der gute König nix wie Ärger gehabt
von seiner Güte und Auslagen, und die hat er natürlich
durch Steuern reinbringen lassen müssen, was böses Blut
erzeugt hat, aber er hat sichs nicht verdrießen lassen. Er
hat eins für sich gehabt, da war Gottes Wort, das war
noch gut. Denn sonst hätts noch geheißen, er tuts für
sich und weil er Gewinnst haben will. So hat er immer ein
gutes Gewissen gehabt, das war ihm die Hauptsach.

to levy a tax on salt back home in Sweden, so his own
subjects are free but they can't afford salt, or, well, the
poor can't afford it, the rich can afford anything, even
when it's taxed and pricey, and even better, the rich get
tax exemptions!

The Chaplain   You shouldn't mock liberty. It's –

The Cook   Who's mocking?

Mother Courage   He isn't mocking anything, he's a
cook, cooks have an intellectual bent, not like preachers.

The Cook   I'm talking about the human body.

Mother Courage   Right.

The Cook   A lovely thing, the human body.

The Chaplain   Created in God's image.

The Cook   You bet. Given half a chance, it'll do a little
jig. It's stubborn, though. The body. Or is that the soul?
Preacher? I get confused.

The Chaplain   I'm sure you do.

The Cook   It's the wanting that makes 'em stubborn, is
my point. So sometimes you have to torture the people –
which by the way adds to the cost of the war, since
contrary to expectations the Poles have preferred to
remain unliberated, the King's tried everything, the rack
and the screw and prisons are expensive, and when the
King discovered they didn't want to be free, even after
torture, he stopped having any fun. But God told our
King to fight, He didn't say it'd be fun, and it isn't much
fun, is it, though since I cook for the General I have table
salt at least, and the rest of it's beyond me, what bodies
want and what bodies get, and it's a good thing the King's
got God going for him. Or else people might suspect that
he's just in it for what he can take out of it. But he's
always had his principles, our King, and with his clear
conscience he doesn't get depressed.

Mutter Courage   Man merkt, Sie sind kein Schwed, sonst würden Sie anders vom Heldenkönig reden.

Der Feldprediger   Schließlich essen Sie sein Brot.

Der Koch   Ich ess nicht sein Brot, sondern ich backs ihm.

Mutter Courage   Besiegt werden kann er nicht, warum, seine Leut glauben an ihn. (*Ernsthaft.*) Wenn man die Großkopfigen* reden hört, führens die Krieg nur aus Gottesfurcht und für alles, was gut und schön is. Aber wenn man genauer hinsieht, sinds nicht so blöd, sondern führn die Krieg für Gewinn. Und anders würden die kleinen Leut wie ich auch nicht mitmachen.

Der Koch   So is es.

Der Feldprediger   Und Sie täten gut als Holländer, sich die Flagg anzusehen, die hier aufgezogen ist, bevor Sie eine Meinung äußern in Polen.

Mutter Courage   Hie gut evangelisch allewege. Prosit!

Kattrin *hat begonnen, mit* **Yvettes** *Hut auf dem Kopf herumzustolzieren,* **Yvettes** *Gang kopierend.*

Plötzlich hört man Kanonendonner und Schüsse. Trommeln. **Mutter Courage**, *der* **Koch** *und der* **Feldprediger** *stürzen hinter dem Wagen vor, die beiden letzteren noch die Gläser in der Hand. Der* **Zeugmeister** *und ein* **Soldat** *kommen zur Kanone gelaufen und versuchen, sie wegzuschieben.*

Mutter Courage   Was ist denn los? Ich muß doch erst meine Wäsch wegtun, ihr Lümmel. (*Sie versucht ihre Wäsche zu retten.*)

Der Zeugmeister   Die Katholischen! Ein Überfall. Wir wissen nicht, ob wir noch wegkommen. (*Zum* **Soldaten**) Bring das Geschütz weg! (*Läuft weiter.*)

Mother Courage   Long live Gustavus Adolphus, the
Hero-King. About whom a certain kind of talk is
unhealthy.

The Chaplain (*to the* **Cook**)   You eat his bread.

The Cook   I don't eat it, I bake it.

Mother Courage   The King will never be defeated, and
why, his people believe in him, and why? Precisely because
everyone knows he's in the war to make a profit. If he
wasn't, little people like me would smell disaster in the war
and steer away from it. If it's business, it makes sense.*

The Cook   Here's to the little people like you.

The Chaplain   Hey, Dutchman, it would be advisable to
cast a glance at the Swedish flag that's flying overhead
before sharing your opinions so liberally.

Mother Courage   No harm done. Nobody here but us
Protestants! Alley-oop!

*They toast and drink, we hear the clink of their glasses. Suddenly
cannon thunder and rifle shots are heard.* **Mother Courage**,
the **Cook** *and the* **Chaplain** *rush around from behind the
wagon, the* **Cook** *and* **Chaplain** *with brandy glasses in hand.*

Mother Courage   What's happened?

The **Quartermaster** *and a* **Soldier** *rush in and begin to wheel
the cannon away, clothes hanging all over it.*

Mother Courage   I have to take the laundry down first,
you idiots.

She scrambles to retrieve her laundry.

The Quartermaster   The Catholics! Attacking! There
wasn't any warning, I don't know if we have time to –

An increase in the sound of fighting, drums and alarms.

(*To the* **Soldier**.) Do something about the cannon!

The **Quartermaster** *runs away. The* **Soldier** *tries with all his
might to move the cannon, which won't budge.*

Der Koch   Um Gottes willen, ich muß zum
Feldhauptmann. Courage, ich komm nächster Tag einmal
herüber zu einer kleinen Unterhaltung. (*Stürzt ab.*)

Mutter Courage   Halt, Sie haben Ihre Pfeif liegen
lassen!

Der Koch (*von weitem*)   Heben Sie sie mir auf! Ich
brauch sie.

Mutter Courage   Grad jetzt, wo wir ein bissel verdient
haben!

Der Feldprediger   Ja, dann geh ich halt auch. Freilich,
wenn der Feind schon so nah heran ist, möchts
gefährlich sein. Selig sind die Friedfertigen, heißts im
Krieg. Wenn ich einen Mantel über hätt.

Mutter Courage   Ich leih keine Mäntel aus, und wenns
das Leben kostet. Ich hab schlechte Erfahrungen
gemacht.

Der Feldprediger   Aber ich bin besonders gefährdet
wegen meinem Glauben.

Mutter Courage (*holt ihm einen Mantel*)   Ich tus gegen
mein besseres Gewissen. Laufen Sie schon.

Der Feldprediger   Schönen Dank, das ist großherzig von
Ihnen, aber vielleicht bleib ich noch besser sitzen hier,
ich möcht Verdacht erregen und den Feind auf mich
ziehn, wenn ich laufend gesehn werd.

Mutter Courage (*zum* **Soldaten**)   Laß sie doch stehn, du
Esel, wer zahlts dir? Ich nehm sie dir in Verwahrung, und
dich kostets Leben.

Der Soldat (*weglaufend*)   Sie können bezeugen, ich habs
versucht.

Mutter Courage   Ich schwörs. (*Sieht ihre Tochter mit dem
Hut.*) Was machst denn du mit dem Hurenhut? Willst du
gleich den Deckel abnehmen, du bist wohl
übergeschnappt? Jetzt, wo der Feind kommt? (*Sie reißt
Kattrin den Hut vom Kopf.*) Sollen sie dich entdecken und

The Cook Better get back to my general, if they haven't shot him* he'll be screaming for dinner. Look for me, Courage, I'll be back for more political debate.

He starts to leave.

Mother Courage You're leaving your pipe!

The Cook (*exiting*) Keep it for me, I'll need it.

Mother Courage Of course, just when we're starting to clear a profit the sky falls in.

The Chaplain I'll be making tracks myself, if the enemy breaks through there's apt to be serious trouble. Blessed are the peaceable, that's my battle cry. I need a big cloak for camouflage.

Mother Courage I'm not lending cloaks or anything else, not if it costs your life. I've gone that route before.

The Chaplain But my religious calling puts me in particular jeopardy.

She hands him a cloak.

Mother Courage This rubs against my better impulses. Now get lost.

The Chaplain Many thanks, it's big-hearted of you, but on further consideration it might be better to settle here for a bit.

Mother Courage (*turning to the* **Soldier** *struggling with the cannon*) Drop it you donkey, who's paying you to do that? I'll watch it for you, it's not worth your life.

The Soldier (*running away*) You can tell them I tried!

Mother Courage I'll swear on the Bible.*

She sees her daughter with **Yvette**'s *hat.*

Mother Courage What're you doing in that hooker's hat? Take that off, are you cracked? Now, with the enemy coming?

She tears the hat off **Kattrin**'s *head.*

zur Hur machen? Und die Schuh hat sie sich angezogen, diese Babylonische! Herunter mit die Schuh! (*Sie will sie ihr ausziehen.*) Jesus, hilf mir, Herr Feldprediger, daß sie den Schuh runterbringt! Ich komm gleich wieder. (*Sie läuft zum Wagen.*)

Yvette (*kommt, sich pudernd*)   Was sagen Sie, die Katholischen kommen? Wo ist mein Hut? Wer hat auf ihm herumgetrampelt? So kann ich doch nicht herumlaufen, wenn die Katholischen kommen. Was denken die von mir? Spiegel hab ich auch nicht. (*Zum* **Feldprediger**) Wie schau ich aus? Ist es zu viel Puder?

Der Feldprediger   Grad richtig.

Yvette   Und wo sind die roten Schuh? (*Sie findet sie nicht, weil* **Kattrin** *die Füße unter den Rock zieht.*) Ich hab sie hier stehnlassen. Ich muß in mein Zelt hinüber, barfuß. Das ist eine Schand! (*Ab.*)

Schweizerkas *kommt gelaufen, eine kleine Schatulle tragend.*

Mutter Courage (*kommt mit den Händen voll Asche. Zu* **Kattrin**)   Da hab ich Asche. (*Zu* **Schweizerkas**) Was schleppst du da?

Schweizerkas   Die Regimentskass.

Mutter Courage   Wirf sie weg! Es hat sich ausgezahlmeistert.

Schweizerkas   Die ist anvertraut. (*Er geht nach hinten.*)

Mother Courage You want them stumbling across you and making you their whore? And you've put on the shoes too, haven't you, you scarlet Babylonian?! Take 'em off, now now now!

Courage tries to yank the shoes off **Kattrin***'s feet. Then she turns to the* **Chaplain***.*

Mother Courage Jesus, help me, Pastor, get her shoes off. I'll be back in a minute.

She runs to the wagon. **Yvette** *comes in, powdering herself.*

Yvette Is it the Catholics? Oh please God let it be the Catholics! Where's my hat? (*She sees the hat on the ground.*) Who stomped on it? I can't run around in that, not if it's Catholics, they're finnicky about costumes.* I gotta get to a mirror. And where are the shoes?

She looks around for them, not seeing them, because **Kattrin** *has hidden her feet under her skirt.*

Yvette They were here when I left them. I'll have to walk back to my tent barefoot. It's mortifying. (*To the* **Chaplain***.*) What do you think? Too heavy with the make-up?

The Chaplain You're perfect.

Yvette *leaves.* **Swiss Cheese** *runs in, carrying a metal cash box.* **Mother Courage** *comes out of the wagon, her hands full of soot.*

Mother Courage (*to* **Kattrin***)* Here. Soot. For you. (To **Swiss Cheese***.*) What're you lugging there?

Swiss Cheese It's the regimental cash box.

Mother Courage Get rid of that! You're not the paymaster any more.*

Swiss Cheese I am. It's my responsibility.

He goes behind the wagon.

Mutter Courage (*zum* **Feldprediger**)   Zieh den
geistlichen Rock ab, Feldprediger, sonst kennen sie dich
trotz dem Mantel. (*Sie reibt* **Kattrin** *das Gesicht ein mit
Asche.*) Halt still! So, ein bissel Dreck, und du bist sicher.
So ein Unglück! Die Feldwachen sind besoffen gewesen.
Sein Licht muß man unter den Scheffel stellen, heißt es.
Ein Soldat, besonders ein katholischer, und ein sauberes
Gesicht, und gleich ist die Hur fertig. Sie kriegen
wochenlang nichts zu fressen, und wenn sie dann
kriegen, durch Plündern, fallen sie über die
Frauenzimmer her. Jetzt mags angehn. Laß dich
anschaun. Nicht schlecht. Wie wenn du im Dreck
gewühlt hättst. Zitter nicht. So kann dir nix geschehn.
(*Zum* **Schweizerkas**.) Wo hast du die Kass gelassen?

Schweizerkas   Ich dacht, ich geb sie in den Wagen.

Mutter Courage (*entsetzt*)   Was, in meinen Wagen? So
eine gottssträfliche Dummheit! Wenn ich einmal
wegschau! Aufhängen tun sie uns alle drei!

Schweizerkas   Dann geb ich sie woanders hin oder
flücht damit.

Mutter Courage   Hier bleibst du, das ist zu spät.

Der Feldprediger (*halb umgezogen nach vorn*)   Um
Himmels willen, die Fahn!

Mutter Courage (*nimmt die Regimentsfahne herunter*)
Bosche moye! Mir fällt die schon gar nicht mehr auf.
Fünfundzwanzig Jahr hab ich die.

Der Kanonendonner wird lauter.

An einem Vormittag, drei Tage später. Die Kanone ist weg.
Mutter Courage, **Kattrin**, *der* **Feldprediger** *und*
Schweizerkas *sitzen bekümmert zusammen beim Essen.*

Schweizerkas   Das ist schon der dritte Tag, daß ich hier
faul herumsitz, und der Herr Feldwebel, wo immer
nachsichtig zu mir gewesen ist, möcht langsam fragen: wo
ist denn der Schweizerkas mit der Soldschatull?

Mutter Courage   Sei froh, daß sie dir nicht auf die Spur
gekommen sind.

Mother Courage (*to the* **Chaplain**)   Take off your clerical get-up, Pastor, they'll see it under the cloak.

She rubs soot all over **Kattrin**'s *face.*

Mother Courage   Hold still! A little filth, a little bit safer. What a disaster! Bet the sentries guarding the camp got drunk. Hide your light under a bushel, just like they say. A soldier sees a girl with a clean face, watch out! When he's done raping her,* he calls for his buddies. (*Looking at* **Kattrin**'s *face.*) That oughta do it. Let me look. Not bad. Like you've been rolling in shit. Don't shiver. Now nothing will happen to you. (*To* **Swiss Cheese**.) Where'd you leave the cash box?

Swiss Cheese   I figured it should go in the wagon.

Mother Courage (*horrified*)   In my wagon? Of all the godforsaken blockheadedness. If I don't watch every second! They'll hang us, all three of us!

Swiss Cheese   Then I'll put it someplace else, or I could take it and run away.

Mother Courage   Stay here, too late for that.

The **Chaplain***, changing his clothes, notices the regimental flag.*

The Chaplain   Oh my goodness, the flag!

Mother Courage *takes down the flag.*

Mother Courage   Holy crap! Blinded by habit! I've flown it for twenty-five years.

The cannons' thunder gets louder.

Mid-morning, three days later. The cannon that had been next to the wagon is gone. **Mother Courage**, **Kattrin**, **Swiss Cheese** *and the* **Chaplain***, nervous, burdened, eating together.*

Swiss Cheese   It's three days now and I'm wasting time sitting around and the Sergeant, who was always nice to me even when I made mistakes, has finally got to be asking himself: where's that Swiss Cheese gone with the regimental cash box?

Mother Courage   Just be glad they haven't come sniffing around here.

Der Feldprediger   Was soll ich sagen? Ich kann auch nicht eine Andacht halten hier, sonst möchts mir schlecht gehn. Wem das Herz voll ist, dem läuft das Maul über, heißts, aber weh, wenns mir überläuft!

Mutter Courage   So ists. Ich hab hier einen sitzen mit einem Glauben und einen mit einer Kass. Ich weiß nicht, was gefährlicher ist.

Der Feldprediger   Wir sind eben jetzt in Gottes Hand.

Mutter Courage   Ich glaub nicht, daß wir schon so verloren sind, aber schlafen tu ich doch nicht nachts. Wenn du nicht wärst, Schweizerkas, wärs leichter. Ich glaub, daß ich mirs gericht hab. Ich hab ihnen gesagt, daß ich gegen den Antichrist bin, den Schweden, wo Hörner aufhat, und daß ichs gesehn hab, das linke Horn ist ein bissel abgeschabt. Mitten im Verhör hab ich gefragt, wo ich Weihkerzen einkaufen kann, nicht zu teuer. Ich habs gut gekonnt, weil dem Schweizerkas sein Vater katholisch gewesen ist und oft drüber Witz gemacht hat. Sie habens mir nicht ganz geglaubt, aber sie haben keine Marketender beim Regiment. So haben sie ein Aug zugedrückt. Vielleicht schlägts sogar zum Guten aus. Wir sind gefangen, aber so wie die Laus im Pelz.

Der Feldprediger   Die Milch ist gut. Was die Quantitäten betrifft, werden wir unsere schwedischen Appetite ja jetzt etwas einschränken müssen. Wir sind eben besiegt.

Mutter Courage   Wer ist besiegt? Die Sieg und Niederlagen der Großkopfigen oben und der von unten fallen nämlich nicht immer zusammen, durchaus nicht. Es gibt sogar Fälle, wo die Niederlag für die Untern eigentlich ein Gewinn ist für sie. Die Ehr ist verloren, aber nix sonst. Ich erinner mich, einmal im Livländischen hat unser Feldhauptmann solche Dresche vom Feind eingesteckt, daß ich in der Verwirrung sogar einen Schimmel aus der Bagage gekriegt hab, der hat mir den Wagen sieben Monat lang gezogen, bis wir gesiegt haben und Revision war. Im allgemeinen kann man sagen, daß uns gemeinen Leuten Sieg und Niederlag teuer zu stehn kommen. Das Beste für uns ist, wenn die Politik nicht recht vom Fleck kommt. (*Zu Schweizerkas:* Iß!)

The Chaplain   Amen. Unobjectionable is our only hope.
He whose heart is full of woe must sing out loud, as they
say, but God and all the apostles forfend I should start
singing now! I don't know any Latin hymns.*

Mother Courage   One's got his cash box and the other's
got an ecclesiastical sense of humour* and I'm stuck
between the two and I don't know which is worse.

The Chaplain   Even now God's watching over us.

Mother Courage   Which explains why I'm not sleeping
well. God and your cash box keep me awake. I think I've
straightened my own position out. I told them I was a
good Catholic and adamantly opposed to Satan, I'd seen
him, Satan, he's a Swede with ram's horns. I stopped to
ask if they knew where I could buy votive candles. I've got
that churchy talk down pat. I know they knew I was lying
but they don't have any commissary wagons, so they
squint a little. It could still work out well for us. We're
prisoners, but so are head lice.

The Chaplain   It's good milk. Albeit available only in
small quantities, we may have to curb our Swedish
appetites. Since we're defeated.

Mother Courage   Victory, defeat,* depends on your
perspective. Defeat is frequently profitable for
underdogs. Honour's lost, but what's that? What works
out best for us is what they call paralysis, a shot here, a
shot there, one step forward, one back, and troops going
no place needing provisions. (*To* **Swiss Cheese**.) Eat!

Schweizerkas   Mir schmeckts nicht. Wie soll der
Feldwebel den Sold auszahlen?

Mutter Courage   Auf der Flucht wird kein Sold
ausgezahlt.

Schweizerkas   Doch, sie haben Anspruch. Ohne Sold
brauchen sie nicht flüchten. Sie müssen keinen Schritt
machen.

Mutter Courage   Schweizerkas, deine Gewissenhaftigkeit
macht mir fast Angst. Ich hab dir beigebracht, du sollst
redlich sein, denn klug bist du nicht, aber es muß seine
Grenzen haben. Ich geh jetzt mit dem Feldprediger eine
katholische Fahn einkaufen und Fleisch. So wie der kann
keiner Fleisch aussuchen, wie im Schlafwandel, so sicher.
Ich glaub, er merkts gute Stückl dran, daß ihm
unwillkürlich das Wasser im Maul zusammenläuft. Nur
gut, daß sie mir meinen Handel erlauben. Ein Händler
wird nicht nach dem Glauben gefragt,* sondern nach
dem Preis. Und evangelische Hosen halten auch warm.

Der Feldprediger   Wie der Bettelmönch gesagt hat, wie
davon die Red war, daß die Lutherischen alles auf den
Kopf stelln werden in Stadt und Land: Bettler wird man
immer brauchen. (**Mutter Courage** *verschwindet im
Wagen.*) Um die Schatull sorgt sie sich doch. Bisher sind
wir unbemerkt geblieben, als gehörten wir alle zum
Wagen, aber wie lang?

Schweizerkas   Ich kann sie wegschaffen.

Der Feldprediger   Das ist beinah noch gefährlicher.
Wenn dich einer sieht! Sie haben Spitzel. Gestern früh ist
einer vor mir aufgetaucht aus dem Graben, wie ich meine
Notdurft verrichtet hab. Ich erschreck und kann grad
noch ein Stoßgebet zurückhalten. Das hätt mich
verraten. Ich glaub, die röchen am liebsten noch am Kot,
obs ein Evangelischer ist. Der Spitzel war so ein kleiner
Verrecker mit einer Bind über einem Aug.

Swiss Cheese   I don't want to eat. How's the Sergeant
going to pay the soldiers?

Mother Courage   They're retreating, they don't get paid
when they're retreating.

Swiss Cheese   If they don't get paid to do it they
shouldn't retreat.

Mother Courage   Swiss Cheese, your conscientiousness
is terrifying. Since you're stupid I decided to raise you to
be honest but really it's getting out of hand. Now I'm
taking the Chaplain to buy a Catholic flag and some
meat. Nobody noses out good meat like the Chaplain,
when there's good meat anywhere in the area you can tell
because there are little spit bubbles in the corners of his
mouth and his lips get shiny. Everything's going to be all
right as long as they let me do business. Protestant pants
cover your ass same as any other.

The Chaplain   Martin Luther met a priest* who was
begging for alms by the side of the road. Luther said to
the beggar priest, 'After I turn the world inside out we
won't need priests!' 'Maybe not,' said the priest, 'but
you'll still need beggars,' and he went on his way.

Mother Courage *has gone into the wagon.*

The Chaplain   That cash box is weighing on her.
Everyone thinks we all belong to the wagon, but how long
before they come to investigate?

Swiss Cheese   I can take it someplace else.

The Chaplain   That could mean trouble for us all if they
catch you doing it. They've got spies everywhere.
Yesterday morning I was relieving myself in an open-air
latrine. I'd just started to squat when a spy jumped up!
Right out of the latrine!

Swiss Cheese   He was in the latrine?*

The Chaplain   Yes! *In* the latrine!

Swiss Cheese   Why was he in the latrine?

The Chaplain   Sniffing out Protestants! Probably sleeps
down there. This one was a little stump of a man with a
patch over his eye. I screamed and almost ejaculated a
prayer, in Swedish, which would have been the end of me.

Mutter Courage (*mit einem Korb aus dem Wagen kletternd*)
Und was hab ich gefunden, du schamlose Person? (*Sie hebt triumphierend rote Stöckelschuhe hoch.*) Die roten Stöckelschuh der Yvette! Sie hat sie kaltblütig gegrapscht. Weil Sie ihr eingeredet haben, daß sie eine einnehmende Person ist! (*Sie legt sie in den Korb.*) Ich geb sie zurück. Der Yvette die Schuh stehlen! Die richt sich zugrund fürs Geld, das versteh ich. Aber du möchtst es umsonst, zum Vergnügen. Ich hab dirs gesagt, du mußt warten, bis Frieden ist. Nur keinen Soldaten! Wart du auf den Frieden mit der Hoffart!

Der Feldprediger   Ich find sie nicht hoffärtig.

Mutter Courage   Immer noch zu viel. Wenn sie ist wie ein Stein in Dalarne, wos nix andres gibt, so daß die Leut sagen: den Krüppel sieht man gar nicht, ist sie mir am liebsten. Solang passiert ihr nix. (*Zu* **Schweizerkas**.) Du läßt die Schatull, wo sie ist, hörst du. Und gib auf deine Schwester acht, sie hats nötig. Ihr bringt mich noch unter den Boden. Lieber einen Sack Flöh hüten.

Sie geht mit dem **Feldprediger** *weg.* **Kattrin** *räumt das Geschirr auf.*

Schweizerkas   Nicht mehr viele Tag, wo man in Hemdärmeln in der Sonne sitzen kann. (**Kattrin** *deutet auf einen Baum.*) Ja, die Blätter sind bereits gelb. (**Kattrin** *fragt ihn mit Gesten, ob er trinken will.*) Ich trink nicht. Ich denk nach. (*Pause.*) Sie sagt, sie schlaft nicht. Ich sollt die Schatull doch wegbringen, ich hab ein Versteck ausgefunden. Hol mir doch ein Glas voll. (*Kattrin geht hinter den Wagen.*) Ich gebs in das Maulwurfsloch am Fluß, bis ichs abhol. Ich hol sie vielleicht schon heut nacht gegen Morgen zu ab und bring sie zum Regiment. Was können die schon in drei Tagen weit geflüchtet sein? Der Herr Feldwebel wird Augen machen. Du hast mich angenehm enttäuscht, Schweizerkas, wird er sagen. Ich vertrau dir die Kass an, und du bringst sie zurück.

Wie **Kattrin** *mit einem Glas voll wieder hinter dem Wagen vorkommt, steht sie vor zwei Männern. Einer davon ist ein Feldwebel, der zweite schwenkt den Hut vor ihr. Er hat eine Binde über dem einen Auge.*

Mother Courage *climbs down from the wagon with a basket.*

Mother Courage And what have I found, you shameless nothing? (*In triumph she holds up the red shoes.*) Yvette's red shoes! She's a cold-blooded thief! (*To the* **Chaplain**.) You led her straight into this, telling her she was comely! (*Putting the shoes in her basket.*) I'm returning them. Stealing Yvette's shoes! She does what she does to make a living, I understand that. But you'll give it for nothing, hoping for a little fun. But until peace comes you have no business having hopes, you hear me? None!

The Chaplain Everyone's entitled to have hopes.*

Mother Courage Not her! I'm her mother, not you! Let her be like a stone in Darlarna. One grey stone among many grey stones as far as the eye can see, and all silent, that's how I want it with her. That way nothing ever happens to her. (*To* **Swiss Cheese**.) Listen up you, leave that cash box right where it is. And keep a close eye on your sister, she needs watching. Raising kids!* It'd be easier turning weasels into house pets.

She leaves with the **Chaplain**. **Kattrin** *clears the dishes from their meal.*

Swiss Cheese Not many days left when people can sit out in the sun in their shirtsleeves.

Kattrin *points to a tree.*

Swiss Cheese That's what I mean, the leaves turned yellow.

Kattrin *gestures to ask him if he wants something to drink.*

Swiss Cheese I won't drink. I have to think.

Pause.

She said she isn't sleeping. I should take the cash box someplace else, I found a secret place for it. All right, now I will have a drink.

Kattrin *goes behind the wagon.*

Der Mit Der Binde   Gott zum Gruß, liebes Fräulein. Haben Sie hier einen vom Quartier des Zweiten Finnischen gesehn?

Kattrin, *sehr erschrocken, läuft weg, nach vorn, den Branntwein verschüttend. Die beiden sehen sich an und ziehen sich zurück, nachdem sie Schweizerkas haben sitzen sehen.*

Schweizerkas (*aus seinem Nachdenken auffahrend*)   Die Hälfte hast du verschüttet. Was machst du für Faxen? Hast du dich am Aug gestoßen? Ich versteh dich nicht. Ich muß auch weg, ich habs beschlossen, es ist das beste. (*Er steht auf. Sie versucht alles, ihn auf die Gefahr aufmerksam zu machen. Er wehrt sie nur ab.*) Ich möcht wissen, was du meinst. Du meinsts sicher gut, armes Tier, kannst dich nicht ausdrücken. Was solls schon machen, daß du den Branntwein verschüttet hast, ich trink noch manches Glas, es kommt nicht auf eins an. (*Er holt aus dem Wagen die Schatulle heraus und nimmt sie unter den Rock.*) Gleich komm ich wieder. Jetzt halt mich aber nicht auf, sonst werd ich bös. Freilich meinst dus gut. Wenn du reden könntest.

Swiss Cheese   There are mole rills down by the river, I'll stick it down into one, then I'll fetch it back. Maybe tonight just before morning and I'll take it to the regiment. It's been three days, how far have they retreated? The Sergeant's eyes are going to bug out of his head. 'Swiss Cheese, I am pleasantly disappointed,' is what he's going to say. 'I trusted you would take care of the regimental cash box and you did.'

Kattrin *is coming from behind the wagon with a glass of brandy when she runs into two men suddenly standing there. One is a* **Sergeant**, *and the other, bowing, sweeps the ground before him with his hat. He wears an eyepatch over one eye.*

The One with the Eyepatch   Nominy dominy, pretty girlie. Seen anyone around here from the HQ of the Second Finnish Regiment?

Kattrin, *badly frightened, runs to* **Swiss Cheese** *at the front of the wagon, spilling brandy, making gestures, including something about an eyepatch. The two men look at one another and, after seeing* **Swiss Cheese**, *they disappear.*

Swiss Cheese (*startled out of a reverie*)   You spilled half of it. Why are you being silly? Did you stab yourself in the eye? I don't understand. I have to go someplace else, I decided, that's what I have to do.

He stands to leave. She frantically tries to explain the danger to him, to stop him. He gets around her.

Swiss Cheese   I wish I knew what you mean. It's something important, you poor mutt, you just can't explain what. Don't worry about the brandy, I'm sure I'll have lots of chances to drink brandy, a little spilt brandy, so what?

He goes into the wagon and returns with the cash box, which he stuffs under his jacket. **Kattrin** *grabs him.*

Swiss Cheese   I'll be back in two shakes. Don't hold on to me, or else I'll have to pinch you. Probably you mean something important. I wish you could talk.

Da sie ihn zurückhalten will, küßt er sie und reißt sich los. Ab.
Sie ist verzweifelt, läuft hin und her, kleine Laute ausstoßend.
Der **Feldprediger** *und* **Mutter Courage** *kommen zurück.*
Kattrin *bestürmt ihre Mutter.*

Mutter Courage   Was denn, was denn? Du bist ja ganz
auseinander. Hat dir jemand was getan? Wo ist der
Schweizerkas? Erzähls ordentlich, Kattrin. Deine Mutter
versteht dich. Was, der Bankert hat die Schatull doch
weggenommen? Ich schlag sie ihm um die Ohren, dem
Heimtücker. Laß dir Zeit und quatsch nicht, nimm die
Händ, ich mag nicht, wenn du wie ein Hund jaulst, was
soll der Feldprediger denken? Dem grausts doch. Ein
Einäugiger war da?

Der Feldprediger   Der Einäugige, das ist ein Spitzel.
Haben sie den Schweizerkas gefaßt? (**Kattrin** *schüttelt den*
Kopf, zuckt die Achseln.) Wir sind aus.

Mutter Courage (*nimmt aus dem Korb eine katholische Fahne,*
die der Feldprediger an der Fahnenstange befestigt)   Ziehens
die neue Fahne auf!

Der Feldprediger (*bitter*)   Hie gut katholisch allerwege.

Man hört von hinten Stimmen. Die beiden Männer bringen
Schweizerkas.

Schweizerkas   Laßt mich los, ich hab nix bei mir.
Verrenk mir nicht das Schulterblatt, ich bin unschuldig.

Der Feldwebel   Der gehört hierher. Ihr kennt euch.

Mutter Courage   Wir? Woher?

Schweizerkas   Ich kenn sie nicht. Wer weiß, wer das ist,
ich hab nix mit ihnen zu schaffen. Ich hab hier ein
Mittag gekauft, zehn Heller hats gekostet. Mag sein, daß
ihr mich da sitzen gesehn habt, versalzen wars auch.

Der Feldwebel   Wer seid ihr, he?

He kisses her and pulls himself away. He leaves. **Kattrin** *runs back and forth, gesticulating frantically, grunting, trying to make words. The* **Chaplain** *and* **Mother Courage** *return.* **Kattrin** *storms around her mother.*

Mother Courage   What then, what then? You're falling into pieces. Did somebody do something to you? Where's Swiss Cheese? (*Trying to calm her.*) One thing, and then the next thing, Kattrin, not all jumbled. Your mother understands you. The biscuit-brains took the money box? I'll twist his ears right off him! Slow down and stop all this flurry, use your hands, I hate it when you moan like a dog, what's the pastor going to think? You'll make his skin crawl. There was a one-eyed man?

The Chaplain   The one with one eye, he's a spy. They arrested Swiss Cheese?

Kattrin *nods 'yes'.*

The Chaplain   It's over.

Mother Courage *takes the Catholic flag out of her basket.*

Mother Courage   Raise the new flag!

The **Chaplain** *affixes it to the flagpole.*

The Chaplain (*bitterly*)   Good Catholics now, root and branches.

Voices are heard. The two men drag in **Swiss Cheese**.

Swiss Cheese   Let me go, I'm not carrying anything. Stop yanking on my shoulder, I didn't do anything wrong.

The Sergeant   He came from here. You know each other.

Mother Courage   We do? From where?

Swiss Cheese   I don't know them. Who knows who they are? I don't know anything about them. I bought my lunch from them, ten hellers it cost me. Maybe you saw me sitting here, too salty to boot.

The Sergeant   Who are you, huh?

Mutter Courage   Wir sind ordentliche Leut. Das ist wahr, er hat hier ein Essen gekauft. Es war ihm zu versalzen.

Der Feldwebel   Wollt ihr etwa tun, als kennt ihr ihn nicht?

Mutter Courage   Wie soll ich ihn kennen? Ich kenn nicht alle. Ich frag keinen, wie er heißt und ob er ein Heid ist; wenn er zahlt, ist er kein Heid. Bist du ein Heid?

Schweizerkas   Gar nicht.

Der Feldprediger   Er ist ganz ordentlich gesessen und hat das Maul nicht aufgemacht, außer wenn er gegessen hat. Und dann muß er.

Der Feldwebel   Und wer bist du?

Mutter Courage   Das ist nur mein Schankknecht. Und ihr seid sicher durstig, ich hol euch ein Glas Branntwein, ihr seid sicher gerannt und erhitzt.

Der Feldwebel   Keinen Branntwein im Dienst. (*Zum* **Schweizerkas.**)   Du hast was weggetragen. Am Fluß mußt dus versteckt haben. Der Rock ist dir so herausgestanden, wie du von hier weg bist.

Mutter Courage   Wars wirklich der?

Schweizerkas   Ich glaub, ihr meint einen andern. Ich hab einen springen gesehn, dem ist der Rock abgestanden. Ich bin der falsche.

Mutter Courage   Ich glaub auch, es ist ein Mißverständnis, das kann vorkommen. Ich kenn mich aus auf Menschen, ich bin die Courage, davon habt ihr gehört, mich kennen alle, und ich sag euch, der sieht redlich aus.

Der Feldwebel   Wir sind hinter der Regimentskass vom Zweiten Finnischen her. Und wir wissen, wie der ausschaut, der sie in Verwahrung hat. Wir haben ihn zwei Tag gesucht. Du bists.

Schweizerkas   Ich bins nicht.

Mother Courage Ordinary people. It's just like he said, he bought lunch. For him it was oversalted.

The Sergeant You want me to believe you don't know each other?

Mother Courage Why should I know him? I don't know everyone. I don't ask names or if someone's a heathen; if you pay up, you're not a heathen. (*To* **Swiss Cheese**.) Are you a heathen?

Swiss Cheese Not at all.

The Chaplain He was an orderly customer and he never opened his mouth, except when he ate. Then you more or less have to.

The Sergeant And who are you?

Mother Courage He serves my liquor. And you're thirsty, he'll fetch you a glass of brandy, you've got to be parched and melting.

The Sergeant No booze when we're working. (*To* **Swiss Cheese**.) You had something with you. You hid it near the river. Your shirt was all puffed out when you left here.

Mother Courage You're sure it was him?

Swiss Cheese Must've been somebody else. I saw a guy run away from here in a big puffy shirt. But that wasn't me.

Mother Courage I agree with him, you're confused, that can happen. I know a good person when I see one, I'm Courage, you've probably heard of me, everybody knows me, and I'm telling you, he seems honest to me.

The Sergeant We're after the cash box of the Second Finnish Regiment. And we know what he looks like, the guy responsible for it. We've been looking for him for two days. You're it.

Swiss Cheese I'm not it.

Der Feldwebel   Und wenn du sie nicht rausrückst, bist du hin, das weißt du. Wo ist sie?

Mutter Courage (*dringlich*)   Er würd sie doch herausgeben, wenn er sonst hin wär. Auf der Stell würd er sagen, ich hab sie, da ist sie, ihr seid die Stärkeren. So dumm ist er nicht. Red doch, du dummer Hund, der Herr Feldwebel gibt dir eine Gelegenheit.

Schweizerkas   Wenn ich sie nicht hab.

Der Feldwebel   Dann komm mit. Wir werdens herausbringen.

Sie führen ihn ab.

Mutter Courage (*ruft nach*)   Er würds sagen. So dumm ist er nicht. Und renkt ihm nicht das Schulterblatt aus! (*Läuft ihnen nach.*)

Am selben Abend. Der **Feldprediger** *und die stumme* **Kattrin** *spülen Gläser und putzen Messer.*

Der Feldprediger   Solche Fäll, wos einen erwischt, sind in der Religionsgeschicht nicht unbekannt. Ich erinner an die Passion von unserm Herrn und Heiland. Da gibts ein altes Lied darüber. (*Er singt das Horenlied.*)

In der ersten Tagesstund
Ward der Herr bescheiden
Als ein Mörder dargestellt
Pilatus dem Heiden.

Der ihn unschuldig fand
On Ursach des Todes
In derhalben von sich sandt
Zum König Herodes.

Umb drei ward der Gottessohn
Mit Geißeln geschmissen
Im sein Haupt mit einer Kron
Von Dornen zurrissen!

The Sergeant   And if you don't hand it over you're dead, you know that. Where is it?

Mother Courage (*urgent*)   Of course he'd give it to you if he knew his life depended on it. Right here, he'd say, I have it, you're stronger than me. He's not that dumb. Do it already, you goose, the Sergeant here is trying to help you.

Swiss Cheese   If I don't have it.

The Sergeant   Let's go, then. We'll help you find it.

The two men drag **Swiss Cheese** *away.*

Mother Courage (*calling after them*)   He'd tell you. He's not that stupid. And don't wrench his shoulder like that!

She runs after them.

Evening of the same day. The **Chaplain** *and dumb* **Kattrin** *are washing glasses and polishing knives.*

The Chaplain   These traps into which one falls, they're not unfamiliar from our Devotional tales. It reminds me a little of the Passion of our Lord and Saviour. There's a very old song about that.

He sings the 'Song of the Hours'.

In the first hour of the day
Our Lord finally knows that
Like a murderer he'll be judged by
Heathen Pontius Pilate.

Pilate shall refuse the blame
Wash his hands in water
Then the innocent condemned
Sent off to the slaughter.

In the third hour God's own son
Flails and scourges flayed him
On his head a thorny crown
That the soldiers made him.

Gekleidet zu Hohn und Spott
Ward er es geschlagen
Und das Kreuz zu seinem Tod
Mußt er selber tragen.

Umb sechs ward er nackt und bloß
An das Kreuz geschlagen
An dem er sein Blut vergoß
Betet mit Wehklagen.

Die Zuseher spotten sein
Auch die bei ihm hingen
Bis die Sonn auch ihren Schein
Entzog solchen Dingen.

Jesus schrie zur neunden Stund
Klaget sich verlassen
Bald ward Gall in seinen Mund
Mit Essig gelassen.

Da gab er auf seinen Geist
Und die Erd erbebet
Des Tempels Vorhang zerreißt
Mancher Fels zerklübet.

Da hat man zur Vesperzeit
Der Schechr Bein zerbrochen
Ward Jesus in seine Seit
Mit eim Speer gestochen.

Doraus Blut und Wasser ran
Sie machtens zum Hohne
Solches stellen sie uns an
Mit dem Menschensohne.

Mutter Courage (*kommt aufgeregt*)   Es ist auf Leben und Tod. Aber der Feldwebel soll mit sich sprechen lassen. Nur, wir dürfen nicht aufkommen lassen, daß es unser Schweizerkas ist, sonst haben wir ihn begünstigt. Es ist nur eine Geldsach. Aber wo nehmen wir das Geld her? War die Yvette nicht da? Ich hab sie unterwegs getroffen, sie hat schon einen Obristen aufgegabelt, vielleicht kauft ihr der einen Marketenderhandel.

Der Feldprediger   Wollen Sie wirklich verkaufen?

Dressed in rags and mockery
They beat him and deride him
And the cross of his own death
He'll drag along beside him.

In the sixth hour, naked, cold
On the cross they staved him
As his blood spilled down he prayed
For his father to save him.

One thief laughed and one thief wept
As he died beside them
While the sun withdrew its light
Hoping thus to hide them.

Jesus screamed by hour nine
Why does God forsake him
In his mouth a bitter gall
Vinegar to slake him.

At last he gave up the ghost
Mountains disassembled
Temple veils were rent in twain
And the whole world trembled.

Dark and sudden night time fell
The mocking crowd was scattered
Jesus's sides were torn by spears
The two thieves' bones were shattered.

Still the blood and water flows
Still their mocking laughter
Thus befell the Son of Man
And many people after.

Mother Courage *comes in, very worried, upset.*

Mother Courage He's strung up between life and death. But the Sergeant's still open to talking. And taking. Only we can't let on that Swiss Cheese is ours, they'll say we helped him. It's just about money. But where are we going to get money? Yvette's snagged herself a colonel, maybe he's interested in getting her started selling merchandise. Where is she? She said she'd hurry.

The Chaplain You're going to sell her the wagon?

Mutter Courage Woher soll ich das Geld für den Feldwebel nehmen?

Der Feldprediger Und wovon wollens leben?

Mutter Courage Das is es.

Yvette Pottier kommt mit einem uralten Obristen.

Yvette (*umarmt* **Mutter Courage**) Liebe Courage, daß wir uns so schnell wiedersehen! (*Flüsternd.*) Er ist nicht abgeneigt. (*Laut.*) Das ist mein guter Freund, der mich berät im Geschäftlichen. Ich hör nämlich zufällig, Sie wollen Ihren Wagen verkaufen, umständehalber. Ich würd reflektieren.

Mutter Courage Verpfänden, nicht verkaufen, nur nix Vorschnelles, so ein Wagen kauft sich nicht leicht wieder in Kriegszeiten.

Yvette (*enttäuscht*) Nur verpfänden, ich dacht verkaufen. Ich weiß nicht, ob ich da Interesse hab. (*Zum Obristen.*) Was meinst du?

Der Obrist Ganz deiner Meinung, Liebe.

Mutter Courage Er wird nur verpfändet.

Yvette Ich dachte, Sie müssen das Geld haben.

Mutter Courage (*fest*) Ich muß das Geld haben, aber lieber lauf ich mir die Füß in den Leib nach einem Angebot, als daß ich gleich verkauf. Warum, wir leben von dem Wagen. Es ist eine Gelegenheit für dich, Yvette, wer weiß, wann du so eine wiederfindest und einen lieben Freund hast, der dich berät, ists nicht so?

Yvette Ja, mein Freund meint, ich sollt zugreifen, aber ich weiß nicht. Wenns nur verpfändet ist ... du meinst doch auch, wir sollten gleich kaufen?

Der Obrist Ich meins auch.

Mutter Courage Da mußt du dir was aussuchen, was zu verkaufen ist, vielleicht findst dus, wenn du dir Zeit laßt, und dein Freund geht herum mit dir, sagen wir eine Woche oder zwei Wochen, könntst du was Geeignetes finden.

Mother Courage   How else get the money the Sergeant's demanding?

The Chaplain   How will you make a living?

Mother Courage   That's it, isn't it?

Yvette *comes in with a decrepit* **Colonel**. *She embraces* **Mother Courage**.

Yvette   Courage, my love, long time no see! (*Whispering.*) It's a go. (*Loud again.*) This is my dear pal and business advisor, Poldi. Poldi, Courage. I hear you're looking to sell your wagon owing to exigent circumstances. It got me thinking.

Mother Courage   Pawn it, not sell it, don't trip over yourself, it's not so easy to find a good wagon in wartime. Two hundred guilders.

Yvette (*disappointed*)   Pawn? I thought it was for sale. (*To the* **Colonel**.) What's your opinion?

The Colonel   Your opinion's my opinion, honey.

Mother Courage   It's only up for pawning.

Yvette   I thought you needed the money.

Mother Courage (*decisively*)   No way around it, the wagon's our life. This is a good thing for you, Yvette, who knows when something like this'll come your way again? You front me the money and when I redeem the pawn, you pocket a tidy profit, you never made such easy money, your nice old pal there agrees with me. (*To the* **Colonel**.) I'm right, huh? What's his name? Mouldy?*

Yvette   Poldi. And he thinks we should keep looking* for something we can buy. Don't you, Poldi?

The Colonel   That's what I think.

Mother Courage   You keep looking then, maybe you'll find something you want, two or three weeks of looking is all it should take, just pray Poldi holds up,* but you better hurry, he looks wobbly to me.

Yvette   Dann können wir ja suchen gehn, ich geh gern
herum und such mir was aus, ich geh gern mit dir
herum, Poldi, das ist ein reines Vergnügen, nicht? Und
wenns zwei Wochen dauert! Wann wollen Sie denn
zurückzahlen, wenn Sie das Geld kriegen?

Mutter Courage   In zwei Wochen kann ich
zurückzahlen, vielleicht in einer.

Yvette   Ich bin mir nicht schlüssig, Poldi, Chéri, berat
mich. (*Sie nimmt den* **Obristen** *auf die Seite.*) Ich weiß, sie
muß verkaufen, da hab ich keine Sorg. Und der
Fähnrich, der blonde, du kennst ihn, will mirs Geld gern
borgen. Der ist verschossen in mich, er sagt, ich erinner
ihn an jemand. Was rätst du mir?

Der Obrist   Ich warn dich vor dem. Das ist kein Guter.
Der nützts aus. Ich hab dir gesagt, ich kauf dir was, nicht,
Haserl?

Yvette   Ich kanns nicht annehmen von dir. Freilich,
wenn du meinst, der Fähnrich könnts ausnützen …
Poldi, ich nehms von dir an.

Der Obrist   Das mein ich.

Yvette   Rätst dus mir?

Der Obrist   Ich rats dir.

Yvette (*zurück zur* **Courage**)   Mein Freund täts mir raten.
Schreiben Sie mir eine Quittung aus und daß der Wagen
mein ist, wenn die zwei Wochen um sind, mit allem
Zubehör, wir gehens gleich durch, die zweihundert
Gulden bring ich später. (*Zum* **Obristen:**) Da mußt du
voraus ins Lager gehn, ich komm nach, ich muß alles
durchgehen, damit nix wegkommt aus meinem Wagen.
(*Sie küßt ihn. Er geht weg. Sie klettert auf den Wagen.*) Stiefel
sinds aber wenige.

Yvette   I'm happy shopping with you, Poldi. You don't mind looking around for a few weeks, do you, so long as we're always together? There are lots of places to look.

The Colonel (*to* **Mother Courage**)   Well, baby girl, my knees go all stiff in this weather,* I –

Mother Courage   I'll pay it back, quick as possible, with interest.

Yvette   I'm all confused, Poldi, *chéri*, advise me.

She takes the **Colonel** *aside.*

Yvette   We should give her the cash, let her pawn it, we'll own the wagon outright in the end, where's she gonna get two hundred guilders from to redeem it? I don't have two hundred guilders, but I can get money from that young blond lieutenant with the enormous feet.* Know who I mean, Poldi? He's always waving it at me!

The Colonel   You don't need him, I told you I'd buy it for you, didn't I, baby bunny?

Yvette   Oh, but it's indecent taking money from someone you love when you aren't married to him, though if in your opinion the lieutenant is inclined to exploit a situation, I'll let you do it.

The Colonel   I insist.

Yvette   I'll find some way to pay you back.

The Colonel   I hate that lieutenant!

Yvette   I know.

She goes back to **Mother Courage**.

Yvette   My friend advises me to accept. Write out a receipt that the wagon's mine, after two weeks, and everything in it, I'll bring your two hundred guilders straight away. (*To the* **Colonel**.) Run back to the camp, I'll be right behind you, I just want to take stock so nothing'll go missing from my wagon.

She kisses the **Colonel** *and he leaves. She climbs up into the wagon.*

Yvette (*inside the wagon*)   You've got boots, but not many.

Mutter Courage   Yvette, jetzt ist keine Zeit, deinen Wagen durchzugehen, wenns deiner ist. Du hast mir versprochen, daß du mit dem Feldwebel redest wegen meinem Schweizerkas, da ist keine Minut zu verlieren, ich hör, in einer Stund kommt er vors Feldgericht.

Yvette   Nur noch die Leinenhemden möcht ich nachzählen.

Mutter Courage (*zieht sie am Rock herunter*)   Du Hyänenvieh, es geht um Schweizerkas. Und kein Wort, von wem das Angebot kommt, tu, als seis dein Liebster in Gottes Namen, sonst sind wir alle hin, weil wir ihm Vorschub geleistet haben.

Yvette   Ich hab den Einäugigen ins Gehölz bestellt, sicher, er ist schon da.

Der Feldprediger   Und es müssen nicht gleich die ganzen zweihundert sein, geh bis hundertfünfzig, das reicht auch.

Mutter Courage Ists Ihr Geld? Ich bitt mir aus, daß Sie sich draußen halten. Sie werden Ihre Zwiebelsupp schon kriegen. Lauf und handel nicht herum, es geht ums Leben. (*Sie schiebt* **Yvette** *weg.*)

Der Feldprediger   Ich wollt Ihnen nix dreinreden, aber wovon wolln wir leben? Sie haben eine erwerbsunfähige Tochter aufm Hals.

Mutter Courage   Ich rechn mit der Regimentskass, Sie Siebengescheiter. Die Spesen werden sie ihm doch wohl bewilligen.

Der Feldprediger   Aber wird sies richtig ausrichten?

Mutter Courage   Sie hat doch ein Interesse daran, daß ich ihre zweihundert ausgeb und sie den Wagen bekommt. Sie ist scharf drauf, wer weiß, wie lang ihr Obrist bei der Stange bleibt. Kattrin, du putzt die Messer, nimm Bimsstein. Und Sie, stehn Sie auch nicht herum wie Jesus am Ölberg, tummeln Sie sich, waschen Sie die Gläser aus, abends kommen mindestens fünfzig Reiter, und dann hör ich wieder: »Ich bin das Laufen nicht

Mother Courage   Yvette, there's no time for that! You
have to go talk to that Sergeant, tell him the money's
coming, there's not a minute to spare.

Yvette (*inside the wagon*)   Let me just take a second count
of these linen shirts.

Mother Courage *grabs hold of* **Yvette'***s skirt and pulls her
down from the wagon.*

Mother Courage   Leave it for now, jackal, or it's over for
Swiss Cheese. And not a word who's making this offer. It
came from your lover, swear that on God's good name,
otherwise we'll all be implicated, his accomplices, we
sheltered him.

Yvette   Calm down, I'll take care of it, One-Eye's
meeting me behind those trees, over there.

The Chaplain   And when you make your first offer, it
doesn't have to be the whole two hundred up front, start
with one hundred and fifty, that's perfectly ample.

Mother Courage (*to the* **Chaplain**)   It's your money?
Please, butt out. You'll still get your soup, now go haggle
somewhere else, this is his life.

She shoos **Yvette** *on her way.*

The Chaplain   Apologies for interfering, but if you give
them the full two hundred, how are you going to live, to
earn money? With your unemployable daughter hanging
around your neck.

Mother Courage   I'm counting on that regimental cash
box, genius. When Swiss Cheese is free he'll bring it back
to us, we can take out money to cover expenses. I'll
redeem the pawn,* we'll get the wagon back when we get
the cashbox. (*To* **Kattrin**.) You, polish the knives, use the
pumice stone. (*To the* **Chaplain**.) And you, leave off
posing like Christ on Mount Olive, wash the glasses, by
evening we'll have fifty suppers to serve.

gewohnt, meine Füß, beir Andacht renn ich nicht.« Ich
denk, sie werden ihn uns herausgeben. Gott sei Dank
sind sie bestechlich. Sie sind doch keine Wölf, sondern
Menschen und auf Geld aus. Die Bestechlichkeit ist bei
die Menschen dasselbe wie beim lieben Gott die
Barmherzigkeit. Bestechlichkeit ist unsre einzige
Aussicht. Solangs die gibt, gibts milde Urteilssprüch, und
sogar der Unschuldige kann durchkommen vor Gericht.

Yvette (*kommt schnaufend*)   Sie wollens nur machen für
zweihundert. Und es muß schnell gehn. Sie habens
nimmer lang in der Hand. Ich geh am besten sofort mit
dem Einäugigen zu meinem Obristen. Er hat gestanden,
daß er die Schatull gehabt hat, sie haben ihm die
Daumenschrauben angelegt. Aber er hat sie in Fluß
geschmissen, wie er gemerkt hat, daß sie hinter ihm her
sind. Die Schatull ist futsch. Soll ich laufen und von
meinem Obristen das Geld holen?

Mutter Courage   Die Schatull ist futsch? Wie soll ich da
meine zweihundert wiederkriegen?

Yvette   Ach, Sie haben geglaubt, Sie können aus der
Schatull nehmen? Da wär ich ja schön hereingelegt
worden. Machen Sie sich keine Hoffnung. Sie müssens
schon zahln, wenn Sie den Schweizerkas zurückhaben
wolln, oder vielleicht soll ich jetzt die ganze Sach
liegenlassen, damit Sie Ihren Wagen behalten können?

Mutter Courage   Damit hab ich nicht gerechnet. Du
brauchst nicht drängen, du kommst schon zum Wagen,
er ist schon weg, ich hab ihn siebzehn Jahr gehabt. Ich
muß nur ein Augenblick überlegen, es kommt ein bissel
schnell, was mach ich, zweihundert kann ich nicht geben,
du hättest doch abhandeln solln. Etwas muß ich in der
Hand haben, sonst kann mich jeder Beliebige in den
Straßengraben schubsen. Geh und sag, ich geb
hundertzwanzig Gulden, sonst wird nix draus, da verlier
ich auch schon den Wagen.

Yvette   Sie werdens nicht machen. Der Einäugige ist
sowieso in Eil und schaut immer hinter sich, so aufgeregt
ist er. Soll ich nicht lieber die ganzen zweihundert geben?

Thank God they're corrupt. They aren't wolves, they're just men after money. Corruption is the human equivalent of God's Mercy. As long as someone's on the take you can buy lighter sentences, so even the innocent have a shot at justice.

Yvette *enters, winded.*

Yvette Two hundred even. I'll go get the money from my Colonel, fast, soon it'll be too late, already he's sentenced to die. They used the thumbscrews, he confessed that he had the cash box. He told them when he saw he was being followed he threw it in the river.

Mother Courage The cash box? He threw it in the . . .

Yvette It's gone. I'm gonna run and get the money from my Colonel.

Mother Courage But if the cash box is gone, how will I get back my two hundred guilders?

Yvette Oh, of course, damn I'm stupid, you were hoping to take it outa that cashbox! I shoulda known you'd find an angle. Well, give that up, you'll have to pay if you want Swiss Cheese back, or maybe you want to forget the whole deal, and you can keep your wagon?

Mother Courage I hadn't anticipated this. Don't panic, you'll get the wagon, it's lost, I had it seventeen years. I need more time to think, what to do, I can't do two hundred, you should've bargained them down. If I'm left without anything, any stranger who wants to can have me in a ditch. Go and tell them I can't do two hundred, I'll give them a hundred twenty guilders, the wagon's lost regardless.

Yvette They're not going to agree. One-Eye's rushing me, he keeps looking with that one eye* to see if someone's watching. He's scared. I have to offer the whole two hundred!

Mutter Courage (*verzweifelt*)   Ich kanns nicht geben. Dreißig Jahr hab ich gearbeitet. Die ist schon fünfundzwanzig und hat noch kein Mann. Ich hab die auch noch. Dring nicht in mich, ich weiß, was ich tu. Sag hundertzwanzig, oder es wird nix draus.

Yvette   Sie müssens wissen. (*Schnell ab.*)

Mutter Courage *sieht weder den* **Feldprediger** *noch ihre Tochter an und setzt sich,* **Kattrin** *beim Messerputzen zu helfen.*

Mutter Courage   Zerbrechen Sie nicht die Gläser, es sind nimmer unsre. Schau auf deine Arbeit, du schneidst dich. Der Schweizerkas kommt zurück, ich geb auch zweihundert, wenns nötig ist. Dein Bruder kriegst du. Mit achtzig Gulden können wir eine Hucke mit Waren vollpacken und von vorn anfangen. Es wird überall mit Wasser gekocht.

Der Feldprediger   Der Herr wirds zum Guten lenken, heißt es.

Mutter Courage   Trocken sollen Sie sie reiben.

Sie putzen schweigend Messer. **Kattrin** *läuft plötzlich schluchzend hinter den Wagen.*

Yvette (*kommt gelaufen*)   Sie machens nicht. Ich hab Sie gewarnt. Der Einäugige hat gleich weggehn wolln, weil es keinen Wert hat. Er hat gesagt, er erwartet jeden Augenblick, daß die Trommeln gerührt werden, dann ist das Urteil gesprochen. Ich hab hundertfünfzig geboten. Er hat nicht einmal mit den Achseln gezuckt. Mit Müh und Not ist er dageblieben, daß ich noch einmal mit Ihnen sprech.

Mutter Courage   Sag ihm, ich geb die zweihundert. Lauf. (**Yvette** *läuft weg. Sie sitzen schweigend. Der* **Feldprediger** *hat aufgehört, die Gläser zu putzen.*) Mir scheint, ich hab zu lang gehandelt.

Von weither hört man Trommeln. Der **Feldprediger** *steht auf und geht nach hinten.* **Mutter Courage** *bleibt sitzen. Es wird dunkel. Das Trommeln hört auf. Es wird wieder hell.* **Mutter Courage** *sitzt unverändert.*

Mother Courage (*despairing*)   I can't! I worked thirty years. She's twenty-five and she hasn't got a husband. She's mine as well. Stop tearing at me, I know what I'm doing. Tell them a hundred twenty and that's that.

Yvette   Your choice.

She leaves. **Mother Courage**, *avoiding looking at the* **Chaplain** *or her daughter, sits and helps* **Kattrin** *with the knives.*

Mother Courage (*to the* **Chaplain**)   Don't break any glasses, they don't belong to us now. (*To* **Kattrin**.) Pay attention, you'll cut yourself. Swiss Cheese will be back, I'll pay the two hundred if that's the only way. You'll get your brother back. With eighty guilders we can provision a rucksack with goods and start over. It's same game everywhere, you want to cook, you cook with water.

The Chaplain   The Lord will steer us right, as they say.

Mother Courage   Dry them carefully.

They scour the knives, silent. Suddenly **Kattrin** *bursts into tears, hurries behind the wagon.* **Yvette** *runs in.*

Yvette   They said no deal. I warned you. One-Eye wants to drop the whole business, he says it's nearly over,* in a minute we're going to hear the drums, the rifles are loaded. I went up to one hundred fifty. He didn't budge, not a flicker. I begged him to wait till I talked to you.

Mother Courage   Tell him I'll pay two hundred. Run.

Yvette *runs out. They sit in silence. The* **Chaplain** *has stopped cleaning the glasses.*

Mother Courage   Seems to me, I haggled too long.

Drums are heard in the distance. The **Chaplain** *stands and goes behind the wagon.* **Courage** *remains seated. It gets dark. The drumroll stops. Then it gets light again.* **Mother Courage** *sits, motionless.* **Yvette** *enters, ashen.*

Yvette (*taucht auf, sehr bleich*)   Jetzt haben Sies geschafft mitn Handel und daß Sie Ihren Wagen behalten. Elf Kugeln hat er gekriegt, sonst nix. Sie verdienens nicht, daß ich mich überhaupt noch um Sie kümmer. Aber ich hab aufgeschnappt, daß sie nicht glauben, die Kass ist wirklich im Fluß. Sie haben einen Verdacht, sie ist hier, überhaupt, daß Sie eine Verbindung mit ihm gehabt haben. Sie wolln ihn herbringen, ob Sie sich verraten, wenn Sie ihn sehn. Ich warn Sie, daß Sie ihn nicht kennen, sonst seid ihr alle dran. Sie sind dicht hinter mir, besser, ich sags gleich. Soll ich die Kattrin weghalten? (**Mutter Courage** *schüttelt den Kopf.*) Weiß sies? Sie hat vielleicht nix gehört von Trommeln oder nicht verstanden.

Mutter Courage   Sie weiß. Hol sie.

Yvette *holt* **Kattrin**, *welche zu ihrer Mutter geht und neben ihr stehenbleibt.* **Mutter Courage** *nimmt sie bei der Hand. Zwei Landsknechte kommen mit einer Bahre, auf der unter einem Laken etwas liegt. Nebenher geht der* **Feldwebel**. *Sie setzen die Bahre nieder.*

Der Feldwebel   Da ist einer, von dem wir nicht seinen Namen wissen. Er muß aber notiert werden, daß alles in Ordnung geht. Bei dir hat er eine Mahlzeit genommen. Schau ihn dir an, ob du ihn kennst. (*Er nimmt das Laken weg.*) Kennst du ihn? (**Mutter Courage** *schüttelt den Kopf.*) Was, du hast ihn nie gesehn, vor er bei dir eine Mahlzeit genommen hat. (**Mutter Courage** *schüttelt den Kopf.*) Hebt ihn auf. Gebt ihn auf den Schindanger. Er hat keinen, der ihn kennt.

Sie tragen ihn weg.

Yvette   Look what you've done with your haggling and hanging on. He got eleven bullets, eleven bullets, it was enough. It's not worth it, worrying about the likes of you. But they don't believe he threw the cash box in the river. They suspect it's been here all along, that you were working with him. So they're bringing him here, maybe you'll give yourself away when you see him. I warn you, you don't know him, or you're all dead. Should I take Kattrin away?

Mother Courage *shakes her head 'no'.*

Mother Courage   She knows. Fetch her.

Yvette *gets* **Kattrin**, *who goes to her mother and stands beside her.* **Mother Courage** *takes her hand. Two soldiers enter with a stretcher on which something is lying, covered with a sheet. The* **Sergeant** *follows. They put the stretcher on the ground.*

The Sergeant   Here's somebody, we don't know his name. It's got to be entered in the record, everything in its place. He bought a meal from you. Look and see if you know him.

He takes the sheet away.

The Sergeant   Know him?

Mother Courage *shakes her head.*

The Sergeant   You never saw him before you served him supper?

Mother Courage *shakes her head.*

The Sergeant   Lift him up. Throw him in the pit. He's got no one who knows him.

They carry him away.

Four

Mutter Courage *singt das Lied von der Großen Kapitulation.*

Vor einem Offizierszelt. **Mutter Courage** *wartet. Ein* **Schreiber** *schaut aus dem Zelt.*

Der Schreiber   Ich kenn Sie. Sie haben einen Zahlmeister von die Evangelischen bei sich gehabt, wo sich verborgen hat. Beschweren Sie sich lieber nicht.

Mutter Courage Doch beschwer ich mich. Ich bin unschuldig, und wenn ichs zulass, schauts aus, als ob ich ein schlechtes Gewissen hätt. Sie haben mir alles mit die Säbel zerfetzt im Wagen und fünf Taler Buß für nix und wieder nix abverlangt.

Der Schreiber   Ich rat Ihnen zum Guten, halten Sie das Maul. Wir haben nicht viel Marketender und lassen Ihnen Ihren Handel, besonders, wenn Sie ein schlechtes Gewissen haben und ab und zu eine Buß zahln.

Mutter Courage Ich beschwer mich.

Der Schreiber   Wie Sie wolln. Dann warten Sie, bis der Herr Rittmeister Zeit hat. (*Zurück ins Zelt.*)

Junger Soldat (*kommt randalierend*)   Bouque la Madonne: Wo ist der gottverdammte Hund von einem Rittmeister, wo mir das Trinkgeld unterschlagt und versaufts mit seine Menscher? Er muß hin sein!

Älterer soldat (*kommt nachgelaufen*)   Halts Maul. Du kommst in Stock!

Four

Mother Courage *sings 'The Song of the Great Capitulation'.*

In front of an officer's tent. **Mother Courage** *is waiting. A* **Clerk** *looks out from inside the tent.*

The Clerk   I know you. You're the one who was hiding that Protestant paymaster. Think twice before you make any complaints.

Mother Courage   I'm making a complaint. I hid nobody, and if I just take what they did to me it'll look like I think I'm guilty of something. They cut my wagon and my entire inventory to ribbons with their sabres, and then they charged me a five-thaler fine, and all for having done nothing, less than nothing.

The Clerk   Listen to what I'm telling you, it's for your own good: we don't have many merchandise wagons, so we'll let you stay in business, provided you assuage your guilty conscience by paying the necessary fines. And keep your mouth shut.

Mother Courage   I want to make a complaint.

The Clerk   Be my guest. Wait here for the Captain's convenience.

He goes back into the tent. A **Young Soldier** *enters, furious. An* **Older Soldier** *is running after him.*

The Young Soldier   By the Holy Virgin's Flowerbush where's that goddamned sonofabitch of a captain who withheld my bonus and then spent it on his whores' bar tab? Time to pay up!

The Older Soldier   Aw Jesus, they're gonna slam you in the stocks!

Junger Soldat   Komm heraus, du Dieb! Ich hau dich zu
Koteletten! Die Belohnung unterschlagen, nachdem ich
in Fluß geschwommen bin, allein vom ganzen Fähnlein,
daß ich nicht einmal ein Bier kaufen kann, ich laß mirs
nicht gefalln. Komm heraus, daß ich dich zerhack!

Älterer soldat   Maria und Josef, das rennt sich ins
Verderben.

Mutter Courage Haben sie ihm kein Trinkgeld gezahlt?

Junger Soldat   Laß mich los, ich renn dich mit nieder, es
geht auf ein Aufwaschen.

Älterer soldat   Er hat den Gaul vom Obristen gerettet
und kein Trinkgeld bekommen. Er ist noch jung und
nicht lang genug dabei.

Mutter Courage Laß ihn los, er ist kein Hund, wo man in
Ketten legen muß. Trinkgeld habn wolln ist ganz
vernünftig. Warum zeichnet er sich sonst aus?

Junger Soldat   Daß der sich besauft drinnen! Ihr seids
nur Hosenscheißer. Ich hab was Besonderes gemacht und
will mein Trinkgeld haben.

Mutter Courage Junger Mensch, brüllen Sie mich nicht
an. Ich hab meine eigenen Sorgen, und überhaupt,
schonen Sie Ihre Stimme, Sie möchten sie brauchen, bis
der Rittmeister kommt, nachher ist er da, und Sie sind
heiser und bringen keinen Ton heraus, und er kann Sie
nicht in Stock schließen lassen, bis Sie schwarz sind.
Solche, wo so brüllen, machen nicht lange, eine halbe
Stunde, und man muß sie in Schlaf singen, so erschöpft
sind sie.

Junger Soldat   Ich bin nicht erschöpft, und von Schlafen
ist keine Red, ich hab Hunger. Das Brot backen Sie aus
Eicheln und Hanfkörnern und sparn damit noch. Der
verhurt mein Trinkgeld, und ich hab Hunger. Er muß hin
sein.

The Young Soldier   Come out, you crook! I'm gonna butcher you! Refusing me my bonus after I was the only one willing to swim that river, the only one in the whole battalion, and I can't even buy a beer for myself. I'm not letting myself get fucked like this.* You come outside now and let me cut your fucking head off!

The **Older Soldier** *restrains the* **Young Soldier**,* *who's trying to get into the tent.*

The Older Soldier   Sweet Christ, he's gonna mess everything up for himself.

Mother Courage   They screwed him out of his bonus?

The Young Soldier   Let go of me or I'll murder you too, he's gonna get hung out to dry, it's gotta happen.

The Older Soldier   He rescued the Colonel's horse but then they didn't give the bonus like they're supposed to. He's young, he hasn't learned.

Mother Courage   Let him loose, he's not a dog, a man doesn't have to be put on a leash. A bonus is a bonus and it's perfectly reasonable to expect to be paid. Why else bother being brave?

The Young Soldier   He's drinking in there! You all shit yourselves for fear of him. I stepped up and stood out and now I get my bonus pay!

Mother Courage   Don't bark at me, son. I've got problems of my own, and anyway you should spare your big fine voice – if all you can do is whisper when the Captain comes out, he won't haul your ass to the stocks. People who shout the way you're shouting are hoarse in half an hour and so exhausted anyone can sing them to sleep.

The Young Soldier   I'm not exhausted and who could sleep this hungry? The bread's made out of acorn mash and hemp seed and now they're cutting back on that. He spent my bonus on whores and I'm starving. He's gonna pay!

Mutter Courage Ich verstehe, Sie haben Hunger. Voriges Jahr hat euer Feldhauptmann euch von die Straßen runterkommandiert und quer über die Felder, damit das Korn niedergetrampelt würd, ich hätt für Stiefel zehn Gulden kriegen können, wenn einer zehn Gulden hätt ausgeben können und ich Stiefel gehabt hätt. Er hat geglaubt, er ist nicht mehr in der Gegend dies Jahr, aber jetzt ist er doch noch da, und der Hunger is groß. Ich versteh, daß Sie einen Zorn haben.

Junger Soldat Ich leids nicht, reden Sie nicht, ich vertrag keine Ungerechtigkeit.

Mutter Courage Da haben Sie recht, aber wie lang? Wie lang vertragen Sie keine Ungerechtigkeit? Eine Stund oder zwei? Sehen Sie, das haben Sie sich nicht gefragt, obwohls die Hauptsach ist, warum, im Stock ists ein Elend, wenn Sie entdecken, jetzt vertragen Sies Unrecht plötzlich.

Junger Soldat Ich weiß nicht, warum ich Ihnen zuhör. Bouque la Madonne, wo ist der Rittmeister?

Mutter Courage Sie hören mir zu, weil Sie schon wissen, was ich Ihnen sag, daß Ihre Wut schon verraucht ist, es ist nur eine kurze gewesen, und Sie brauchten eine lange, aber woher nehmen?

Junger Soldat Wollen Sie etwa sagen, wenn ich das Trinkgeld verlang, das ist nicht billig?

Mutter Courage Im Gegenteil. Ich sag nur, Ihre Wut ist nicht lang genug, mit der können Sie nix ausrichten, schad. Wenn Sie eine lange hätten, möcht ich Sie noch aufhetzen. Zerhacken Sie den Hund, möcht ich Ihnen dann raten, aber was, wenn Sie ihn dann gar nicht zerhacken, weil Sie schon spüren, wie Sie den Schwanz einziehn. Dann steh ich da, und der Rittmeister hält sich an mich.

Mother Courage   I get it, you're hungry. I remember last
year when your general ordered you guys to march back
and forth across the cornfields – I could've sold boots for
ten guilders a pair if I'd had any boots to sell. He planned
to be elsewhere by now, but here he is, a year later,
bogged down, and there's no corn and everyone's
starving. I get it, you're angry.

The Young Soldier   Stop talking to me, I don't give a shit
about any of that, I won't let myself be treated unfairly.

Mother Courage   How long?* How long will you refuse
to be treated unfairly? An hour, two? See, never occurs to
you to ask yourself that, and that's the first thing you
should ask, 'cause it's no good figuring it out later, after
all the skin on your back has been flayed off with the
whipping you'll get for insubordination, after the whip's
blistered all the skin off you and you're raw and bleeding,
in chains praying for death it hurts so bad, then it's a
little late to realise that maybe, on second thoughts,
actually you can live with being treated unfairly.

The Young Soldier   Why am I listening to you? By the
Holy Mother's Bush! CAPTAIN!

Mother Courage   I'll tell you why you're listening: I'm
right and you know it, your fury's just a lightning bolt
that splits the air,* bright, noisy, then BANG! – all over. It
was short-lived anger, when what you needed was long-
burning rage, but where would you get something like
that?

The Young Soldier   You're saying I don't have a right to
get paid what I'm owed?

Mother Courage   Just the opposite. You have a right, but
you have a short-lived anger and that'll never get you
what you want. If you had long-lasting rage, I'd cheer you
on. Hack the sonofabitch to death, I'm right behind you,
but what if you cool down smack in the middle of it, and
he doesn't get hacked up, because your hard-on's gone
all of a sudden? There I am, standing there, you've slunk
off and the Captain blames me.

Älterer soldat Sie haben ganz recht, er hat nur einen Rappel.

Junger Soldat So, das will ich sehn, ob ich ihn nicht zerhack. (*Er zieht sein Schwert.*) Wenn er kommt, zerhack ich ihn.

Der Schreiber (*guckt heraus*)   Der Herr Rittmeister kommt gleich. Hinsetzen.

Der **junge Soldat** *setzt sich hin.*

Mutter Courage Er sitzt schon. Sehn Sie, was hab ich gesagt. Sie sitzen schon. Ja, die kennen sich aus in uns und wissen, wie sies machen müssen. Hinsetzen! und schon sitzen wir. Und im Sitzen gibts kein Aufruhr. Stehen Sie lieber nicht wieder auf, so wie Sie vorhin gestanden haben, stehen Sie jetzt nicht wieder. Vor mir müssen Sie sich nicht genieren, ich bin nicht besser, was nicht gar. Uns haben sie allen unsre Schneid abgekauft. Warum, wenn ich aufmuck, möchts das Geschäft schädigen. Ich werd Ihnen was erzähln von der Großen Kapitulation. (*Sie singt das Lied von der Großen Kapitulation.*)

Einst, im Lenze meiner jungen Jahre
Dacht auch ich, daß ich was ganz Besondres bin.
(Nicht wie jede beliebige Häuslertochter, mit meinem
Aussehn und Talent und meinem Drang nach
Höherem!)
Und bestellte meine Suppe ohne Haare
Und von mir, sie hatten kein Gewinn.
(Alles oder nix, jedenfalls nicht den Nächstbesten,
jeder is seines Glückes Schmied, ich laß mir keine
Vorschriften machen!)

The Older Soldier You're right, he'll settle down, he just went a little crazy.

The Young Soldier You'll see, I'm gonna cut his throat.

He draws his sword.

As soon as he sets his foot out here I'm gonna do it.

The **Clerk** *comes out.*

The Clerk The Captain'll be out soon. Sit.

The **Young Soldier** *sits.*

Mother Courage They say sit, he sits. Like I said. Sitting pretty. They know us so well, what makes us tick. Sit! And we sit. And sitting people don't make trouble.

The **Young Soldier** *starts to stand.*

Mother Courage Better not stand up again, you won't be standing the way you did before.

He sits back down.

Mother Courage Hope you're not embarrassed on my account, I'm not better than you, worse if anything. We had gumption. They bought it, all of it. Why kick, might hurt business. It's called the Great Capitulation.

She sings 'The Song of the Great Capitulation'.

> Back when I was young, fresh as grass and innocent,
> Any day, I'd fly away on butterfly wings.

(*Speaking.*) Not just a peddler's daughter, me with my good looks and my talent and my longing for a better life!

Singing.

> If my soup was cold, or the meat they served me wasn't
>   succulent,
> Back it went, it's worth the wait for nicer things.

(*Speaking.*) All or nothing, next best is no good at all, everyone makes her own luck, I don't take orders from anyone.

Doch vom Dach ein Star
Pfiff: wart paar Jahr!
  Und du marschierst in der Kapell
  Im Gleichschritt, langsam oder schnell
  Und bläsest deinen kleinen Ton:
  Jetzt kommt er schon.
  Und jetzt das Ganze schwenkt!
  Der Mensch denkt: Gott lenkt
  Keine Red davon!

Und bevor das Jahr war abgefahren
Lernte ich zu schlucken meine Medizin.
(Zwei Kinder aufm Hals und bei dem Brotpreis und
was alles verlangt wird!)
Als sie einmal mit mir fix und fertig waren
Hatten sie mich auf dem Arsch und auf den Knien.
(Man muß sich stelln mit den Leuten, eine Hand
wäscht die andre, mit dem Kopf kann man nicht durch
die Wand.)
  Und vom Dach der Star
  Pfiff: noch kein Jahr!
  Und sie marschiert in der Kapell
  Im Gleichschritt, langsam oder schnell
  Und bläset ihren kleinen Ton:
  Jetzt kommt er schon.
  Und jetzt das Ganze schwenkt!
  Der Mensch denkt: Gott lenkt
  Keine Red davon!

Viele sah ich schon den Himmel stürmen
Und kein Stern war ihnen groß und weit genug.
(Der Tüchtige schafft es, wo ein Wille ist, ist ein Weg,
wir werden den Laden schon schmeißen.)

Singing.

Birdsong up above:
Push comes to shove.
Soon you fall down from the grandstand
And join the players in the band
Who tootle out that melody:
Wait, wait and see.
And then: it's all downhill.
Your fall was God's will.
Better let it be.

But within a year, I would eat what I was served.
And I learned, you smile and take your medicine.

(*Speaking.*) Two kids hanging on my neck and the price of
bread and everything it takes from you.

Singing.

I'd accepted that I only got the shit that I deserved.
On my ass, or on my knees, I took it with a grin.

(*Speaking.*) You have to learn to make deals with people,
one hand washes the other one, your head's not hard
enough to knock over a wall.

Singing.

Birdsong from above:
Push comes to shove.
Soon you fall down from your grandstand
And join the players in the band
Who tootle out that melody:
Wait, wait and see.
And then: it's all downhill.
Your fall was God's will.
Better let it be.

Many folk I've known planned to scale the highest peak.
Off they go, the starry sky high overhead.

(*Speaking.*) To the victor the spoils, where there's a will
there's a way, at least act like you own the store.

Doch sie fühlten bald beim Berg-auf-Berge-Türmen
Wie doch schwer man schon an einem Strohhut trug.
(Man muß sich nach der Decke strecken!)
  Und vom Dach der Star
  Pfeift: wart paar Jahr!
  Und sie marschiern mit der Kapell
  Im Gleichschritt, langsam oder schnell
  Und blasen ihren kleinen Ton:
  Jetzt kommt er schon.
  Und jetzt das Ganze schwenkt!
  Der Mensch denkt: Gott lenktKeine Red davon!

(**Mutter Courage** *zu dem* **jungen Soldaten**) Darum denk
ich, du solltest dableiben mitn offnen Schwert, wenns dir
wirklich danach ist und dein Zorn ist groß genug, denn
du hast einen guten Grund, das geb ich zu, aber wenn
dein Zorn ein kurzer ist, geh lieber gleich weg!

Junger Soldat   Leck mich am Arsch! (*Er stolpert weg, der*
ältere Soldat *ihm nach.*)

Der Schreiber (*steckt den Kopf heraus*)   Der Rittmeister ist
gekommen. Jetzt können Sie sich beschweren.

Mutter Courage   Ich habs mir anders überlegt. Ich
beschwer mich nicht. (*Ab.*)

Singing.

> Stone by stone you climb, but your efforts only leave you
>   worn and weak,
> Broken down, you barely make it back to bed.

(*Speaking.*) If the shoe fits, wear it.

Singing.

> From the God of Love:
> Push comes to shove.
> And you fall down from that grandstand
> And join the players in the band
> Who tootle out that melody:
> Wait, wait and see.
> And then: it just goes downhill.
> Who knows? It's God's will.
> Best to leave it be.

(*Speaking, to the* **Young Soldier**.) Stay here with your sword ready if your anger is great enough, because you're in the right, I know you are, but if your anger's only a flash, better to run away.

The Young Soldier   Go fuck yourself in hell.

He stumbles out, the **Older Soldier** *following him. The* **Clerk** *sticks his head out of the tent.*

The Clerk   The Captain's ready. You can make your complaint now.

Mother Courage   I've thought it over. I'm not complaining.

She leaves.

Interval.

Five

Zwei Jahre sind vergangen. Der Krieg überzieht immer weitere Gebiete. Auf rastlosen Fahrten durchquert der kleine Wagen der Courage Polen, Mähren, Bayern, Italien und wieder Bayern. 1631. Tillys Sieg bei Magdeburg kostet **Mutter Courage** *vier Offiziershemden.*

Mutter Courages *Wagen steht in einem zerschossenen Dorf. Von weither dünne Militärmusik. Zwei* **Soldaten** *am Schanktisch, von* **Kattrin** *und* **Mutter Courage** *bedient. Der eine hat einen Damenpelzmantel umgehängt.*

Mutter Courage   Was, zahlen kannst du nicht? Kein Geld, kein Schnaps. Siegesmärsch spielen sie auf, aber den Sold zahlen sie nicht aus.

Soldat Meinen Schnaps will ich. Ich bin zu spät zum Plündern gekommen. Der Feldhauptmann hat uns beschissen und die Stadt nur für eine Stunde zum Plündern freigegeben. Er ist kein Unmensch, hat er gesagt; die Stadt muß ihm was gezahlt haben.

Der Feldprediger (*kommt gestolpert*)   In dem Hof da liegen noch welche. Die Bauernfamilie. Hilf mir einer. Ich brauch Leinen.

Der zweite **Soldat** *geht mit ihm weg.* **Kattrin** *gerät in große Erregung und versucht ihre Mutter zur Herausgabe von Leinen zu bringen.*

Mutter Courage Ich hab keins. Meine Binden hab ich ausverkauft beim Regiment. Ich zerreiß für die nicht meine Offiziershemden.

Der Feldprediger (*zurückrufend*)   Ich brauch Leinen, sag ich.

Mutter Courage (**Kattrin** *den Eintritt in den Wagen verwehrend, indem sie sich auf die Treppe setzt*)   Ich gib nix. Die zahlen nicht, warum, die haben nix.

Der Feldprediger (*über einer Frau, die er hergetragen hat*) Warum seid ihr dageblieben im Geschützfeuer?

Five

Two years have gone by. The war has expanded over ever wider territory. **Mother Courage**'s *little wagon travels ceaselessly, crossing Poland, Moravia, Bavaria, Italy, and Bavaria again. 1631. Tilly's victory at Magdeburg costs* **Mother Courage** *four officers' shirts.*

Mother Courage's *wagon has set up in a village that's been wrecked by cannon fire. Military marches sound in the distance. Two* **Soldiers** *stand at the wagon's bar, served by* **Kattrin** *and* **Mother Courage**. *One of the* **Soldiers** *has a woman's fur coat draped over his shoulders.*

Mother Courage   Why can't you pay? No money, no schnapps. If I'm hearing a victory march, the soldiers ought to have enough back pay to pay a bar tab.

Soldier   C'mon, schnapps! I was delayed and I missed the looting. The General only allowed one hour of looting, one hour for a whole city! It'd be inhuman to allow more, he said; the city must've bribed him, the treacherous fuck.*

The **Chaplain** *stumbles in.*

The Chaplain   In the farmyard, they're lying there. A family. Somebody help me. I need linen.

The **Second Soldier** *goes with him.* **Kattrin**, *agitated, beseeches her mother to bring out linen.*

Mother Courage   I'm out. I sold every bandage in stock to the regiment. What should I do, tear up good officers' shirts* to bandage farmers?

The Chaplain (*calling from offstage*)   I said I need linen.

Mother Courage *sits on the steps to the wagon so* **Kattrin** *can't go in.*

Mother Courage   I'm giving nothing. They'll never pay, and here's why, because they've got nothing.

The **Chaplain** *is bent over a woman he's carried from the yard.*

The Chaplain (*to the woman*)   Why did you stay after the shooting started?

Die Bauersfrau (*schwach*)   Hof.

Mutter Courage   Die und weggehen von was! Aber jetzt soll ich herhalten. Ich tus nicht.

Erster Soldat   Das sind Evangelische. Warum müssen sie evangelisch sein?

Mutter Courage   Die pfeifen dir aufn Glauben. Denen ist der Hof hin.

Zweiter Soldat   Die sind gar nicht evangelisch. Die sind selber katholisch.

Erster Soldat   Wir können sie nicht herausklauben bei der Beschießung.

Ein Bauer (*den der* **Feldprediger** *bringt*)   Mein Arm ist hin.

Der Feldprediger   Wo ist das Leinen?

Alle sehen auf **Mutter Courage**, *die sich nicht rührt.*

Mutter Courage   Ich kann nix geben. Mit all die Abgaben, Zöll, Zins und Bestechungsgelder! (**Kattrin** *hebt, Gurgellaute ausstoßend, eine Holzplanke auf und bedroht ihre Mutter damit.*) Bist du übergeschnappt? Leg das Brett weg, sonst schmier ich dir eine, Krampen! Ich gib nix, ich mag nicht, ich muß an mich selber denken. (*Der* **Feldprediger** *hebt sie von der Wagentreppe auf und setzt sie auf den Boden; dann kramt er Hemden heraus und reißt sie in Streifen.*) Meine Hemden! Das Stück zu einem halben Gulden! Ich bin ruiniert!

Aus dem Hause kommt eine schmerzliche Kinderstimme.

Der Bauer Das Kleine is noch drin!

The Farmer's Wife (*very weak*)   Farm.

Mother Courage   Them let go of what's theirs? Oh no, never! And I should be left holding the bill. Not me, no way.

First Soldier   Too bad they wouldn't convert.

Mother Courage   They would have if anyone'd asked.* They'd whistle any tune you wanted. The farm's everything to farmers.

Second Soldier   Anyway, not a one of them is Protestant. These are Catholics, same as us.

First Soldier   That's the trouble with artillery shells, they're indiscriminate.

The **Chaplain** *has carried the* **Farmer** *from the yard.*

Farmer   My arm's ripped open.

The Chaplain   Where's the linen?

Everyone looks at **Mother Courage** *who doesn't move.*

Mother Courage   Taxes, tolls, penalties and payoffs! I can't spare a thing.

Growling, **Kattrin** *picks up a plank and threatens her mother with it.*

Mother Courage   Have you snapped your tether? You put that plank down now or I'll slap your face off you, you cramp! I'm giving nothing, no one can make me, I've got myself to think about.

The **Chaplain** *lifts her off the steps and puts her on the ground. He goes into the wagon and comes out with linen shirts, which he proceeds to tear into strips.*

Mother Courage   Oh not my shirts! That's half a guilder I paid per. I'm ruined!

A baby is heard screaming in terror inside the house.

The Farmer   Baby's still inside!

Kattrin *rennt hinein.*

Der Feldprediger (*zur Frau*)   Bleib liegen! Es wird schon herausgeholt.

Mutter Courage   Haltet sie zurück, das Dach kann einfallen.

Der Feldprediger   Ich geh nicht mehr hinein.

Mutter Courage (*hin und her gerissen*)   Aasens nicht mit meinem teuren Leinen!

Der zweite **Soldat** *hält sie zurück.* **Kattrin** *bringt einen Säugling aus der Trümmerstätte.*

Mutter Courage Hast du glücklich wieder einen Säugling gefunden zum Herumschleppen? Auf der Stell gibst ihn der Mutter, sonst hab ich wieder einen stundenlangen Kampf, bis ich ihn dir herausgerissen hab, hörst du nicht? (*Zum zweiten* **Soldaten**.) Glotz nicht, geh lieber dort hinter und sag ihnen, sie sollen mit der Musik aufhören, ich seh hier, daß sie gesiegt haben. Ich hab nur Verluste von eure Sieg.

Der Feldprediger (*beim Verbinden*)   Das Blut kommt durch.

Kattrin *wiegt den Säugling und lallt ein Wiegenlied.*

Mutter Courage   Da sitzt sie und ist glücklich in all dem Jammer, gleich gibst es weg, die Mutter kommt schon zu sich. (*Sie entdeckt den ersten* **Soldaten**, *der sich über die Getränke hergemacht hat und jetzt mit der Flasche wegwill.*) Pschagreff! Du Vieh, willst du noch weitersiegen? Du zahlst.

Erster Soldat   Ich hab nix.

Mutter Courage (*reißt ihm den Pelzmantel ab*)   Dann laß den Mantel da, der ist sowieso gestohlen.

Der Feldprediger   Es liegt noch einer drunten.

Kattrin *rushes into the house. The* **Farmer's Wife** *tries to sit up, the* **Chaplain** *restrains her.*

The Chaplain (*to the* **Farmer's Wife**)   Stay, stay, they've gone in to get it.

Mother Courage   Stop her, the roof might collapse.

The Chaplain   I'm not going in there again.

Mother Courage   Leave off my poor linen, you jackass.

Kattrin *emerges from the rubble, carrying an infant.*

Mother Courage   Oh what luck, who's found herself another suckling to haul around? You give it back to its mother one-two-three before you get attached and I have to spend hours pulling it away, you hear me? (*To the* **Second Soldier**.) Stop gawping, go tell them they can stop that music, I don't need to hear about it, I can see they've had a victory. I've had only losses from your victory.

The **Chaplain** *is bandaging wounds.*

The Chaplain   This isn't stopping the bleeding.

Kattrin *rocks the baby, singing a cradle song in her thick inarticulate way.*

Mother Courage   Look at her, joy sitting in the midst of misery, now give it back, its mother's coming to.

She grabs the **First Soldier***, who's been pouring himself drinks and is now trying to get away with the whole bottle.*

Mother Courage   Pay up, pig, no victories for you here, animal! Pay up.

First Soldier   With what?

She tears the fur coat off his shoulders.

Mother Courage   Leave me the coat, which anyway you stole somewhere.

The Chaplain   Someone's still inside.

Six

Vor der Stadt Ingolstadt in Bayern wohnt die Courage dem Begräbnis des gefallenen kaiserlichen **Feldhauptmanns** *Tilly bei. Es finden Gespräche über Kriegshelden und die Dauer des Krieges statt. Der* **Feldprediger** *beklagt, daß seine Talente brachliegen, und die stumme* **Kattrin** *bekommt die roten Schuhe. Man schreibt das Jahr 1632.*

Im Innern eines Marketenderzeltes, mit einem Ausschank nach hinten zu. Regen. In der Ferne Trommeln und Trauermusik. Der **Feldprediger** *und der* **Regimentsschreiber** *spielen ein Brettspiel.* **Mutter Courage** *und ihre Tochter machen Inventur.*

Der Feldprediger Jetzt setzt sich der Trauerzug in Bewegung.

Mutter Courage Schad um den Feldhauptmann – zweiundzwanzig Paar von die Socken –, daß er gefalln ist, heißt es, war ein Unglücksfall. Es war Nebel auf der Wiesen, der war schuld. Der Feldhauptmann hat noch einem Regiment zugerufen, sie solln todesmutig kämpfen, und ist zurückgeritten, in dem Nebel hat er sich aber in der Richtung geirrt, so daß er nach vorn war und er mitten in der Schlacht eine Kugel erwischt hat – nur noch vier Windlichter zurück. (*Von hinten ein Pfiff. Sie geht zum Ausschank.*) Eine Schand, daß ihr euch vom Begräbnis von eurem toten Feldhauptmann drückt! (*Sie schenkt aus.*)

Der Schreiber Man hätts Geld nicht vorm Begräbnis auszahln solln. Jetzt besaufen sie sich, anstatt daß sie zum Begräbnis gehen.

Der Feldprediger (*zum* **Schreiber**) Müssen Sie nicht zum Begräbnis?

Der Schreiber Ich hab mich gedrückt, wegn Regen.

Mutter Courage Bei Ihnen ists was andres, Ihnen möchts die Uniform verregnen. Es heißt, sie haben ihm natürlich die Glocken läuten wollen

Six

Near the Bavarian city of Ingolstadt **Mother Courage** *observes the funeral of the fallen Imperial Field Marshal Tilly. Discussions take place regarding war heroes and the duration of the war. The* **Chaplain** *complains that he's wasting his talents, and dumb* **Kattrin** *gets the red shoes. The year's recorded: 1632.*

Inside a canteen tent **Mother Courage** *has set up. A bar in the back is open to serve people outside. Rain. Drumrolls and sad music in the distance. The* **Chaplain** *and the* **Regimental Secretary** *are playing a board game.* **Mother Courage** *and her daughter are taking stock.*

The Chaplain   The funeral cortege has set forth.

Mother Courage   Too bad about the Field Marshal – twenty-two pairs of socks – he was up at the front before the battle, inspiring yet another regiment, don't fear death and that sort of thing, then he headed back to HQ but there was fog on the meadows and he got turned around and ended up in the middle of the slaughter and he caught a musket ball in the gut – we've only got four lanterns left.

Someone outside whistles and **Mother Courage** *goes to tend the bar.*

Mother Courage   You guys are shameless, he was your Field Marshal and you're skipping his funeral!

She serves them drinks.

The Regimental Secretary   It was a mistake, paying them before the funeral. Now instead of attending, they're all getting soused.

The Chaplain (*to the* **Regimental Secretary**)   Shouldn't you be at the funeral?

The Regimental Secretary   I wanted to go but it's raining.

Mother Courage   You've got an excuse, the rain'd ruin your uniform. They're saying they wanted to ring church

zum Begräbnis, aber es hat sich herausgestellt, daß die
Kirchen weggeschossen waren auf seinen Befehl, so daß
der arme Feldhauptmann keine Glocken hören wird,
wenn sie ihn hinabsenken. Anstatt dem wolln sie drei
Kanonenschüsse abfeuern, daß es nicht gar zu nüchtern
wird – siebzehn Leibriemen.

Rufe Vom Ausschank   Wirtschaft! Ein Branntwein!

Mutter Courage   Ersts Geld! Nein, herein kommt ihr
mir nicht mit eure Dreckstiefeln in mein Zelt! Ihr könnt
draußen trinken, Regen hin, Regen her. (*Zum* **Schreiber**.)
Ich laß nur die Chargen herein. Der Feldhauptmann hat
die letzte Zeit Sorgen gehabt, hör ich. Im Zweiten
Regiment solls Unruhen gegeben haben, weil er keinen
Sold ausgezahlt, sondern gesagt hat, es is ein
Glaubenskrieg, sie müssens ihm umsonst tun.

Trauermarsch. Alle sehen nach hinten.

Der Feldprediger   Jetzt defilierens vor der hohen Leich.

Mutter Courage   Mir tut so ein Feldhauptmann oder
Kaiser leid, er hat sich vielleicht gedacht, er tut was
übriges und was, wovon die Leut reden, noch in
künftigen Zeiten, und kriegt ein Standbild, zum Beispiel
er erobert die Welt, das is ein großes Ziel für einen
Feldhauptmann, er weiß es nicht besser. Kurz, er rackert
sich ab, und dann scheiterts am gemeinen Volk, was
vielleicht ein Krug Bier will und ein bissel Gesellschaft,
nix Höheres. Die schönsten Plän sind schon zuschanden
geworden durch die Kleinlichkeit von denen, wo sie
ausführen sollten, denn die Kaiser selber können ja nix
machen, sie sind angewiesen auf die Unterstützung von
ihre Soldaten und dem Volk, wo sie grad sind, hab ich
recht?

Der Feldprediger (*lacht*)   Courage, ich geb Ihnen recht,
bis auf die Soldaten. Die tun, was sie können. Mit denen
da draußen zum Beispiel, die ihren Branntwein im Regen
saufen, getrau ich mich hundert Jahr einen Krieg nach
dem andern zu machen und zwei auf einmal, wenns sein
muß, und ich bin kein gelernter Feldhauptmann.

bells for the funeral, the way you ought to, but the Field Marshal blew up every steeple in Ingolstadt, so no bells for the poor bastard as his coffin's dropped down to the worms. They'll fire off the cannons, just to keep it from getting too sober – seventeen bullet belts.

Calls from outside, men at the bar:

Voices Outside COME ON! SERVICE! BRANDY!!

Mother Courage Show me your money first. And no one comes inside, you're not mucking up my tent with your filthy boots. You'll drink outside, rain rain go away.* (*To the* **Regimental Secretary**.) Only commissioned officers get in. On a memorable occasion such as this* you want classier company.

A funeral march. Everyone looks outside.

The Chaplain They're filing past the estimable corpse.

Mother Courage It grieves me in a special way when it's a field marshal or a king who dies, someone who dreamed of doing things that'll still be talked about ages hence, whose strivings fell flat all because big dreamers need common people to do the sweaty work, and common people have no aspirations, a cold mug of beer in some friendly saloon and they're happy. Look at those men out there, drinking brandy in the rain. It's pathetic is what it is, that tiny-mindedness.

The Chaplain Oh, they're not so bad. Soldiers. They do what they're told.* They'll fight for a hundred more years if they're ordered to. Two hundred years. Tell 'em to do it and they'll fight for ever.

Mutter Courage   Dann meinen Sie nicht, daß der Krieg ausgehn könnt?

Der Feldprediger   Weil der Feldhauptmann hin ist? Sein Sie nicht kindisch. Solche finden sich ein Dutzend, Helden gibts immer.

Mutter Courage   Sie, ich frag Sie das nicht nur aus Hetz, sondern weil ich mir überleg, ob ich Vorrät einkaufen soll, was grad billig zu haben sind, aber wenn der Krieg ausgeht, kann ich sie dann wegschmeißen.

Der Feldprediger   Ich versteh, daß Sies ernst meinen. Es hat immer welche gegeben, die gehn herum und sagen: »Einmal hört der Krieg auf.« Ich sag: daß der Krieg einmal aufhört, ist nicht gesagt. Es kann natürlich zu einer kleinen Paus kommen. Der Krieg kann sich verschnaufen müssen, ja er kann sogar sozusagen verunglücken. Davor ist er nicht gesichert, es gibt ja nix Vollkommenes allhier auf Erden. Einen vollkommenen Krieg, wo man sagen könnt: an dem ist nix mehr auszusetzen, wirds vielleicht nie geben. Plötzlich kann er ins Stocken kommen, an was Unvorhergesehenem, an alles kann kein Mensch denken. Vielleicht ein Übersehn, und das Schlamassel ist da. Und dann kann man den Krieg wieder aus dem Dreck ziehn! Aber die Kaiser und Könige und der Papst wird ihm zu Hilf kommen in seiner Not. So hat er im ganzen nix Ernstliches zu fürchten, und ein langes Leben liegt vor ihm.

Ein Soldat *singt vor der Schenke:*

> Ein Schnaps, Wirt, schnell, sei g'scheit!
> Ein Reiter hat kein Zeit.
> Muß für sein Kaiser streiten.

Einen doppelten, heut ist Festtag!

Mutter Courage   Wenn ich Ihnen traun könnt …

Der Feldprediger   Denken Sie selber! Was sollt gegen den Krieg sein?

Mother Courage   Think the war will end now?

The Chaplain   Why? Because a field marshal died? Don't be silly. Food's scarce, not field marshals.*

Mother Courage   Seriously, for me it's not a casual question, I could really beef up the inventory, I've got cash and prices are low, but then if the war ends, no demand, I'll be sunk.

The Chaplain   Very well then, my earnest opinion. There are always people who run around and say, 'Some day the war will end.' I say no one can say whether the war will end. There will of course be brief pauses, intermissions if you will. The war might meet with an accident, same as the Field Marshal. There are risks in every enterprise, the earth is under heaven and nothing's perfect upon it. Wars get stuck in ruts, no one saw it coming, no one can think of everything, maybe there's been short-sighted planning and all at once your war's a big mess. But the Emperor or the King or the Pope reliably provides what's necessary to get it going again. This war's got no significant worries as far as I can see, a long life lies ahead of it.

A **Soldier** *is singing at the bar.*

The Soldier (*singing*)
  A schnapps, landlord, and fast!
  A soldier's never last!
  His fists are even faster!*

(*Speaking.*) Make mine a double, today's a holiday!

Mother Courage   I must be getting tired, or it's the rain or the funeral or something, uncertainty's never bothered me before.*

The Chaplain   What's uncertain? What will ever stop the war?

Der Soldat *singt hinten:*

Dein Brust, Weib, schnell, sei g'scheit!
Ein Reiter hat kein Zeit.
Er muß gen Mähren reiten.

Der Schreiber (*plötzlich*)   Und der Frieden, was wird aus
ihm? Ich bin aus Böhmen und möcht gelegentlich heim.

Der Feldprediger   So, möchten Sie? Ja, der Frieden! Was
wird aus dem Loch, wenn der Käs gefressen ist?

Der Soldat *singt hinten:*

Trumpf aus, Kamrad, sei g'scheit!
Ein Reiter hat kein Zeit.
Muß kommen, solang sie werben.

Dein Spruch, Pfaff, schnell, sei g'scheit!
Ein Reiter hat kein Zeit.
Er muß fürn Kaiser sterben.

Der Schreiber   Auf die Dauer kann man nicht ohne
Frieden leben.

Der Feldprediger   Ich möcht sagen, den Frieden gibts
im Krieg auch, er hat seine friedlichen Stelln. Der Krieg
befriedigt nämlich alle Bedürfniss, auch die friedlichen
darunter, dafür ist gesorgt, sonst möcht er sich nicht
halten können. Im Krieg kannst du auch kacken wie im
tiefsten Frieden, und zwischen dem einen Gefecht und
dem andern gibts ein Bier, und sogar auf dem Vormarsch
kannst du ein'n Nicker machen, aufn Ellbogen, das ist
immer möglich, im Straßengraben. Beim Stürmen kannst
du nicht Karten spieln, das kannst du beim Akkerpflügen
im tiefsten Frieden auch nicht, aber nach dem Sieg gibts
Möglichkeiten. Dir mag ein Bein abgeschossen werden,
da erhebst du zuerst ein großes Geschrei, als wärs was,
aber dann beruhigst du dich oder kriegst Schnaps, und
am End hüpfst du wieder herum, und der Krieg ist nicht
schlechter dran als vorher. Und was hindert dich, daß du
dich vermehrst inmitten all dem Gemetzel, hinter einer
Scheun oder woanders, davon bist du nie auf die Dauer
abzuhalten, und dann hat der Krieg deine Sprößlinge

The Soldier (*singing*)
Your tits, girl, show 'em fast!
A soldier's heart is vast!
But please don't tell the pastor!

The Regimental Secretary (*abruptly*)   And peace,
whatever happened to that? I'm from Bohemia and I
want to go home.

The Chaplain   Oh, yes, peace indeed. It's the hole in the
cheese, we search high and low for it after we've eaten.

The Soldier (*singing*)
Your cards, comrades, and fast!
A soldier's not tight-assed!
He smiles at disaster!

Your prayer, good priest, and fast!
A soldier's die is cast!
He's mincemeat for his master!

The Regimental Secretary   People can't live without
peace.

The Chaplain   True, but just because there's war doesn't
mean there's no peace, war has its moments of peace.
War satisfies every human need, even for peace, it's got to
or why else would we have wars? You can take a dump in
wartime exactly as you do when things are peaceful, and
between one battle and the next have a beer. Even when
you're dog weary on the march you can prop your head
up on your elbows and catch a nap in a ditch. While it's
true that in the thick of battle you can't play cards, you
can't do that in the thick of peacetime either, when
you're ploughing furrows in the field, hour by hour day
after day – after a battle, at least, if you win, there are
possibilities. Your leg's shot up, maybe, and first thing you
scream, then you calm down, then a glass of schnapps,
then in the end you're hopping about like a regular flea
and the war's still the war, unperturbed by your
misadventure. And what's to stop you from multiplying in
the midst of slaughter, behind a barn or anyplace,
breeding like maggots in raw meat,* nothing stops that,
and then the war takes the kids you produce and on and

und kann mit ihnen weiterkommen. Nein, der Krieg
findet immer einen Ausweg, was nicht gar. Warum soll er
aufhörn müssen?

*Kattrin hat aufgehört zu arbeiten und starrt auf den
Feldprediger.*

Mutter Courage   Da kauf ich also die Waren. Ich verlaß
mich auf Sie. (**Kattrin** *schmeißt plötzlich einen Korb mit
Flaschen auf den Boden und läuft hinaus.*) Kattrin! (*Lacht.*)
Jesses, die wart doch auf den Frieden. Ich hab ihr
versprochen, sie kriegt einen Mann, wenn Frieden wird.
(*Sie läuft ihr nach.*)

Der Schreiber (*aufstehend*)   Ich hab gewonnen, weil Sie
geredet haben. Sie zahln.

Mutter Courage (*herein mit* **Kattrin**)   Sei vernünftig, der
Krieg geht noch ein bissel weiter, und wir machen noch
ein bissel Geld, da wird der Friede um so schöner. Du
gehst in die Stadt, das sind keine zehn Minuten, und
holst die Sachen im Goldenen Löwen, die wertvollern,
die andern holn wir später mitm Wagen, es ist alles
ausgemacht, der Herr Regimentsschreiber begleitet dich.
Die meisten sind beim Begräbnis vom Feldhauptmann,
da kann dir nix geschehn. Machs gut, laß dir nix
wegnehmen, denk an deine Aussteuer!

Kattrin *nimmt eine Leinwand über den Kopf und geht mit dem*
Schreiber.

Der Feldprediger   Können Sie sie mit dem Schreiber
gehn lassen?

Mutter Courage   Sie is nicht so hübsch, daß sie einer
ruinieren möcht.

Der Feldprediger   Wie Sie so Ihren Handel führn und
immer durchkommen, das hab ich oft bewundert. Ich
verstehs, daß man Sie Courage geheißen hat.

on it goes on and on and on. No, war always finds a way. Why should it ever end?

Kattrin *has stopped working. She's holding a basket full of bottles and is staring at the* **Chaplain**.

Mother Courage   OK, I'm buying more goods. On your say-so.

Kattrin *suddenly throws the basket to the ground and runs off.*

Mother Courage   Kattrin! (*Laughing.*) Jesus, she's waiting for peace. I promised her she'd get a husband when peace arrives.

Mother Courage *runs after her. The* **Regimental Secretary** *stands up.*

The Regimental Secretary   While you chattered I paid attention to the game. I win. Pay up.

Mother Courage *returns with* **Kattrin**.

Mother Courage   A little more war, a little more money, peace'll be sweeter for the wait. You go to town, ten minutes' walk, get our package at the Golden Lion, the pricey things, the rest we'll pick up with the wagon. They expect you, and the Regimental Secretary here will accompany you. Most everyone's at the Field Marshal's funeral, nothing can happen to you. Hang tight to the package, anyone says they'll help carry it no thanks, think about your trousseau.

Kattrin *covers her head with a scarf and leaves with the* **Regimental Secretary**.

The Chaplain   You think it's a good idea, letting her go with him?

Mother Courage   She should be so pretty that a man like him pays attention to her.

The Chaplain   Often I sit back and watch you, amazed. Your quick mind, your indomitable spirit, it's the right name for you, Courage.

Mutter Courage Die armen Leut brauchen Courage.
Warum, sie sind verloren. Schon daß sie aufstehn in der
Früh, dazu gehört was in ihrer Lag. Oder daß sie einen
Acker umpflügen, und im Krieg! Schon daß sie Kinder in
die Welt setzen, zeigt, daß sie Courage haben, denn sie
haben keine Aussicht. Sie müssen einander den Henker
machen und sich gegenseitig abschlachten, wenn sie
einander da ins Gesicht schaun wolln, das braucht wohl
Courage. Daß sie einen Kaiser und einen Papst dulden,
das beweist eine unheimliche Courage, denn die kosten
ihnen das Leben. (*Sie setzt sich nieder, zieht eine kleine Pfeife
aus der Tasche und raucht.*) Sie könnten ein bissel
Kleinholz machen.

Der Feldprediger (*zieht widerwillig die Jacke aus und bereitet
sich vor zum Kleinholzmachen*) Ich bin eigentlich
Seelsorger und nicht Holzhacker.

Mutter Courage Ich hab aber keine Seel. Dagegen
brauch ich Brennholz.

Der Feldprediger Was ist das für eine Stummelpfeif?

Mutter Courage Halt eine Pfeif.

Der Feldprediger Nein, nicht »halt eine«, sondern eine
ganz bestimmte.

Mutter Courage So?

Der Feldprediger Das ist die Stummelpfeif von dem
Koch vom Oxenstjerna-Regiment.

Mutter Courage Wenn Sies wissen, warum fragen Sie
dann erst so scheinheilig?

Mother Courage   You're talkative today. I'm not
courageous. Only poor people need courage.* Why,
because they're hopeless. To get out of bed each
morning, or plough a potato field in wartime, or bring
kids with no prospects into the world – to live poor, that
takes courage. Consider how easily and often they
murder each other, they need courage just to look one
another in the face. They trudge along, uncomplainingly
carrying the Emperor and his heavy throne and the Pope
and his stone cathedral,* they stagger, starving, bearing
the whole thundering weight of the great wealth of the
wealthy on their broad stupid backs, and is that courage?
Must be, but it's perverted courage, because what they
carry on their backs will cost them their lives.

She sits, takes a small pipe from a pocket, lights it and smokes.

You could be chopping up kindling.

The **Chaplain** *reluctantly takes off his coat, picks up a hatchet
and a bundle of branches, and starts chopping kindling,
standing over a chopping block, hacking the branches into
smaller sticks.*

The Chaplain   I'm a pastor, not a woodcutter.

Mother Courage   I don't have a soul so I don't need a
pastor. I have a stove, and it needs firewood.

The Chaplain   Where'd you get that stubby little pipe?

Mother Courage   It's a pipe, who knows?

The Chaplain   It's not a pipe, or rather not just a pipe,
it's special.

Mother Courage   Is it?

The Chaplain   It's the stubby little pipe of the cook from
the Oxenstjerna Regiment.

Mother Courage   If you know, why're you asking,
hypocrite?

Der Feldprediger   Weil ich nicht weiß, ob Sie sich bewußt sind, daß Sie grad die rauchen. Hätt doch sein können, Sie fischen nur so in Ihren Habseligkeiten herum, und da kommt Ihnen irgendeine Stummelpfeif in die Finger, und Sie nehmen sie aus reiner Geistesabwesenheit.

Mutter Courage   Und warum sollts nicht so sein?

Der Feldprediger   Weils nicht so ist. Sie rauchen sie bewußt.

Mutter Courage   Und wenn ich das tät?

Der Feldprediger   Courage, ich warn Sie. Es ist meine Pflicht. Sie werden den Herrn kaum mehr zu Gesicht kriegn, aber das ist nicht schad, sondern Ihr Glück. Er hat mir keinen verläßlichen Eindruck gemacht. Im Gegenteil.

Mutter Courage   So? Er war ein netter Mensch.

Der Feldprediger   So, das nennen Sie einen netten Menschen? Ich nicht. Ich bin weit entfernt, ihm was Böses zu wolln, aber nett kann ich ihn nicht nennen. Eher einen Donschuan, einen raffinierten. Schauen Sie die Pfeif an, wenn Sie mir nicht glauben. Sie müssen zugeben, daß sie allerhand von seinem Charakter verrät.

Mutter Courage   Ich seh nix. Gebraucht ist sie.

Der Feldprediger   Durchgebissen ist sie halb. Ein Gewaltmensch. Das ist die Stummelpfeif von einem rücksichtslosen Gewaltmenschen, das sehn Sie dran, wenn Sie noch nicht alle Urteilskraft verloren haben.

Mutter Courage   Hacken Sie mir nicht meinen Hackpflock durch.

Der Feldprediger   Ich hab Ihnen gesagt, ich bin kein gelernter Holzhacker. Ich hab Seelsorgerei studiert. Hier werden meine Gaben und Fähigkeiten mißbraucht zu körperlicher Arbeit. Meine von Gott verliehenen Talente kommen überhaupt nicht zur Geltung. Das ist eine Sünd. Sie haben mich nicht predigen hörn. Ich kann ein Regiment nur mit einer Ansprach so in Stimmung versetzen, daß es den Feind wie eine Hammelherd

The Chaplain   Because I don't know whether you pay attention to what you smoke. Could be you just fish around in your pockets like some people do and any stumpy grubby snub of a pipe your fingers come across, you'll pop it in your mouth from sheer absent-mindedness.

Mother Courage   As long as I can suck smoke out of it, I'm not fussy.

The Chaplain   Perhaps, only I don't think so. Not you. You know what you're smoking.

Mother Courage   This is going somewhere?

The Chaplain   Listen to me, Courage. It's my obligation as your minister. It's hardly likely you'll meet up with that character again, and you know what character I mean, but that's luck not loss.

Mother Courage   Seemed nice enough to me. Who cares what you think?

The Chaplain   Good, you think he was nice, I think he wasn't, I think he's maybe not actually evil, but nice, definitely not. A Don Juan, exceedingly well-oiled. Take a look at that pipe, it exposes him, his personality.

Mother Courage   I'm looking at it.

The Chaplain   The stem of which has been half chewed through. As if a rat had attacked it.* The gnawed-upon pipe of a boorish violent rat of a man, you can see it for yourself if you haven't lost your last lick of horse sense.

Mother Courage   You're really going to town with that hatchet.

The Chaplain   I'm not trained to do this, I'm trained to preach. I went to divinity school. My gifts, my abilities are squandered on physical activity. It's an inappropriate application of God-given talents. Which is sinful. You never heard me preach. I can so intoxicate a battalion they think the enemy army's a grazing flock of fine fat mutton.

ansieht. Ihr Leben ist ihnen wie ein alter verstunkener
Fußlappen, den sie wegwerfen in Gedanken an den
Endsieg. Gott hat mir die Gabe der Sprachgewalt verliehen.
Ich predig, daß Ihnen Hören und Sehen vergeht.

Mutter Courage   Ich möcht gar nicht, daß mir Hören
und Sehen vergeht. Was tu ich da?

Der Feldprediger   Courage, ich hab mir oft gedacht, ob
Sie mit Ihrem nüchternen Reden nicht nur eine
warmherzige Natur verbergen. Auch Sie sind ein Mensch
und brauchen Wärme.

Mutter Courage   Wir kriegen das Zelt am besten warm,
wenn wir genug Brennholz haben.

Der Feldprediger   Sie lenken ab. Im Ernst, Courage, ich
frag mich mitunter, wie es wär, wenn wir unsere
Beziehung ein wenig enger gestalten würden. Ich mein,
nachdem uns der Wirbelsturm der Kriegszeiten so
seltsam zusammengewirbelt hat.

Mutter Courage   Ich denk, sie ist eng genug. Ich koche
Ihnens Essen, und Sie betätigen sich und machen zum
Beispiel Brennholz.

Der Feldprediger (*tritt auf sie zu*)   Sie wissen, was ich mit
»enger« mein; das ist keine Beziehung mit Essen und
Holzhacken und solche niedrigen Bedürfnisse. Lassen
Sie Ihr Herz sprechen,* verhärten Sie sich nicht.

Mutter Courage   Kommen Sie nicht mitn Beil auf mich
zu. Das wär mir eine zu enge Beziehung.

Der Feldprediger   Ziehen Sies nicht ins Lächerliche. Ich
bin ein ernster Mensch und hab mir überlegt, was ich sag.

Mutter Courage   Feldprediger, sein Sie gescheit. Sie sind
mir sympathisch, ich möcht Ihnen nicht den Kopf
waschen müssen. Auf was ich aus bin, ist, mich und
meine Kinder durchbringen mit meinem Wagen. Ich
betracht ihn nicht als mein, und ich hab auch jetzt
keinen Kopf für Privatgeschichten. Eben jetzt geh ich ein
Risiko ein mit Einkaufen, wo der Feldhauptmann gefalln
ist und alles vom Frieden redet. Wo wolln Sie hin, wenn

When I preach, a soldier's life's no more to him than an old *fershtunkeneh** footwrap he casts away as he marches off to glory. God gave me a mighty tongue. When I preach people fall dumb and go blind.

Mother Courage   Jesus, that's sort of terrifying.

The Chaplain   Courage, I've been waiting for this opportunity to talk to you.

Mother Courage   Maybe if we're quiet* we'll hear more funeral music.

The Chaplain   Beneath your customarily brusque and businesslike manner you're human, a woman, you need warmth.

Mother Courage   I'm warm, and all it takes is a steady supply of chopped wood.

The Chaplain   Kindling aside, Courage, shouldn't we make our relationship a closer one? I mean, consider how the whirligig of war has whirled us two together.

Mother Courage   I think we've whirled close as we're ever going to get. I cook, you eat what I cook, you do this and that and when you feel like it you chop kindling.

The **Chaplain** *moves towards her.*

The Chaplain   You know perfectly well that when I use the word 'close' I don't mean cooking or eating or kindling.

Mother Courage   Don't come at me waving that axe.

The Chaplain   I'm not a figure of fun. You make me a figure of fun. I'm a man with his dignity and I'm tendering you a considered, legitimate proposal. I'm proposing! Respond to my proposal!

Mother Courage   Give it a rest, Pastor. We get along, don't make me dunk your head in a pail. I want nothing more than for me and my children to get through all this with our wagon. I have nothing to give anyone, and anyway there's no room inside me for private dramas. It's drama enough, stocking up with the Field Marshal fallen

ich ruiniert bin? Sehen Sie, das wissen Sie nicht. Hacken
Sie uns das Brennholz, dann haben wir abends warm, das
ist schon viel in diese Zeiten. Was ist das?

Sie steht auf. Herein **Kattrin**, *atemlos, mit einer Wunde über
Stirn und Auge. Sie schleppt allerlei Sachen, Pakete, Lederzeug,
eine Trommel usw.*

Mutter Courage   Was ist, bist du überfalln worden? Aufn
Rückweg? Sie ist aufn Rückweg überfalln worden! Wenn
das nicht der Reiter gewesen ist, der sich bei mir besoffen
hat! Ich hätt dich nie gehn lassen solln. Schmeiß das
Zeug weg! Das ist nicht schlimm, die Wund ist nur eine
Fleischwund. Ich verbind sie dir, und in einer Woche ist
sie geheilt. Sie sind schlimmer als die Tier. (*Sie verbindet
die Wunde.*)

Der Feldprediger   Ich werf ihnen nix vor. Daheim haben
sie nicht geschändet. Schuld sind die, wo Krieg anstiften,
sie kehren das Unterste zuoberst in die Menschen.

Mutter Courage   Hat dich der Schreiber nicht
zurückbegleitet? Das kommt davon, daß du eine
anständige Person bist, da schern sie sich nicht drum. Die
Wund ist gar nicht tief, da bleibt nix zurück. So, jetzt ists
verbunden. Du kriegst was, sei ruhig. Ich hab dir
insgeheim was aufgehoben, du wirst schauen. (*Sie kramt
aus einem Sack die roten Stöckelschuhe der Pottier heraus.*) Was,
da schaust du? Die hast du immer wolln. Da hast du sie.
Zieh sie schnell an, daß es mich nicht reut. (*Sie hilft ihr die
Schuhe anziehen.*) Nix bleibt zurück, wenngleich mirs nix
ausmachen möcht. Das Los von denen, wo ihnen
gefallen, ist das schlimmste. Die ziehn sie herum, bis sie
kaputt sind. Wen sie nicht mögen, die lassen sie am
Leben. Ich hab schon solche gesehn, wo hübsch im
Gesicht gewesen sind, und dann haben sie bald so
ausgeschaut, daß einen Wolf gegraust hat. Nicht hinter
einen Alleebaum können sie gehn, ohne daß sie was
fürchten müssen, sie haben ein grausliches Leben. Das ist
wie mit die Bäum, die graden, luftigen werden abgehaun
für Dachbalken, und die krummen dürfen sich ihres
Lebens freun. Das wär also nix als ein Glück. Die Schuh
sind noch gut, ich hab sie eingeschmiert aufgehoben.

and everyone talking about peace. If my business folds, where would you be? Look, you hesitate, you don't know. If you make kindling we'll be warm come evening, and that's a lot, these days. (*She stands up.*) What's that?

Kattrin *enters, a large cut across her forehead and over an eye. She carries many packages, leather goods, a drum and other things as well.*

Mother Courage What, what, did somebody attack you? On your way back? Someone attacked her on the way back! Bet it was that soldier who was getting drunk! I shouldn't have sent you. Drop those things! It's not so terrible, a bad scratch. I'll bandage you up and in a week you're healed. They're not human, none of 'em, every one of them's swine.

She bandages **Kattrin***'s wounds.*

The Chaplain Blame the ones who start the wars. They don't rape back home.

Mother Courage I'll blame who I want and the hell they don't. Why didn't the Regimental Secretary walk you back? Probably he figured an upstanding person such as yourself wouldn't get bothered by anyone. The wound's not deep, it won't leave a mark. Done and done, wrapped tight. You just rest, calm yourself. I've got a secret something to show you, you'll see.

She gets a sack from which she takes **Yvette***'s red shoes.*

Mother Courage All right, look! See? You've been dreaming about them. They're yours. Put them on quick, before I have second thoughts. You won't be scarred, though there are worse things than that. If you're pretty you've got to be afraid of what's hiding behind every bush, your life's a nightmare. It's the ones no one wants who manage to have a life, like with trees, the tall beautiful trees get felled for roof beams, but the crippled and crooked trees get overlooked and go on living. You have to know how to recognise good luck. The shoes are ready to be worn, I've been shining them on the sly.

Kattrin *läßt die Schuhe stehen und kriecht in den Wagen.*

Der Feldprediger   Hoffentlich ist sie nicht verunstaltet.

Mutter Courage   Eine Narb wird bleiben. Auf den
Frieden muß die nimmer warten.

Der Feldprediger   Die Sachen hat sie sich nicht nehmen
lassen.

Mutter Courage   Ich hätts ihr vielleicht nicht
einschärfen solln. Wenn ich wüßt, wie es in ihrem Kopf
ausschaut! Einmal ist sie eine Nacht ausgeblieben, nur
einmal in all die Jahr. Danach ist sie herumgegangen wie
vorher, hat aber stärker gearbeitet. Ich konnt nicht
herausbringen, was sie erlebt hat. Ich hab mir eine
Zeitlang den Kopf zerbrochen. (*Sie nimmt die von* **Kattrin**
gebrachten Waren auf und sortiert sie zornig.) Das ist der
Krieg! Eine schöne Einnahmequell!

Man hört Kanonenschüsse.

Der Feldprediger   Jetzt begraben sie den
Feldhauptmann. Das ist ein historischer Augenblick.

Mutter Courage   Mir ist ein historischer Augenblick, daß
sie meiner Tochter übers Aug geschlagen haben. Die ist
schon halb kaputt, einen Mann kriegt sie nicht mehr,
und dabei so ein Kindernarr, stumm ist sie auch nur
wegen dem Krieg, ein Soldat hat ihr als klein was in den
Mund geschoppt. Den Schweizerkas seh ich nicht mehr,
und wo der Eilif ist, das weiß Gott. Der Krieg soll
verflucht sein.

Kattrin *leaves the shoes and crawls into the wagon.*

The Chaplain Hopefully she won't be disfigured.

Mother Courage It'll scar. Peace will never come for her.

The Chaplain She didn't let them take your merchandise.

Mother Courage I shouldn't have made such a fuss about that, maybe. I wish I knew what it looked like inside her head! She stayed out all night just once in all these years. After that she stumped around the way she does, only she started to work herself till she dropped, every day. She'd never tell me about it, what adventures she'd had. I clubbed my forehead with my fists for a long time over that one.

She picks up the goods **Kattrin** *dropped and angrily inspects them.*

Mother Courage War! A great way to make a living!

Cannon fire.

The Chaplain Now they're burying the Field Marshal. A moment in history.

Mother Courage The only history I know is today's the day they hit my daughter in the eye. She's more than halfway to done-for now, no husband for her now, and her such a great fool for children, she's mute because of the war, that too, when she was little a soldier stuffed something in her mouth. I'll never see Swiss Cheese again, and where Eilif is only God knows. It's a curse, this fucking war.

Seven

Mutter Courage *auf der Höhe ihrer geschäftlichen Laufbahn.*

Landstraße. Der **Feldprediger**, **Mutter Courage** *und ihre Tochter* **Kattrin** *ziehen den Planwagen, an dem neue Waren hängen.* **Mutter Courage** *trägt eine Kette mit Silbertalern.*

Mutter Courage   Ich laß mir den Krieg von euch nicht madig machen. Es heißt, er vertilgt die Schwachen, aber die sind auch hin im Frieden. Nur, der Krieg nährt seine Leut besser. (*Sie singt.*)

> Und geht er über deine Kräfte
> Bist du beim Sieg halt nicht dabei.
> Der Krieg ist nix als die Geschäfte
> Und statt mit Käse ists mit Blei.
> Und was möcht schon Seßhaftwerden nützen? Die
> Seßhaften sind zuerst hin. *Singt.*
> So mancher wollt so manches haben
> Was es für manchen gar nicht gab:
> Er wollt sich schlau ein Schlupfloch graben
> Und grub sich nur ein frühes Grab.
> Schon manchen sah ich sich abjagen
> In Eil nach einer Ruhestatt –
> Liegt er dann drin, mag er sich fragen
> Warums ihm so geeilet hat.

Sie ziehen weiter.

Seven

Mother Courage *at the height of her business career.*

A highway. The **Chaplain** *and* **Kattrin** *are pulling the wagon, festooned with new wares.* **Mother Courage** *walks alongside, wearing a necklace made of silver thalers.*

Mother Courage   I won't let you knock the war. Everyone says the weak are exterminated, but the weak don't fare any better in peacetime. War feeds its people better.

She sings:

It overwhelms all opposition,
It needs to grow or else it dies.
What else is war but competition,
A profit-building enterprise?

(*Speaking.*) You can't hide from it. The ones who hide are the first it finds.

War isn't nice, you hope to shirk it,
You hope you'll find someplace to hide.
But if you've courage you can work it,
And put a tidy sum aside.
The refugees? Oh sure, I've seen 'em,
The thousands fleeing from the war!
They've not a scrap of bread between 'em.
I wonder what they're running for?

The spring has come, and winter's dead.
The snow has gone, so draw a breath!
Let Christian souls crawl out of bed,
Pull on their socks and conquer death!

They keep pulling.

Eight

Im selben Jahr fällt der Schwedenkönig Gustav Adolf in der Schlacht bei Lützen. Der Frieden droht **Mutter Courages** *Geschäft zu ruinieren. Der Courage kühner Sohn vollbringt eine Heldentat zu viel und findet ein schimpfliches Ende.*

Feldlager. Ein Sommermorgen. Vor dem Wagen stehen eine **alte Frau** *und ihr* **Sohn**. *Der Sohn schleppt einen großen Sack mit Bettzeug.*

Mutter Courages Stimme (*aus dem Wagen*) Muß das in aller Herrgottsfrüh sein?

Der Junge Mann Wir sind die ganze Nacht zwanzig Meilen hergelaufen und müssen noch zurück heut.

Mutter Courages Stimme Was soll ich mit Bettfedern? Die Leut haben keine Häuser.

Der Junge Mann Wartens lieber, bis Sie sie sehn.

Die Alte Frau Da ist auch nix. Komm!

Der Junge Mann Dann verpfänden sie uns das Dach überm Kopf für die Steuern. Vielleicht gibt sie drei Gulden, wenn du das Kreuzel zulegst. (*Glocken beginnen zu läuten.*) Horch, Mutter!

Stimmen (*von hinten*) Frieden! Der Schwedenkönig ist gefallen!

Mutter Courage (*steckt den Kopf aus dem Wagen. Sie ist noch unfrisiert*) Was ist das für ein Geläut mitten in der Woch?

Der Feldprediger (*kommt unterm Wagen vorgekrochen*) Was schrein sie?

Mutter Courage Sagen Sie mir nicht, daß Friede ausgebrochen ist, wo ich eben neue Vorrät eingekauft hab.

Der Feldprediger (*nach hinten rufend*) Ists wahr, Frieden?

Eight

In the same year the Swedish king, Gustavus Adolphus, falls in the Battle of Lützen. Peace threatens to ruin **Mother Courage***'s business. Her brave son does one heroic deed too many and comes to an ignominious end.*

An army camp. A summer's morning. Outside the wagon, an **Old Woman** *and a* **Young Man**, *her son, are waiting. The son is carrying a heavy mattress.*

Mother Courage's Voice (*inside the wagon*)   Does it have to be so goddamned early?

The Young Man   We've been walking all night, twenty miles, we have to get back today.

Mother Courage's Voice (*inside the wagon*)   Who's buying mattresses? People don't have houses.

The Young Man   Come look at it.

The Old Woman   She doesn't want it, no one does. Let's go home.

The Young Man   Home's forfeit if we can't pay the taxes. She'll give us at least three guilders for the bed if we include your crucifix.

Bells start ringing.

The Young Man   Listen, Mama!

Offstage Voices   Peace! The Swedish king is dead!

Mother Courage *sticks her head out of the wagon. Her hair's an uncombed mess.*

Mother Courage   What's with the bells? It's Wednesday!

The **Chaplain** *crawls out from under the wagon.*

The Chaplain   What's the shouting about?

Mother Courage   Don't tell me peace has broken out, I've just replenished my entire stock.

The Chaplain (*shouting to the rear*)   Is it peace?

Stimme   Seit drei Wochen, heißts, wir habens nur nicht erfahren.

Der Feldprediger (*zur* **Courage**)   Warum solln sie sonst die Glocken läuten?*

Stimme   In der Stadt sind schon ein ganzer Haufen Lutherische mit Fuhrwerken angekommen, die haben die Neuigkeit gebracht.

Der Junge Mann   Mutter, es ist Frieden. Was hast?

Die alte Frau ist zusammengebrochen.

Mutter Courage (*zurück in den Wagen*)   Marandjosef! Kattrin, Friede! Zieh dein Schwarzes an! Wir gehn in Gottesdienst. Das sind wir dem Schweizerkas schuldig. Obs wahr ist?

Der Junge Mann   Die Leut hier sagens auch. Es ist Frieden gemacht worden. Kannst du aufstehn? (*Die* **alte Frau** *steht betäubt auf.*) Jetzt bring ich die Sattlerei wieder in Gang. Ich versprech dirs. Alles kommt in Ordnung. Vater kriegt sein Bett wieder. Kannst du laufen? (*Zum* **Feldprediger**.) Schlecht ist ihr geworden. Das ist die Nachricht. Sie hats nicht geglaubt, daß es noch Frieden wird. Vater hats immer gesagt. Wir gehn gleich heim.

Beide ab.

Mutter Courages Stimme   Gebt ihr einen Schnaps!

Der Feldprediger   Sie sind schon fort.

Mutter Courages Stimme   Was ist im Lager drüben?

Der Feldprediger   Sie laufen zusammen. Ich geh hinüber. Soll ich nicht mein geistliches Gewand anziehn?

Mutter Courages Stimme   Erkundigen Sie sich erst genauer, vor Sie sich zu erkennen geben als Antichrist. Ich bin froh übern Frieden, wenn ich auch ruiniert bin. Wenigstens zwei von den Kindern hätt ich also durchgebracht durch den Krieg. Jetzt werd ich meinen Eilif wiedersehn.

A Voice   The war was over three weeks ago, they're saying, it took three weeks for the news to get here!

Another Voice   In town, a whole heap of Lutherans arrived in their carts, they brought the news with them.

The Young Man   Ma, it's peace!

The **Old Woman** *collapses. Her son rushes to her.*

The Young Man   Ma? MA!

Mother Courage *goes back inside the wagon.*

Mother Courage   Mary and Joseph! Kattrin, it's peace! Put your black dress on! We'll go find a Protestant church. We should pray for Swiss Cheese. I can't believe it!

The Young Man   They wouldn't be saying it if it wasn't true. They made peace. (*To his mother.*) Can you stand up?

The **Old Woman** *stands.*

The Young Man   I'll start making saddles again, I'll open up the shop. I promise you. Everything will go back to what it was. We'll bring back Daddy's bedding. Can you walk? (*To the* **Chaplain**.) It hit her hard. The news. She decided long ago the war would last for ever. (*To his mother.*) Daddy always said otherwise. Let's get home.

The mother and son leave.

Mother Courage (*inside the wagon*)   Give the old woman a schnapps!

The Chaplain   Gone. Gone.

Mother Courage (*inside the wagon*)   What're they up to in the camp?

The Chaplain   There's a huge crowd. I'll go over. Think I should put on my evangelical garb?

Mother Courage (*inside the wagon*)   If it was me, I'd inquire a little more precisely as to the state of things before I went into a Catholic army camp dressed as the Antichrist. I'm so happy it's peace, I don't care if I'm ruined. At least two of my children survived the war, I saw to that. Bet I'll see my Eilif soon.

Der Feldprediger   Und wer kommt da die Lagergass herunter? Wenn das nicht der Koch vom Feldhauptmann ist!

Der Koch (*etwas verwahrlost und mit einem Bündel*)   Wen seh ich? Den Feldprediger!

Der Feldprediger   Courage, ein Besuch!

Mutter Courage *klettert heraus.*

Der Koch   Ich habs doch versprochen, ich komm, sobald ich Zeit hab, zu einer kleinen Unterhaltung herüber. Ich hab Ihren Branntwein nicht vergessen, Frau Fierling.

Mutter Courage   Jesus, der Koch vom Feldhauptmann! Nach all die Jahr! Wo ist der Eilif, mein Ältester?

Der Koch   Ist der noch nicht da? Der ist vor mir weg und wollt auch zu Ihnen.

Der Feldprediger   Ich zieh mein geistliches Gewand an, wartets. (*Ab hinter den Wagen.*)

Mutter Courage   Da kann er jede Minute eintreffen. (*Ruft in den Wagen.*) Kattrin, der Eilif kommt! Hol ein Glas Branntwein fürn Koch, Kattrin! (*Kattrin zeigt sich nicht.*) Gib ein Büschel Haar drüber, und fertig! Herr Lamb ist kein Fremder. (*Holt selber den Branntwein.*) Sie will nicht heraus, sie macht sich nix ausn Frieden. Er hat zu lang auf sich warten lassen. Sie haben sie über das eine Aug geschlagen, man siehts schon kaum mehr, aber sie meint, die Leut stiern auf sie.

Der Koch   Ja, der Krieg!

The **Cook** *enters, haggard, carrying a bundle.*

The Chaplain   And look what peace already dragged in. It's the General's cook!

The Cook   What's this apparition I see before me?* The Holy Ghost? No, it's the General's chaplain, same as ever, pale as a snail's sticky underbelly!

The Chaplain   Courage, a visitor!

Mother Courage *climbs down from the wagon.*

Mother Courage   The General's cook. After all these years.

The Cook   At the first opportunity, as promised, a visit, a little intelligent conversation, some unforgettable brandy, Mrs Fierling, a man's only as good as his word.

Mother Courage   Where's Eilif, my eldest?

The Cook   He left before I did, on his way here same as me. Funny he isn't here yet, he's so robust.

The Chaplain   I'm putting on my pastoral vestments, don't say anything interesting till I get back.

He goes behind the wagon.

Mother Courage   He's robust but he dawdles. He'll show up any minute, I can feel it! (*Calling into the wagon.*) Kattrin, Eilif's coming! Bring the cook a glass of brandy, Kattrin!

Kattrin *doesn't come out.*

Mother Courage (*calling into the wagon*)   Comb your bangs down over it, it's enough already! Mr Lamb isn't a stranger.

She gets the brandy herself.

She won't come out, what does peace mean to her? It took its time coming and it came too late. They hit her, right above the eye, you can barely see the scar now, but to her mind people stare.

The Cook   War.

Er und **Mutter Courage** *setzen sich.*

Mutter Courage   Koch, Sie treffen mich im Unglück. Ich bin ruiniert.

Der Koch   Was? Das ist aber ein Pech.

Mutter Courage   Der Friede bricht mirn Hals. Ich hab auf den Feldprediger sein Rat neulich noch Vorrät eingekauft. Und jetzt wird sich alles verlaufen, und ich sitz auf meine Waren.

Der Koch   Wie können Sie auf den Feldprediger hörn? Wenn ich damals Zeit gehabt hätt, aber die Katholischen sind zu schnell gekommen, hätt ich Sie vor dem gewarnt. Das ist ein Schmalger. So, der führt bei Ihnen jetzt das große Wort.

Mutter Courage   Er hat mirs Geschirr gewaschen und ziehn helfen.

Der Koch   Der, und ziehn! Er wird Ihnen schon auch ein paar von seine Witz erzählt haben, wie ich den kenn, der hat eine ganz unsaubere Anschauung vom Weib, ich hab mein Einfluß umsonst bei ihm geltend gemacht. Er ist unsolid.

Mutter Courage   Sind Sie solid?

Der Koch   Wenn ich nix bin, bin ich solid. Prost!

Mutter Courage   Das ist nix, solid. Ich hab nur einen gehabt, Gott sei Dank, wo solid war. So hab ich nirgends schuften müssen, er hat die Decken von die Kinder verkauft im Frühjahr, und meine Mundharmonika hat er unchristlich gefunden. Ich find, Sie empfehln sich nicht, wenn Sie eingestehn, Sie sind solid.

Der Koch   Sie haben immer noch Haare auf die Zähn, aber ich schätz Sie drum.

Mutter Courage   Sagen Sie jetzt nicht, Sie haben von meine Haar auf die Zähn geträumt!

Der Koch   Ja, jetzt sitzen wir hier, und Friedensglocken und Ihr Branntwein, wie nur Sie ihn ausschenken, das ist ja berühmt.

They sit.

Mother Courage You're showing up at an unlucky moment for me, Cook. Ruined. I took the Chaplain's advice and I've overstocked, forked over all my cash for goods I'll be sitting on, the troops'll be packing up and heading home.

The Cook A woman your age listening to a preacher? For shame. I meant to warn you back when to give that dried-up-twig of a chaplain a wide berth but there wasn't time, and you – you fell for his big words.

Mother Courage I fell for nothing. He's chief dishwasher and assistant drayhorse and that's it.

The Cook You must be hard up for drayhorses. He tell you any of his sideways jokes, he's sort of got a careless opinion of women, I tried to use my influence for moral improvements but in vain, the man's absolutely unsolid.

Mother Courage You're solid, huh?

The Cook If I'm anything, I'm solid. (*Toasting her.*) *Skol!*

Mother Courage *Prosit!*

The Cook *A votre santé!*

Mother Courage Mud in yer eye. I've only been with one solid man, thank God. Soon as spring arrived for a little extra pocket money he stripped the blankets from the kids' beds, then he told me my harmonica wasn't a Christian instrument.

The Cook I like a woman who knows how to handle a harmonica.*

Mother Courage Maybe later, if the mood strikes me, I might play a snatch.

The Cook Here we sit, together again, and the bells are chiming peace, peace peace . . . And then there's your indelible brandy, your unimpeachable hospitality.

Mutter Courage Ich halt nix von Friedensglocken im Moment. Ich seh nicht, wie sie den Sold auszahln wolln, wo im Rückstand ist, und wo bleib ich dann mit meinem berühmten Branntwein? Habt ihr denn ausgezahlt bekommen?

Der Koch (*zögernd*) Das nicht grad. Darum haben wir uns aufgelöst. Unter diese Umständ hab ich mir gedacht, was soll ich bleiben, ich besuch inzwischen Freunde. Und so sitz ich jetzt Ihnen gegenüber.

Mutter Courage Das heißt, Sie haben nix.

Der Koch Mit dem Gebimmel könnten sie wirklich aufhören, nachgerad. Ich käm gern in irgendeinen Handel mit was. Ich hab keine Lust mehr, denen den Koch machen. Ich soll ihnen aus Baumwurzeln und Schuhleder was zusammenpantschen, und dann schütten sie mir die heiße Suppe ins Gesicht. Heut Koch, das ist ein Hundeleben. Lieber Kriegsdienst tun, aber freilich, jetzt ist ja Frieden. (*Da der* **Feldprediger** *auftaucht, nunmehr in seinem alten Gewand.*) Wir reden später darüber weiter.

Der Feldprediger Es ist noch gut, nur paar Motten waren drin.

Der Koch Ich seh nur nicht, wozu Sie sich die Müh machen. Sie werden doch nicht wieder eingestellt, wen sollten Sie jetzt anfeuern, daß er seinen Sold ehrlich verdient und sein Leben in die Schanz schlägt? Ich hab überhaupt mit Ihnen noch ein Hühnchen zu rupfen, weil Sie die Dame zu einem Einkauf von überflüssigen Waren geraten haben unter der Angabe, der Krieg geht ewig.

Der Feldprediger (*hitzig*) Ich möcht wissen, was Sie das angeht?

Der Koch Weils gewissenlos ist, so was! Wie können Sie sich in die Geschäftsführung von andern Leuten einmischen mit ungewünschten Ratschlägen?

Der Feldprediger Wer mischt sich ein? (*Zur* **Courage**.) Ich hab nicht gewußt, daß Sie eine so enge Freundin von dem Herrn sind und ihm Rechenschaft schuldig sind.

Mother Courage   Did you get paid before you deserted?

The Cook (*hesitantly*)   Not exactly, no, they've been out of cash all year. So I didn't desert, non-payment of our salaries inspired us to dissolve our regiment on our own authority.

Mother Courage   You're broke.

The Cook   Oh really you know, they could stop that fucking din. I'm not broke, I'm between money, looking for something to which I can apply these capable hands, I've lost my appetite as it were for army cooking, they give me roots and boots for the soup pot then they throw the consequences piping hot in my face. I begged to be transferred to the infantry, and now, peacetime.

The **Chaplain** *appears in his pastor's coat.*

The Cook (*to* **Mother Courage**)   Later.

The Chaplain   Apart from the occasional moth hole, it's perfectly presentable.

The Cook   But not worth the effort, putting it on. No more soldiers to inflame. And I have another chicken to pluck with you, if you've the time, because thanks to you this lady purchased surplus goods under the illusion you peddled her that the war will go on eternally.

The Chaplain (*heatedly*)   I'm going to have to ask you how this is any concern of yours?

The Cook   It's unscrupulous, what you did! Interfering in the way other people manage their affairs with unasked-for advice.

The Chaplain   I interfered? Who says I interfered? (*To* **Mother Courage**.) Did you say I interfered?

Mother Courage   Don't get excited, the Cook's entitled to his personal opinion.

The Chaplain   I didn't know you owed him perusal of your accounts.*

Mutter Courage   Regen Sie sich nicht auf, der Koch sagt nur seine Privatmeinung, und Sie können nicht leugnen, daß Ihr Krieg eine Niete war.

Der Feldprediger   Sie sollten sich nicht am Frieden versündigen, Courage! Sie sind eine Hyäne des Schlachtfelds.

Mutter Courage   Was bin ich?

Der Koch   Wenn Sie meine Freundin beleidigen, kriegen Sies mit mir zu tun.

Der Feldprediger   Mit Ihnen red ich nicht. Sie haben mir zu durchsichtige Absichten. (*Zur* **Courage**.) Aber wenn ich Sie den Frieden entgegennehmen seh wie ein altes verrotztes Sacktuch, mit Daumen und Zeigefinger, dann empör ich mich menschlich; denn dann seh ich, Sie wollen keinen Frieden, sondern Krieg, weil Sie Gewinne machen, aber vergessen Sie dann auch nicht den alten Spruch: »Wer mitn Teufel frühstücken will, muß ein langen Löffel haben!«

Mutter Courage   Ich hab nix fürn Krieg übrig, und er hat wenig genug für mich übrig. Ich verbitt mir jedenfalls die Hyäne, wir sind geschiedene Leut.

Der Feldprediger   Warum beklagen Sie sich dann übern Frieden, wenn alle Menschen aufatmen? Wegen paar alte Klamotten in Ihrem Wagen?!

Mutter Courage   Meine Waren sind keine alte Klamotten, sondern davon leb ich, und Sie habens bisher auch.

Der Feldprediger   Also vom Krieg! Aha!

Der Koch (*zum* **Feldprediger**)   Als erwachsener Mensch hätten Sie sich sagen müssen, daß man keinen Rat gibt. (*Zur* **Courage**.) In der Lag können Sie jetzt nix Besseres mehr tun, als gewisse Waren schnell losschlagen, vor die Preis ins Aschgraue sinken. Ziehn Sie sich an und gehn Sie los, verliern Sie keine Minut!

Mutter Courage   Das ist ein ganz vernünftiger Rat. Ich glaub, ich machs.

Der Feldprediger   Weil der Koch es sagt!

Mother Courage I owe him quatsch, and I owe you quatsch, and his point is your war was a bust, and he's got a point. You ruined me.

The Chaplain The way you talk about peace, Courage, it's a sin. You're a hyena of the battlefields.

Mother Courage I'm what?

The Cook He who insults my friend deals with me.

The Chaplain I wasn't talking to you. You have transparent intentions. (*To* **Mother Courage**.) But when I see you picking up peace disdainfully betwixt your thumb and forefinger as if it were a, a, a snot-rag, my humanity's affronted; I see you as you are, a woman who hates peace and loves war, as long as you can make money off it, but don't forget the old saying, 'If you want to dine with the Devil bring a long spoon!'

Mother Courage I didn't ask the war to linger and it didn't linger any longer than it wanted to. And anybody calls me a hyena is looking for a divorce.

The Chaplain The whole world's finally, finally able to draw a deep breath and you alone, you, carping about peace because, because what, because of that load of tattery antiquated crap in your wagon?!

Mother Courage My wares aren't crap, and I survived by selling them, and you survived by leeching off me.

The Chaplain By leeching off war! My point! Right!

The Cook (*to the* **Chaplain**) Adults should neither give nor receive advice, according to someone or other. Who probably knew what he was talking about. (*To* **Mother Courage**.) Sell quick before prices fall much farther. Dress up and get going, there isn't a second to spare!

Mother Courage Sharp thinking. I like it, I'll do it.

The Chaplain On his say-so?

Mutter Courage   Warum haben Sies nicht gesagt? Er hat recht, ich geh besser auf den Markt. (*Sie geht in den Wagen.*)

Der Koch   Einen für mich, Feldprediger. Sie sind nicht geistesgegenwärtig. Sie hätten sagen müssen: *ich* soll Ihnen ein Rat gegeben haben? Ich hab höchstens politisiert! Mit mir sollten Sie sich nicht hinstelln. So ein Hahnenkampf paßt sich nicht für Ihr Gewand!

Der Feldprediger   Wenn Sie nicht das Maul halten, ermord ich Sie, ob sich das paßt oder nicht.

Der Koch (*seine Stiefel ausziehend und sich die Fußlappen abwickelnd*)   Wenn Sie nicht ein so gottloser Lump geworden wären, könntens jetzt im Frieden leicht wieder zu einem Pfarrhaus kommen. Köch wird man nicht brauchen, zum Kochen ist nix da, aber geglaubt wird immer noch, da hat sich nix verändert.

Der Feldprediger   Herr Lamb, ich muß Sie bitten, mich hier nicht hinauszudrängeln. Seit ich verlumpt bin, bin ich ein besserer Mensch geworden. Ich könnt ihnen nicht mehr predigen.

Yvette Pottier *kommt, in Schwarz, aufgetakelt, mit Stock. Sie ist viel älter, dicker und sehr gepudert. Hinter ihr ein Bedienter.*

Yvette   Holla, ihr Leut! Ist das bei Mutter Courage?

Der Feldprediger   Ganz recht. Und mit wem haben wir das Vergnügen?

Yvette   Mit der Obristin Starhemberg, gute Leut. Wo ist die Courage?

Der Feldprediger (*ruft in den Wagen*) Die Obristin Starhemberg möcht Sie sprechen!

Stimme Der Mutter Courage   Ich komm gleich!

Mother Courage   Better his than yours! Anyone asks, I'm off to the market.

She goes into the wagon.

The Cook   Score one for me, Pastor. You don't think quick on your feet. You should have said, 'When did I ever advise you? A little political hypothesising was all it was!' You're outflanked. Cockfighting doesn't suit men who're dressed like that.

The Chaplain   If you don't shut up, whether or not it suits my clothes, I'm going to murder you.

*The **Cook** takes his shoes off and unwinds the rags wrapped around his feet.*

The Cook   If the war hadn't turned you into the secular wreck I see before me, you could've found a parsonage to settle in, what with peace and all. No one needs a cook when there's no food, but folks still believe in things they can't see, nothing changes that.

The Chaplain   Mr Lamb, please, I'm asking you, don't push me out. I am a wreck, you're right, I've been brought low, humiliated, debased. But I . . . I like myself better now. Even if you handed me a nice metropolitan pulpit with a sinecure, I don't think I could preach. Washing bottles is better work than saving souls,* the bottles come clean. Tell her to keep me.

Yvette *comes in, dressed in black, but bedizened, walking with a cane. She's much older, fatter, and she wears gobs of make-up. A serving man walks behind her. The **Cook** turns away and busies himself with something.*

Yvette   Hey hey, everyone! Is this Mother Courage's?

The Chaplain   Is, was, and always will be.*

Yvette   Where's Courage? Could you please announce that she has a guest, Madame Colonel Starhemberg.

The Chaplain (*calling into the wagon*)   Madame Colonel Starhemberg wants to speak with you!

Mother Courage (*from inside*)   Be right out!

Yvette   Ich bin die Yvette!

Stimme Der Mutter Courage   Ach, die Yvette!

Yvette   Nur nachschaun, wies geht! (*Da der* **Koch** *sich entsetzt herumgedreht hat.*) Pieter!

Der Koch   Yvette!

Yvette   So was! Wie kommst denn du da her?

Der Koch   Im Fuhrwerk.

Der Feldprediger   Ach, ihr kennts euch? Intim?

Yvette   Ich möchts meinen. (*Sie betrachtet den* **Koch**.) Fett.

Der Koch   Du gehörst auch nicht mehr zu die Schlanksten.

Yvette   Jedenfalls schön, daß ich dich treff, Lump. Da kann ich dir sagen, was ich über dich denk.

Der Feldprediger   Sagen Sies nur genau, aber warten Sie, bis die Courage heraußen ist.

Mutter Courage (*kommt heraus, mit allerlei Waren*)   Yvette! (*Sie umarmen sich.*) Aber warum bist du in Trauer?

Yvette   Stehts mir nicht? Mein Mann, der Obrist, ist vor ein paar Jahr gestorben.

Mutter Courage   Der Alte, wo beinah mein Wagen gekauft hätt?

Yvette   Sein älterer Bruder.

Yvette   I'm Yvette!

Mother Courage (*excited, from inside*)   Aaaaccchh! Yvette!

Yvette   Popped over to see what's up!

The **Cook** *turns around.*

Yvette   Pieter!

The Cook   Yvette!

Yvette   Holy shit! Since when! How come you're here?

The Cook   As opposed to where?

The Chaplain   How well do you know each other?

Yvette   Too well!

She gives the **Cook** *the once-over.*

Yvette   Fat!

The Cook   You've been slimmer yourself.

Yvette   You're fat and I'm fat and how-de-do, you scalded hog. How many years has it been I've been waiting to tell you what I think of you?

The Chaplain   Many, many years, from the look of it, but if you could wait just a minute longer and start telling him when Courage is here.

Mother Courage *comes out of the wagon, hauling merchandise.*

Mother Courage   Yvette!

They embrace.

You're in mourning?

Yvette   Looks nice, huh? My husband the Colonel died a few years back.

Mother Courage   The old guy who wanted to buy you my wagon?

Yvette   No, his father!*

Mutter Courage Da stehst dich ja nicht schlecht! Wenigstens eine, wos im Krieg zu was gebracht hat.

Yvette Auf und ab und wieder auf ists halt gegangen.

Mutter Courage Reden wir nicht Schlechtes von die Obristen, sie machen Geld wie Heu!

Der Feldprediger (*zum* **Koch**) Ich möcht an Ihrer Stell die Schuh wieder anziehn. (*Zu* **Yvette**.) Sie haben versprochen, Sie sagen, was Sie über den Herrn denken, Frau Obristin.

Der Koch Yvette, mach keinen Stunk hier.

Mutter Courage Das ist ein Freund von mir, Yvette.

Yvette Das ist der Pfeifenpieter.

Der Koch Laß die Spitznamen! Ich heiß Lamb.

Mutter Courage (*lacht*) Der Pfeifenpieter! Wo die Weiber verrückt gemacht hat! Sie, Ihre Pfeif hab ich aufbewahrt.

Der Feldprediger Und draus geraucht!

Yvette Ein Glück, daß ich Sie vor dem warnen kann. Das ist der schlimmste, wo an der ganzen flandrischen Küste herumgelaufen ist. An jedem Finger eine, die er ins Unglück gebracht hat.

Der Koch Das ist lang her. Das ist schon nimmer wahr.

Yvette Steh auf, wenn eine Dame dich ins Gespräch zieht! Wie ich diesen Menschen geliebt hab! Und zu gleicher Zeit hat er eine kleine Schwarze gehabt mit krumme Bein, die hat er auch ins Unglück gebracht, natürlich.

Mother Courage   You look nice all right, not bad, not bad at all! At least somebody got something out of the war.

Yvette   Touch and go,* that's how I do it, up and down and up and down and etcetera.

Mother Courage   Yeah, but you hooked a colonel and we have to hand it to those colonels, they made hay.

The Chaplain (*to the* **Cook**)   Heaven forfend I offer advice, but you might want to consider getting back in your boots. (*To* **Yvette**.) Madame Colonel, you had something you were about to say about this barefoot man.

The Cook   Don't make a stink, Yvette.

Mother Courage   Yvette, let me introduce you to a friend of mine.

Yvette   No, no, let me introduce you! Courage, meet Piping Pieter.

Mother Courage (*laughing*)   Piping Pieter!

The Cook   An old nickname, forget it.

Mother Courage   Who made the girls throw their skirts over their heads!

The Cook   My name's Lamb.

Mother Courage   Look, I hung on to your pipe.

The Chaplain   Rarely took it out of her mouth.

Yvette   Fling his poxy pipe away, Courage, this is the nastiest fish ever to wash up on the Flanders shore. Every one of his fingers has brought misery to a different miserable girl.

The Cook   Years ago. A man can change.

Yvette   Stand up when a lady talks to you, poodle. God how I loved this man!*

Der Koch   Dich hab ich jedenfalls eher ins Glück
gebracht, wies scheint.

Yvette   Halt das Maul, traurige Ruin! Aber hüten Sie
sich vor ihm, so einer bleibt gefährlich auch im Zustand
des Verfalls!

Mutter Courage (*zu* **Yvette**)   Komm mit, ich muß mein
Zeug losschlagen, vor die Preis sinken. Vielleicht hilfst du
mir beim Regiment mit deine Verbindungen. (*Ruft in den
Wagen.*) Kattrin, es ist nix mit der Kirch, stattdem geh ich
aufn Markt. Wenn der Eilif kommt, gebts ihm was zum
Trinken. (*Ab mit* **Yvette**.)

Yvette (*im Abgehn*)   Daß mich so was wie dieser Mensch
einmal vom graden Weg hat abbringen können! Ich habs
nur meinem guten Stern zu danken, daß ich dennoch in
die Höh gekommen bin. Aber daß ich dir jetzt das
Handwerk gelegt hab, wird mir dereinst oben
angerechnet, Pfeifenpieter.

Der Feldprediger   Ich möcht unsrer Unterhaltung das
Wort zugrund legen: Gottes Mühlen mahlen langsam.
Und Sie beschweren sich über meinen Witz!

Der Koch   Ich hab halt kein Glück. Ich sags, wies ist: ich
hab auf eine warme Mahlzeit gehofft. Ich bin
ausgehungert, und jetzt reden die über mich, und sie
bekommt ein ganz falsches Bild von mir. Ich glaub, ich
verschwind, bis sie zurück ist.

Der Feldprediger   Ich glaub auch.

The Cook   I was the best thing ever happened to you, I helped you find your calling.

Yvette   Shut your mouth, you tragic disaster! (*To* **Mother Courage**.) After he disappeared and left me, um, broken-hearted, I found four other girls in town in a similar condition, and it was a very small town! Maybe you're thinking time and dissipation has ground down his teeth and horns, but you listen to me, be careful, there's danger in the ruins. If he's here hoping to hitch a ride on your wagon, show him the highway and bless his scabby backside with your boot!

Mother Courage (*to* **Yvette**)   You come with me to the market, I've got to unload this stuff before the prices hit bottom. You must know the whole regiment, tell me who to talk to. (*Calling into the wagon.*) Never mind church, Kattrin, I'm going to market. As soon as Eilif shows, give him something to drink.

She leaves with **Yvette**. *As they go,* **Yvette** *says:*

Yvette   It amazes me, a picked-over carcass of a man like you was enough to overturn my apple cart. I've got my lucky star to thank, I got every fucking apple back, and then some! I've saved this woman from the catastrophe of your company, and that'll go down to my credit in the world to come. And now, at very long last, Piping Pieter, you can kiss my ass!

They leave.

The Chaplain   I suddenly find my tongue freed, I can sermonise again! I take as our text today: 'The mills of God grind slowly. And they grind small.'

The Cook   I never had a lucky star. It's just . . . well, I'd hoped there might be a warm meal. I'm starving. I haven't had food in two days. Now they're clucking about me, and she'll form a more-or-less completely false impression. It discombobulates me, a woman's cold shoulder. I'll leave before she's back.

The Chaplain   Better part of valour. Amen.

Der Koch   Feldprediger, mir hangt der Frieden schon wieder zum Hals heraus. Die Menschheit muß hingehn durch Feuer und Schwert,* weil sie sündig ist von Kindesbeinen an. Ich wollt, ich könnt dem Feldhauptmann, wo Gott weiß wo ist, wieder einen fetten Kapaun braten, in Senfsoße mit bissel gelbe Rüben.

Der Feldprediger   Rotkohl. Zum Kapaun Rotkohl.

Der Koch   Das ist richtig, aber er hat gelbe Rüben wolln.

Der Feldprediger   Er hat nix verstanden. F

Der Koch   Sie habens immer wacker mitgefressen.

Der Feldprediger   Mit Widerwillen.

Der Koch   Jedenfalls müssen Sie zugeben, daß das noch Zeiten warn.

Der Feldprediger   Das würd ich eventuell zugeben.

Der Koch   Nachdem Sie sie eine Hyäne geheißen haben, sinds für Sie hier keine Zeiten mehr. Was stiern Sie denn?

Der Feldprediger   Der Eilif! (*Von* **Soldaten** *mit Picketten gefolgt, kommt* **Eilif** *daher. Seine Hände sind gefesselt. Er ist kalkweiß.*) Was ist denn mit dir los?

Eilif   Wo ist die Mutter?

Der Feldprediger   In die Stadt.

Eilif   Ich hab gehört, sie ist am Ort. Sie haben erlaubt, daß ich sie noch besuchen darf.

Der Koch (*zu den* **Soldaten**)   Wo führt ihr ihn denn hin?

Ein Soldat   Nicht zum Guten.

Der Feldprediger   Was hat er angestellt?

Der Soldat   Bei einem Bauern ist er eingebrochen. Die Frau ist hin.

Der Feldprediger   Wie hast du das machen können?

Eilif   Ich hab nix andres gemacht als vorher auch.

The Cook Peace is as heavy as a millstone. I miss the General, you know, God knows where he is, I could be basting a fat roasted capon with mustard sauce, served with yellow carrots.

The Chaplain Red cabbage. Red cabbage with a capon.

The Cook I know, I know, but he insisted on carrots.

The Chaplain The man was an appalling ignoramus.

The Cook You never mentioned that when you were sitting next to him stuffing your face.

The Chaplain I swallowed my pride.

The Cook You swallowed more than that. Who knew we'd long for those days?

The Chaplain Nostalgic for the war. Peace seems less hospitable, somehow.

The Cook You're finished here same as me, you called her a hyena. You – what are you staring at?

The Chaplain I think it's Eilif.

A grim contingent of **Soldiers** *with pikes leading* **Eilif**, *whose hands are tied. He's chalk-white.*

The Chaplain What's happened?

Eilif Where's my mother?

The Chaplain In town.

Eilif I heard she was here. They let me come to see her.

The Cook (*to the* **Soldiers**) Where are you taking him?

A Soldier Noplace good.

The Chaplain What did he do?

The Soldier He broke into a farmhouse. The wife – (*Gestures to indicate she's dead.*)

The Chaplain You did that? How could you do that?

Eilif Same as I've always done.

Der Koch   Aber im Frieden.

Eilif   Halt das Maul. Kann ich mich hinsetzen, bis sie kommt?

Der Soldat   Wir haben keine Zeit.

Der Feldprediger   Im Krieg haben sie ihn dafür geehrt, zur Rechten vom Feldhauptmann ist er gesessen. Da wars Kühnheit! Könnt man nicht mit dem Profos reden?

Der Soldat   Das nutzt nix. Einem Bauern sein Vieh nehmen, was wär daran kühn?

Der Koch   Das war eine Dummheit!

Eilif   Wenn ich dumm gewesen wär, dann wär ich verhungert, du Klugscheißer.

Der Koch   Und weil du klug warst, kommt dir der Kopf herunter.

Der Feldprediger   Wir müssen wenigstens die Kattrin herausholen.

Eilif   Laß sie drin! Gib mir lieber einen Schluck Schnaps.

Der Soldat   Zu dem hats keine Zeit, komm!

Der Feldprediger   Und was solln wir deiner Mutter ausrichten?

Eilif   Sag ihr, es war nichts anderes, sag ihr, es war dasselbe. Oder sag ihr gar nix.

Die **Soldaten** *treiben ihn weg.*

Der Feldprediger   Ich geh mit dir deinen schweren Weg.

Eilif   Ich brauch keinen Pfaffen.

Der Feldprediger   Das weißt du noch nicht. (*Er folgt ihm.*)

Der Koch (*ruft ihnen nach*)   Ich werds ihr doch sagen müssen, sie wird ihn noch sehn wollen!

Der Feldprediger   Sagen Sie ihr lieber nix. Höchstens, er war da und kommt wieder, vielleicht morgen. Inzwischen bin ich zurück und kanns ihr beibringen.

The Cook   But it's peacetime. You can't –

Eilif   Shut up. Can I sit till she comes back?

The Soldier   We don't have time for that.

The Chaplain   During the war he got medals for things like this, he was fearless, they said, brave, he was summoned to sit at the General's right hand. Couldn't we talk to your commander?

The Soldier   Why bother? Stealing some farmer's cow, that's brave?

The Cook   It was idiotic!

Eilif   If I was an idiot I'd have starved long before this, you asshole.

The Cook   So you used your brains and now they're going to cut your head off.

The Chaplain   At least let's get Kattrin.

Eilif   No! Don't! Leave her. Give me a taste of schnapps.

The Soldier   You don't have time for that, come on!

The Chaplain   What should we tell your mother?

Eilif   Tell her it wasn't different. Tell her it was the same. Or don't tell her anything.

The **Soldiers** *shove him and he starts to walk.*

The Chaplain   I'll walk with you on your hard path.

Eilif   I don't need you, black crow.

The Chaplain   You don't know what you may need.

The **Soldiers** *shove* **Eilif** *again and they leave. The* **Chaplain** *follows them.*

The Cook (*calling after the* **Chaplain**)   I have to tell her, she'll want to see him!

The Chaplain   Better not say anything. Or he was here and he'll be back, tomorrow possibly. When I get back I'll find some way to explain.

Hastig ab. Der **Koch** *schaut ihnen kopfschüttelnd nach, dann geht er unruhig herum. Am Ende nähert er sich dem Wagen.*

Der Koch Holla! Wolln Sie nicht rauskommen? Ich versteh ja, daß Sie sich vorm Frieden verkrochen haben. Ich möchts auch. Ich bin der Koch vom Feldhauptmann, erinnern Sie sich an mich? Ich frag mich, ob Sie bissel was zu essen hätten, bis Ihre Mutter zurückkommt. Ich hätt grad Lust auf ein Speck oder auch Brot, nur wegen der Langeweil. (*Er schaut hinein.*) Hat die Deck überm Kopf.

Hinten Kanonendonner.

Mutter Courage (*kommt gelaufen, sie ist außer Atem und hat ihre Waren noch*) Koch, der Frieden ist schon wieder aus! Schon seit drei Tag ist wieder Krieg. Ich hab mein Zeug noch nicht losgeschlagen gehabt, wie ichs erfahrn hab. Gott sei Dank! In der Stadt schießen sie sich mit die Lutherischen. Wir müssen gleich weg mitn Wagen. Kattrin, packen! Warum sind Sie betreten? Was ist los?

Der Koch Nix.

Mutter Courage Doch, es ist was. Ich sehs Ihnen an.

Der Koch Weil wieder Krieg ist wahrscheinlich. Jetzt kanns bis morgen abend dauern, bis ich irgendwo was Warmes in Magen krieg.

Mutter Courage Das ist gelogen, Koch.

Der Koch Der Eilif war da. Er hat nur gleich wieder wegmüssen.

Mutter Courage War er da? Da werden wir ihn aufn Marsch sehn. Ich zieh mit die Unsern jetzt. Wie sieht er aus?

Der Koch Wie immer.

The **Chaplain** *runs off after them. The* **Cook** *watches them leave, shakes his head, then finally goes to the wagon. He calls in.*

The Cook   Hey! Don't you want to come out? I understand you, I think, peace comes and you crawl under the rug. Me too. It's terrifying. I was the General's cook, remember? I'm asking myself if maybe there's a scrap left over from your breakfast, just to tide me over till your mother returns? A little ham or some bread, we might have a bit of a wait.

He looks inside.

She's thrown the blanket over her head.

In the distance, cannonfire. **Mother Courage** *runs in, still carrying all her wares, out of breath.*

Mother Courage   Cook! Peace is finished! The war's been back on three whole days. I was just about to sell at a loss when I heard the news! Thank God! In town they're shooting at the Lutherans and the Lutherans are shooting back. We've got to get on our way with the wagon. Kattrin, pack! (*To the* **Cook**.) Look me in the eye. What's the matter?

The Cook   Nothing.

Mother Courage   Bullshit, it's something, something's wrong.

The Cook   War's started up, maybe that's it. And it'll probably be tomorrow evening before I get hot food in my stomach.

Mother Courage   You're lying, Cook.

The Cook   Eilif was here. He couldn't stay.

Mother Courage   He was here? Then we'll find him on the march. From now on I'm pulling right behind the soldiers, like I was official, it's safer. Did he look all right?

The Cook   As always.

Mutter Courage   Der wird sich nie ändern. Den hat der Krieg mir nicht wegnehmen können. Der ist klug. Helfen Sie mir beim Packen? (*Sie beginnt zu packen.*) Hat er was erzählt? Steht er sich gut mitn Hauptmann? Hat er was von seine Heldentaten berichtet?

Der Koch (*finster*)   Eine hat er, hör ich, noch einmal wiederholt.

Mutter Courage   Sie erzählens mir später, wir müssen fort. (**Kattrin** *taucht auf.*) Kattrin, der Frieden ist schon wieder herum. Wir ziehn weiter. (*Zum* **Koch**.) Was ist mit Ihnen?

Der Koch   Ich laß mich anwerben.

Mutter Courage   Ich schlag Ihnen vor ... wo ist der Feldprediger?

Der Koch   In die Stadt mit dem Eilif.

Mutter Courage   Dann kommen Sie ein Stückl mit, Lamb. Ich brauch eine Hilf.

Der Koch   Die Geschicht mit der Yvette ...

Mutter Courage   Die hat Ihnen nicht geschadet in meinen Augen. Im Gegenteil. Wos raucht, ist Feuer, heißts. Kommen Sie also mit uns?

Der Koch   Ich sag nicht nein.

Mutter Courage   Das Zwölfte is schon aufgebrochen. Gehens an die Deichsel. Da is ein Stück Brot. Wir müssen hintenrum, zu den Lutherischen. Vielleicht seh ich den Eilif schon heut nacht. Das ist mir der liebste von allen. Ein kurzer Friede wars, und schon gehts weiter. (*Sie singt, während der* **Koch** *und* **Kattrin** *sich vorspannen.*)

Mother Courage   He's always the same as always, smart. That one the war couldn't take from me. Help me pack?

She starts packing. The **Cook** *helps.*

Mother Courage   Did he have any news? Is he still the General's favourite? Any more heroism?

The Cook (*grim*)   Yes, apparently, only recently.

Mother Courage   Tell me about it once we're under way.

Kattrin *comes out of the wagon and takes her place at the axle shaft, ready to pull.*

Mother Courage   Peace is already over, Kattrin. We're on the move again. (*To the* **Cook**.) And you?

The Cook   Find my regiment, sign up.

Mother Courage   You could do that I guess or . . . Where's his Holiness?

The Cook   He went towards town with Eilif.

Mother Courage   Come along, Lamb, for a bit. I need a helper.

The Cook   All that stuff Yvette was saying . . .

Mother Courage   Didn't do you discredit in my eyes. The opposite. I've always admired vitality;* don't worry as much as I used to over the shape it chooses to take. Interested?

The Cook   I'm not saying no.

Mother Courage   The Twelfth Regiment's already headed out. Take hold and pull. Here's a slice of bread. We'll have to go the long way around to catch up with the Lutherans. I might see Eilif this very night. I love him best of all. It was a short peace. Let's get going.

Kattrin *and the* **Cook** *in harness start to pull the wagon while* **Mother Courage** *sings:*

Von Ulm nach Metz, von Metz nach Mähren!
Mutter Courage ist dabei!
Der Krieg wird seinen Mann ernähren
Er braucht nur Pulver zu und Blei.
Von Blei allein kann er nicht leben
Von Pulver nicht, er braucht auch Leut!
Müßts euch zum Regiment begeben
Sonst steht er um! So kommt noch heut!

Nine

Schon sechzehn Jahre dauert nun der große Glaubenskrieg. Über die Hälfte seiner Bewohner hat Deutschland eingebüßt. Gewaltige Seuchen töten, was die Metzeleien übriggelassen haben. In den ehemals blühenden Landstrichen wütet der Hunger. Wölfe durchstreifen die niedergebrannten Städte. Im Herbst 1634 begegnen wir der Courage im deutschen Fichtelgebirge, abseits der Heerstraße, auf der die schwedischen Heere ziehen. Der Winter in diesem Jahr kommt früh und ist streng. Die Geschäfte gehen schlecht, so daß nur Betteln übrigbleibt. Der Koch bekommt einen Brief aus Utrecht und wird verabschiedet.

Vor einem halbzerfallenen Pfarrhaus. Grauer Morgen im Frühwinter. Windstöße. **Mutter Courage** *und der* **Koch** *in schäbigen Schafsfellen am Wagen.*

Der Koch   Es ist alles dunkel, noch niemand auf.

Mutter Courage   Aber ein Pfarrhaus. Und zum Glockenläuten muß er aus den Federn kriechen. Dann hat er eine warme Supp.

Mother Courage (*singing*)
From Ulm to Metz . . .

The Cook (*singing*)
                                        . . . from Metz to Mähren!*

Mother Courage (*singing*)
The goddamned army's on its feet!
What if the land is burnt and barren?

The Cook (*singing*)
The war needs men, and men must eat!

Mother Courage (*singing*)
The war will feed you steel and fire
If you sign up for bloody deeds!
It's only blood that wars require!
So come and feed it what it needs!

Nine

The great war of religion has been going on for sixteen years. Over half the inhabitants of Germany have perished. Widespread plague kills those the war spares. In once fertile countries, famine. Wolves prowl through the burnt-out cities. In the autumn of 1634 we meet **Courage** *in the German mountains called Fichtelgebirge, off the route of the Swedish army. Winter this year has come early and is severe. Business is terrible, and begging is all that remains. The* **Cook** *gets a letter from Utrecht and is bid farewell.*

Outside a half-ruined parsonage. Grey morning in early winter. Wind is blasting. **Mother Courage** *and the* **Cook** *in ratty sheepskins, the wagon nearby.*

The Cook   It's pitch black, nobody's up.

Mother Courage   It's a parsonage. The bells will have to be rung and the Father's got to crawl to it. Then he'll have hot soup.

Der Koch Woher, wenns ganze Dorf verkohlt ist, wie wir gesehn haben.

Mutter Courage Aber es ist bewohnt, vorhin hat ein Hund gebellt.

Der Koch Wenn der Pfaff hat, gibt er nix.

Mutter Courage Vielleicht, wenn wir singen …

Der Koch Ich habs bis oben auf. (*Plötzlich.*) Ich hab einen Brief aus Utrecht, daß meine Mutter an der Cholera gestorben ist, und das Wirtshaus gehört mir. Da ist der Brief, wenns nicht glaubst. Ich zeig ihn dir, wenns dich auch nix angeht, was meine Tante über meinen Lebenswandel schmiert.

Mutter Courage (*liest den Brief*) Lamb, ich bin das Herumziehn auch müd. Ich komm mir vor wien Schlachterhund, ziehts Fleisch für die Kunden und kriegt nix davon ab. Ich hab nix mehr zu verkaufen, und die Leut haben nix, das Nix zu zahln. Im Sächsischen hat mir einer in Lumpen ein Klafter Pergamentbänd aufhängen wolln für zwei Eier, und fürn Säcklein Salz hätten sie mir im Württembergischen ihren Pflug abgelassen. Wozu pflügen? Es wachst nix mehr, nur Dorngestrüpp. Im Pommerschen solln die Dörfler schon die jüngern Kinder aufgegessen haben, und Nonnen haben sie bei Raubüberfäll erwischt.

Der Koch Die Welt stirbt aus.

Mutter Courage Manchmal seh ich mich schon durch die Höll fahrn mit mein Planwagen und Pech verkaufen oder durchn Himmel, Wegzehrung ausbieten an irrende Seelen. Wenn ich mit meine Kinder, wo mir verblieben sind, eine Stell fänd, wo nicht herumgeschossen würd, möcht ich noch ein paar ruhige Jahr haben.

The Cook You're talking nonsense, the village was burnt to the ground.

Mother Courage Someone's living here, there was a dog barking.

The Cook If the parson's got anything, he won't give it away.

Mother Courage Maybe if we sing something.

The Cook I've had more than my share of this. (*He takes a letter from his pocket.*) A letter from Utrecht, my mother's dead from cholera, her inn belongs to me now. Read the letter if you don't believe me.

He proffers the letter, **Mother Courage** *reaches to take it, he snatches it back.*

The Cook From my aunt, the handwriting's a little primitive. But . . . there's stuff about what a wretched little bastard I always was, that's family matters, skip that, read here, the salient part.

He hands her the letter, which she takes and reads. She stops reading, looks at him.

Mother Courage Lamb, I can't take the open road any more either. Look at us begging. My whole life, I never begged before. I feel like a slaughterhouse dog, red meat for paying customers but nothing for me. I have nothing to sell any more and no one has anything to pay with. In Saxony one of those raggedy beggars offered me a parcel of precious books wrapped in greaseproof parchment, just for two eggs, and for a little bag of salt in Würtenburg they wanted to give me their plough. What's the use of ploughing? Nothing grows but nettles. In Pomerania I've heard there's villagers so ravenous they've eaten little children.*

The Cook The world's dying.

Mother Courage Sometimes I see myself pulling that wagon through the streets of hell, selling burning pitch. Or making a living in purgatory, offering my wares to the wandering souls till the last trumpet blast. If me and my children could find a place where no one's shooting, I wouldn't mind a few years' rest, a few years of calm.

Der Koch   Wir könnten das Wirtshaus aufmachen. Anna, überleg dirs. Ich hab heut nacht meinen Entschluß gefaßt, ich geh mit dir oder ohne dich nach Utrecht zurück, und zwar heut.

Mutter Courage   Ich muß mit der Kattrin reden. Es kommt bissel schnell, und ich faß meine Entschlüss ungern in der Kält und mit nix im Magen. Kattrin! (**Kattrin** *klettert aus dem Wagen.*) Kattrin, ich muß dir was mitteilen. Der Koch und ich wolln nach Utrecht. Er hat eine Wirtschaft dort geerbt. Da hättst du ein festen Punkt und könntest Bekanntschaften machen. Eine gesetzte Person möcht mancher schätzen, das Aussehn ist nicht alles. Ich wär auch dafür. Ich vertrag mich mitn Koch. Ich muß für ihn sagen: er hat ein Kopf fürs Geschäft. Wir hätten unser gesichertes Essen, das wär fein, nicht? Und du hast deine Bettstatt, das paßt dir, wie? Auf der Straß ist kein Leben auf die Dauer. Du möchtst verkommen. Verlaust bist schon. Wir müssen uns entscheiden, warum, wir könnten mit den Schweden ziehn, nach Norden, sie müssen dort drüben sein. (*Sie zeigt nach links.*) Ich denk, wir entschließen uns, Kattrin.

Der Koch   Anna, ich möcht ein Wort mit dir allein haben.

Mutter Courage   Geh in den Wagen zurück, Kattrin.

Kattrin *klettert zurück.*

Der Koch   Ich hab dich unterbrochen, weil das ist ein Mißverständnis von deiner Seit, seh ich. Ich hab gedacht, das müßt ich nicht eigens sagen, weils klar ist. Aber wenn nicht, muß ich dirs halt sagen, daß du die mitnimmst, davon kann keine Rede sein. Ich glaub, du verstehst mich.

Kattrin *steckt hinter ihnen den Kopf aus dem Wagen und lauscht.*

Mutter Courage   Du meinst, ich soll die Kattrin zurücklassen?

The Cook We could make a go of it at the inn. Give it serious consideration, Anna. Last night I made my final decision, I'm going to Utrecht with you or alone, today.

Mother Courage I have to talk it over with Kattrin. It's a little abrupt, and I'm usually averse to making big decisions when I'm freezing and there's nothing in my belly. Kattrin!

Kattrin *climbs down from the wagon.*

Mother Courage Kattrin, we have to talk about something. The Cook and I want to go to Utrecht. He's inherited an inn. You'd have a home, make acquaintances. There are many men who'd want a competent somebody who helped run an inn, good looks aren't everything. It's a good deal. The Cook and I get along. I will say this about him: he tucks his head between his shoulders and goes about his business. We'd know where our next meal came from, and when to expect it, that'd be a change, huh, nice? And your own bed, you'd sleep better, right? Finally, life on the road isn't life. Look at us, you're falling apart. Lice are eating you alive. We have to decide, all right, Utrecht or, or we could just keep on, go where the Swede soldiers are, the army up north. (*She gestures vaguely to the left.*) We could go find the army again, but . . . I think we'll go with Cook, Kattrin.

The Cook Anna, I have to talk to you alone.

Mother Courage Go back in the wagon, Kattrin.

Kattrin *climbs back into the wagon.*

The Cook I interrupted you because you didn't understand me. I thought I was clear but I guess I wasn't, so: you can't bring her. I think that's clear enough.

Kattrin *positions herself inside so she can listen.*

Mother Courage What do you mean, leave Kattrin?

Der Koch   Wie denkst du dirs? Da ist kein Platz in der
Wirtschaft. Das ist keine mit drei Schankstuben. Wenn
wir zwei uns auf die Hinterbein stelln, können wir unsern
Unterhalt finden, aber nicht drei, das ist ausgeschlossen.
Die Kattrin kann den Wagen behalten.

Mutter Courage   Ich hab mir gedacht, sie kann in
Utrecht einen Mann finden.

Der Koch   Daß ich nicht lach! Wie soll die einen Mann
finden? Stumm und die Narb dazu! Und in dem Alter?

Mutter Courage   Red nicht so laut!

Der Koch   Was ist, ist, leis oder laut. Und das ist auch ein
Grund, warum ich sie nicht in der Wirtschaft haben
kann. Die Gäst wolln so was nicht immer vor Augen
haben. Das kannst du ihnen nicht verdenken.

Mutter Courage   Halts Maul. Ich sag, du sollst nicht so
laut sein.

Der Koch   Im Pfarrhaus ist Licht. Wir können singen.

Mutter Courage   Koch, wie könnt sie allein mitn Wagen
ziehn? Sie hat Furcht vorm Krieg. Sie verträgts nicht. Was
die für Träum haben muß! Ich hör sie stöhnen nachts.
Nach Schlachten besonders. Was sie da sieht in ihre
Träum, weiß ich nicht. Die leidet am Mitleid. Neulich hab
ich bei ihr wieder einen Igel versteckt gefunden, wo wir
überfahren haben.

Der Koch   Die Wirtschaft ist zu klein. (*Er ruft.*) Werter
Herr, Gesinde und Hausbewohner! Wir bringen zum
Vortrag das Lied von Salomon, Julius Cäsar und andere
große Geister, denens nicht genützt hat. Damit ihr seht,
auch wir sind ordentliche Leut und habens drum schwer,
durchzukommen, besonders im Winter.

> Ihr saht den weisen Salomon
> Ihr wißt, was aus ihm wurd.
> Dem Mann war alles sonnenklar

The Cook   Think. There's not enough room for her. It's not a big place. If we screw our hind legs to the floor we might keep it open and running, but three people, the inn can't support that. Kattrin can take over the wagon.

Mother Courage   I was thinking she'd find a husband in Utrecht.

The Cook   That's a laugh! Dumb, a scarred face, and old as she is?

Mother Courage   Don't talk so loud!

The Cook   What is, is, loud or soft. And come to think of it, there's the paying guests at the inn, who'd want to look up from supper and see that waiting to clear the table? How do you think this could work?

Mother Courage   I said shut up, I said don't talk so loud.

The Cook   Someone's lit a candle in the parsonage. Let's sing.

Mother Courage   Cook, how'd she pull that wagon on her own? She's frightened by the war. She couldn't manage. The dreams she must have! I hear her groaning nights. After battles especially. What she sees in those dreams, I can't imagine. She suffers because she pities. A few days back I found a hedgehog we'd killed, the wagon, an accident. She'd hidden it in her blanket.

The Cook   The inn's too small. (*Shouting.*) Worthy gentlemen, servants, and all who dwell within! In the hope of procuring a little leftover food, we will now give you a lecture in the form of a song, the Song of Solomon, Julius Caesar and other men possessed of a gigantic spirit, which proved to be of little use to them. All of this so you can see that we're decent obedient people and we are having a hard time getting by, especially this winter!

He sings:

> No doubt you've heard of Solomon,
> The wisest man on earth!
> He saw with perfect clarity,

Er verfluchte die Stunde seiner Geburt
Und sah, daß alles eitel war.
Wie groß und weis war Salomon!
Und seht, da war es noch nicht Nacht
Da sah die Welt die Folgen schon:
Die Weisheit hatte ihn so weit gebracht!
Beneidenswert, wer frei davon!

Alle Tugenden sind nämlich gefährlich auf dieser Welt,
wie das schöne Lied beweist, man hat sie besser nicht und
hat ein angenehmes Leben und Frühstück, sagen wir,
eine warme Supp. Ich zum Beispiel hab keine und möcht
eine, ich bin ein Soldat, aber was hat meine Kühnheit
mir genutzt in all die Schlachten, nix, ich hunger und
wär besser ein Hosenscheißer geblieben und daheim.
Denn warum?

Ihr saht den kühnen Cäsar dann
Ihr wißt, was aus ihm wurd.
Der saß wien Gott auf dem Altar
Und wurde ermordet, wie ihr erfuhrt
Und zwar, als er am größten war.
Wie schrie der laut: Auch du, mein Sohn!
Denn seht, da war es noch nicht Nacht
Da sah die Welt die Folgen schon:
Die Kühnheit hatte ihn so weit gebracht!
Beneidenswert, wer frei davon!

(*Halblaut.*) Sie schaun nicht mal heraus. (*Laut.*) Werter
Herr, Gesinde und Hausbewohner! Sie möchten sagen,
ja, die Tapferkeit ist nix, was seinen Mann nährt,
versuchts mit der Ehrlichkeit! Da möchtet ihr satt werden
oder wenigstens nicht ganz nüchtern bleiben. Wie ists
damit?

He would spit on the cursed hour of his birth
And say that all was vanity.
How deep and wise was Solomon!
And see, before the night descends,
He longed to taste oblivion!
He started wise but as a fool he ends.
Oh, wisdom's fine; we're glad we've none.

(*Shouting.*) All virtues are dangerous in a world like this,
as our beautiful song shows, you're better off having an
easy life and breakfast, in our opinion, hot soup. I, for
instance, I've got none and I'd like some, I'm a soldier,
but what use was it to me, my bravery in all those battles,
nix, nil, starvation, and if I'd stayed home shitting myself
I'd be better off. This is why:

Sings:

Then Julius Caesar, mighty one,
Raised high his royal rod,
So brave he tore the world apart,
So they voted and changed their Caesar to a God,
Then drove a dagger through his heart.
How loud he screamed: 'You too, my son!'
And see, before the night descends,
His reign had only just begun,
So brave, but screaming out in fear he ends.
Brave hearts are grand! We're fine with none.

(*Muttering.*) They're hiding in there, the bastards.
(*Shouting.*) Worthy gentlemen, servants and the whole
household! You aren't responding, you're sitting in there
by your fire, and maybe you're saying to yourself, sure,
bravery's not much when you need a hot meal, I agree,
but maybe if you were honest you wouldn't be so bad off!
Maybe if you were honest someone would feed you or at
least not leave you completely sober.

Let's test this proposition!

Sings:

Ihr kennt den redlichen Sokrates
Der stets die Wahrheit sprach:
Ach nein, sie wußten ihm keinen Dank
Vielmehr stellten die Obern böse ihm nach
Und reichten ihm den Schierlingstrank.
Wie redlich war des Volkes großer Sohn!
Und seht, da war es noch nicht Nacht
Da sah die Welt die Folgen schon:
Die Redlichkeit hat ihn so weit gebracht!
Beneidenswert, wer frei davon!

Ja, da heißts selbstlos sein und teilen, was man hat, aber
wenn man nix hat? Denn die Wohltäter habens vielleicht
auch nicht leicht, das sieht man ein, nur, man brauchet
halt doch was. Ja, die Selbstlosigkeit ist eine seltene
Tugend, weil sie sich nicht rentiert.

Der heilige Martin, wie ihr wißt
Ertrug nicht fremde Not.
Er sah im Schnee ein armen Mann
Und er bot seinen halben Mantel ihm an
Da frorn sie allebeid zu Tod.
Der Mann sah nicht auf irdischen Lohn!
Und seht, da war es noch nicht Nacht
Da sah die Welt die Folgen schon:
Selbstlosigkeit hat ihn so weit gebracht!
Beneidenswert, wer frei davon!

Und so ists mit uns! Wir sind ordentliche Leut, halten
zusammen, stehln nicht, morden nicht, legen kein Feuer!
Und so kann man sagen, wir sinken immer tiefer, und das
Lied bewahrheitet sich an uns, und die Suppen sind rar,
und wenn wir anders wären und Dieb und Mörder,
möchten wir vielleicht satt sein! Denn die Tugenden
zahln sich nicht aus, nur die Schlechtigkeiten, so ist die
Welt und müßt nicht so sein!

And Socrates, that paragon,
Who always told the truth –
They mixed a bitter poison drink
Made of hemlock; they said he's done things to our youth
And now we hate the way they think!
His truth was a phenomenon.
And see, before his night descends,
No longer dazzled by the sun,
He pays his bills and with a sip, he ends.
Truths are lovely; we know none.

(*Shouting.*) You still don't want to give, and it's not
surprising, who wants to give anyone anything? Sure, they
tell us to give unto others, but what if you've got nothing
to give? And the ones who give are left empty-handed,
and that can't feel very good either, and that's why
sacrifice is the rarest of all the virtues, because in the end
it makes everyone feel like crap.

Sings:

St Martin sang his benison,
His pity flowereth.
He met a man lost in the snows
Who was freezing, so Martin shared with him his clothes.
Of course the two men froze to death.
The pearly gates no doubt he won!
And see, before the night descends,
So kind beyond comparison!
Warm-hearted but beneath the ice he ends.
Oh, pity's great; thank God we've none.

(*Shouting.*) And that's how it is with us! Law-abiding
people, loyal to each other, we don't steal, murder or
burn down houses! And like the song says, down we're
going, deeper in the hole, and soup's a rare commodity,
and if we were thieves and murderers we might eat! So if
you've no food for us you better pray our patience holds
out, because we know! It's not virtue that pays in this
world, but wickedness, that's how the world is and it
shouldn't be that way!

Hier seht ihr ordentliche Leut
Haltend die zehn Gebot.
Es hat uns bisher nichts genützt:
Ihr, die am warmen Ofen sitzt
Helft lindern unsre große Not!
Wie kreuzbrav waren wir doch schon!
Und seht, da war es noch nicht Nacht
Da sah die Welt die Folgen schon:
Die Gottesfurcht hat uns so weit gebracht!
Beneidenswert, wer frei davon!

Stimme (*von oben*)   Ihr da! Kommt herauf! Eine
Brennsupp könnt ihr haben.

Mutter Courage   Lamb, ich könnt nix hinunterwürgen.
Ich sag nicht, was du sagst, is unvernünftig, aber wars
dein letztes Wort? Wir haben uns gut verstanden.

Der Koch   Mein letztes. Überlegs dir.

Mutter Courage   Ich brauch nix zu überlegen. Ich laß
sie nicht hier.

Der Koch   Das wär recht unvernünftig, ich könnts aber
nicht ändern. Ich bin kein Unmensch, nur, das Wirtshaus
ist ein kleines. Und jetzt müssen wir hinauf, sonst ist das
auch nix hier, und wir haben umsonst in der Kält
gesungen.

Mutter Courage   Ich hol die Kattrin.

Der Koch   Lieber steck oben was für sie ein. Wenn wir
zu dritt anrücken, kriegen sie einen Schreck.

Beide ab.

Aus dem Wagen klettert **Kattrin**, *mit einem Bündel. Sie sieht
sich um, ob die beiden fort sind. Dann arrangiert sie auf dem
Wagenrad eine alte Hose vom* **Koch** *und einen Rock ihrer
Mutter nebeneinander, so, daß es leicht gesehen wird. Sie ist
damit fertig und will mit ihrem Bündel weg, als* **Mutter
Courage** *aus dem Haus zurückkommt.*

Sings:

> At last our final yarn's been spun.
> We ask you, gentle souls,
> What use our loving heaven's been?
> While you sit safe and soft within,
> We stand without, with empty bowls.
> God's love has left us here, undone.
> And see, before the night descends
> The way the meek are overrun.
> Our virtues led us to our wretched ends.
> And folk do better who have none.

A Voice From Above (*inside the house*)   You out there!
Come inside! We'll give you some hot marrow stew.

Mother Courage   I'd choke on anything I tried to
swallow now, Lamb. I can't argue with anything you've
said but is it your final word? We've always had a good
understanding.

The Cook   My last word. Take some time to decide.

Mother Courage   I don't need it. I'm not leaving her
here.

The Cook   That's pure senselessness, but nothing I can
do about it. I'm not a monster, it's a small inn. Let's go
inside before there's no more soup, we'll have sung in
the cold in vain.

Mother Courage   I'll get Kattrin.

The Cook   Come get it and bring it out to her. If it's
three of us tramping in, they might get scared.

They go into the house. **Kattrin** *climbs down from the wagon,
carrying a bundle. She looks to make sure the others have gone
in. She drapes, over a wheel of the wagon where it can't be
missed, one of her mother's skirts, and then atop the skirt, an old
pair of the* **Cook**'s *pants. As she's leaving with her bundle,*
Mother Courage *comes out of the house, carrying a bowl of hot
soup.*

Mutter Courage (*mit einem Teller Suppe*)   Kattrin! Bleibst
stehn! Kattrin! Wo willst du hin, mit dem Bündel? Bist du
von Gott und alle guten Geister verlassen? (*Sie untersucht
das Bündel.*) Ihre Sachen hat sie gepackt! Hast du
zugehört? Ich hab ihm gesagt, daß nix wird aus Utrecht,
seinem dreckigen Wirtshaus, was solln wir dort? Du und
ich, wir passen in kein Wirtshaus. In dem Krieg is noch
allerhand für uns drin. (*Sie sieht die Hose und den Rock.*)
Du bist ja dumm. Was denkst, wenn ich das gesehn hätt,
und du wärst weggewesen? (*Sie hält Kattrin fest, die weg
will.*) Glaub nicht, daß ich ihm deinetwegen den Laufpaß
gegeben hab. Es war der Wagen, darum. Ich trenn mich
doch nicht vom Wagen, wo ich gewohnt bin, wegen dir
ists gar nicht, es ist wegen dem Wagen. Wir gehn die
andere Richtung, und dem Koch sein Zeug legen wir
heraus, daß ers find, der dumme Mensch. (*Sie klettert
hinauf und wirft noch ein paar Sachen neben die Hose.*) So,
der ist draus aus unserm Geschäft, und ein andrer
kommt mir nimmer rein. Jetzt machen wir beide weiter.
Der Winter geht auch rum, wie alle andern. Spann dich
ein, es könnt Schnee geben.

*Sie spannen sich beide vor den Wagen, drehen ihn um und
ziehen ihn weg. Wenn der* **Koch** *kommt, sieht er verdutzt sein
Zeug.*

Mother Courage Kattrin! Wait! Kattrin! Stop! What's the bundle and where are you off to? Have you turned your back on God and all his angels?

She grabs the bundle away from **Kattrin** *and opens it.*

Mother Courage She's packed her belongings! You heard? I told him to fuck himself, with the shitty tiny tavern and Utrecht, what would we do in Utrecht? We don't know anything about innkeeping. The war's still got a great deal in store for us.

She sees the skirt and pants.

Mother Courage You're an idiot. What do you think I'd have done, seeing that and you just gone?

Kattrin *tries to go, but* **Mother Courage** *won't let her.*

Mother Courage Don't be so quick, it wasn't for your sake I handed him his walking papers. It's the wagon. I'm never giving up that wagon. It's mine, it's what I'm used to, it's not about you in the least. We'll go now, we'll go the opposite direction of Utrecht and find the army and leave the Cook's stuff here where he'll trip over it, the stupid man.

She climbs up and then throws out a few things to lie near the trousers.

Mother Courage There, the partnership's dissolved, and I'm not taking anyone else into the business ever. We'll both go on. The winter will be over some day, like all the other winters. Get in the harness, snow's coming.

They strap themselves into the harnesses, turn the wagon in another direction and pull it away. The **Cook** *comes out of the house. He sees his things on the ground. And stands there, dumbstruck.*

Ten

Das ganze Jahr 1635 ziehen **Mutter Courage** *und ihre Tochter* **Kattrin** *über die Landstraßen Mitteldeutschlands, folgend den immer zerlumpteren Heeren.*

Landstraße. **Mutter Courage** *und* **Kattrin** *ziehen den Planwagen. Sie kommen an einem Bauernhaus vorbei, aus dem eine* **Stimme** *singt.*

Die Stimme
Uns hat eine Ros ergetzet
Im Garten mittenan
Die hat sehr schön geblühet
Haben sie im März gesetzet
    Und nicht umsonst gemühet.
    Wohl denen, die ein Garten han.
    Sie hat so schön geblühet.
    Und wenn die Schneewind wehen
    Und blasen durch den Tann
    Es kann uns wenig g'schehen
    Wir habens Dach gerichtet
    Mit Moos und Stroh verdichtet.
    Wohl denen, die ein Dach jetzt han
    Wenn solche Schneewind wehen.

Mutter Courage *und* **Kattrin** *haben eingehalten, um zuzuhören, und ziehen dann weiter.*

Ten

The entire year 1635 **Mother Courage** *and her daughter* **Kattrin** *pull across central German highways, following behind ever more ragged armies.*

A highway. **Mother Courage** *and* **Kattrin** *are pulling the wagon. They come to a small farmhouse. Someone inside is singing.* **Mother Courage** *and* **Kattrin** *stop to listen.*

A Voice Inside (*singing*)
We've got a rosebush glowing
Within our garden wall.
When April winds come calling
They set the blossoms blowing
And petals will go falling,
All white and red the petals fall
When April winds come calling.

When wild geese go flying
Before the winter storm,
The autumn roses dying,
Our roof's in need of fixing!
Of moss and straw we're mixing
The stuff to keep the parlour warm
For when wild geese go flying.

Mother Courage *and* **Kattrin** *start to pull again.*

Eleven

Januar 1636. Die kaiserlichen Truppen bedrohen die evangelische Stadt Halle. Der Stein beginnt zu reden. **Mutter Courage** *verliert ihre Tochter und zieht allein weiter. Der Krieg ist noch lange nicht zu Ende.*

Der Planwagen steht zerlumpt neben einem Bauernhaus mit riesigem Strohdach, das sich an eine Felswand anlehnt. Es ist Nacht. Aus dem Gehölz treten ein **Fähnrich** *und drei* **Soldaten** *in schwerem Eisen.*

Der Fähnrich   Ich will keinen Lärm haben. Wer schreit, dem haut den Spieß hinauf.

Erster Soldat   Aber wir müssen sie herausklopfen, wenn wir einen Führer haben wollen.

Der Fähnrich   Das ist kein unnatürlicher Lärm, Klopfen. Da kann eine Kuh sich an die Stallwand wälzen.

Die Soldaten klopfen an die Tür des Bauernhauses. Eine Bäuerin öffnet. Sie halten ihr den Mund zu. Zwei **Soldaten** *hinein.*

Männerstimme Drinnen   Ist was?

Die **Soldaten** *bringen* **einen Bauern** *und seinen* **Sohn** *heraus.*

Der Fähnrich (*deutet auf den Wagen, in dem* **Kattrin** *aufgetaucht ist*)   Da ist auch noch eine. (*Ein* **Soldat** *zerrt sie heraus.*) Seid ihr alles, was hier wohnt?

Die Bauersleute   Das ist unser Sohn, und das ist eine Stumme, ihre Mutter ist in die Stadt, einkaufen, für ihren Warenhandel, weil viele fliehn und billig verkaufen. Es sind fahrende Leut, Marketender.

Der Fähnrich   Ich ermahn euch, daß ihr euch ruhig verhaltet, sonst, beim geringsten Lärm, gibts den Spieß über die Rübe. Und ich brauch einen, der uns den Pfad zeigt, wo auf die Stadt führt. (*Deutet auf den* **jungen Bauern**.) Du, komm her!

Eleven

January 1636. Imperial troops threaten the Protestant city of Halle. The stone begins to speak. **Mother Courage** *loses her daughter and continues alone. The war goes on, no sign that it will end.*

The wagon, beaten up, stand forlornly alongside a farmhouse with a huge thatched roof which leans against a cliff. It's night. A **Lieutenant** *and three* **Soldiers** *in heavy armour step out of the nearby woods.*

The Lieutenant   I don't want any noise. Somebody even looks like shouting, gut 'em.

One of the **Soldiers** *knocks on the door of the house. A* **Farm Woman** *comes out. He covers her mouth with his hand. The other two* **Soldiers** *go into the house. They come out with the* **Farmer** *and his* **Son**. **Kattrin** *has put her head out of the wagon to see what's happening. The* **Lieutenant** *points at her.*

The Lieutenant   There's someone else.

One of the **Soldiers** *pulls* **Kattrin** *out of the wagon.*

The Lieutenant   Who else lives here?

The Farmer   That's our son.

The Farmer's Wife   She's a dumb girl.

The Farmer   Her mother's marketing in town.

The Farmer's Wife   For their provisioning business, salespeople, people are fleeing and they're hunting bargains.

The Farmer   They're migrants.

The Lieutenant   All right, enough, you have to stay quiet, all of you, the first noise from any of you I'm going to tell my boys to shove bayonets through your thick stupid country-ass heads. I need one of you to show us the path into town. (*Pointing to the* **Farmer's Son**.) You.

Der Junge Bauer Ich weiß keinen Pfad nicht.

Zweiter Soldat (*grinsend*) Er weiß keinen Pfad nicht.

Der Junge Bauer Ich dien nicht die Katholischen.

Der Fähnrich (*zum zweiten* **Soldaten**) Gib ihm den Spieß in die Seit!

Der Junge Bauer (*auf die Knie gezwungen und mit dem Spieß bedroht*) Ich tus nicht ums Leben.

Erster Soldat Ich weiß was, wie er klug wird. (*Er tritt auf den Stall zu.*) Zwei Küh und ein Ochs. Hör zu: wenn du keine Vernunft annimmst, säbel ich das Vieh nieder.

Der Junge Bauer Nicht das Vieh!

Die Bäuerin (*weint*) Herr Hauptmann, verschont unser Vieh, wir möchten sonst verhungern.

Der Fähnrich Es ist hin, wenn er halsstarrig bleibt.

Erster Soldat Ich fang mit dem Ochsen an.

Der Junge Bauer (*zum Alten*) Muß ichs tun? (*Die* **Bäuerin** *nickt.*) Ich tus.

Die Bäuerin Und schönen Dank, Herr Hauptmann, daß Sie uns verschont haben, in Ewigkeit, Amen.

Der **Bauer** *hält die* **Bäuerin** *von weiterem Danken zurück.*

Erster Soldat Hab ich nicht gleich gewußt, daß der Ochs ihnen über alles geht!

Geführt von dem **jungen Bauern**, *setzen der* **Fähnrich** *und die* **Soldaten** *ihren Weg fort.*

The Farmer's Son   I don't know where the path is.

Second Soldier (*grinning*)   Doesn't know where his dick is.* Fucking peasants.

The Farmer's Son   There's no path for Catholics.

The Lieutenant (*to the* **Second Soldier**)   You gonna take that from him?

The **Soldiers** *force the* **Farmer's Son** *to his knees and the* **Second Soldier** *holds a bayonet to his throat.*

The Farmer's Son   Cut my throat. I won't help you.

First Soldier (*to his comrades*)   Watch this.

The **First Soldier** *goes to the barn door and looks in.*

First Soldier   Two cows and an ox. Before the army I was a butcher's apprentice.*

The Farmer's Son   Don't!

The Farmer's Wife (*crying*)   Captain, please, leave our animals alone.

The Lieutenant   Help us out or we'll eat your ox. (*Indicating the* **Farmer's Son**.) Hope you didn't raise stubborn children.

First Soldier   Wish I'd brought my bone saw. Here goes.

The Farmer's Son (*to his father*)   What do I do?

The **Farmer's Wife** *looks at her son.*

The Farmer's Son (*to the* **Soldiers**)   All right, all right. Let's go.

The Farmer's Wife   And many thanks, Captain, for not butchering them, for ever and amen.

The **Farmer** *stops his wife from continuing to thank the* **Lieutenant**.

First Soldier   It's the ox before everything, then the cows, then their kid, farm priorities.

The **Lieutenant** *and the* **Soldiers** *leave, led by the* **Farmer's Son**.

Der Bauer   Ich möcht wissen, was die vorhaben. Nix Gutes.

Die Bäuerin   Vielleicht sinds nur Kundschafter. – Was willst?

Der Bauer (*eine Leiter ans Dach stellend und hinaufkletternd*) Sehn, ob die allein sind. (*Oben.*) Im Gehölz bewegt sichs. Bis zum Steinbruch hinab seh ich was. Und da sind auch Gepanzerte in der Lichtung. Und eine Kanon. Das ist mehr als ein Regiment. Gnade Gott der Stadt und allen, wo drin sind.

Die Bäuerin   Ist Licht in der Stadt?

Der Bauer   Nix. Da schlafens jetzt. (*Er klettert herunter.*) Wenn die eindringen, stechen sie alles nieder.

Die Bäuerin   Der Wachtposten wirds rechtzeitig entdecken.

Der Bauer   Den Wachtposten im Turm oben aufm Hang müssen sie hingemacht haben, sonst hätt der ins Horn gestoßen.

Die Bäuerin   Wenn wir mehr wären …

Der Bauer   Mit dem Krüppel allein hier oben …

Die Bäuerin   Wir können nix machen, meinst …

Der Bauer   Nix.

Die Bäuerin   Wir können nicht hinunterlaufen, in der Nacht.

Der Bauer   Der ganze Hang hinunter ist voll von ihnen. Wir könnten nicht einmal ein Zeichen geben.

Die Bäuerin   Daß sie uns hier oben auch umbringen?

Der Bauer   Ja, wir können nix machen.

The Farmer   What're they planning? Nothing good.

The Farmer's Wife   Probably they're just scouting around –

The **Farmer** *has got a ladder and is propping it against the wall of the house.*

The Farmer's Wife   What in God's name?

The Farmer   I want to see how many. (*He climbs up to the roof.*) The woods are full of 'em. To the quarry. I can see armoured men in the clearing, and there's cannons, it's more than a regiment. God help the city and everyone in it.

The Farmer's Wife   Any lights on?

The Farmer   None. Everyone's sleeping. (*He climbs down.*) They'll kill everyone.

The Farmer's Wife   The town sentries.

The Farmer   Probably killed the men in the watchtower by the cliffs, or else we'd have heard their horns.

The Farmer's Wife   If we had a few more of us . . .

The Farmer   More than just us all the way up here, us and this cripple.

The Farmer's Wife   What should we do then? Anything?

The Farmer   Nothing.

The Farmer's Wife   Even if we dared to, it's night and we couldn't run.

The Farmer   They're all over the hill like ants.

The Farmer's Wife   So there's no way to signal?

The Farmer   Not unless you want to get killed.

Die Bäuerin (*zu* **Kattrin**)   Bet, armes Tier, bet! Wir können nix machen gegen das Blutvergießen. Wenn du schon nicht reden kannst, kannst doch beten. Er hört dich, wenn dich keiner hört. Ich helf dir. (*Alle knien nieder,* **Kattrin** *hinter den Bauersleuten.*) Vater unser, der du bist im Himmel, hör unser Gebet, laß die Stadt nicht umkommen mit alle, wo drinnen sind und schlummern und ahnen nix. Erweck sie, daß sie aufstehn und gehn auf die Mauern und sehn, wie sie auf sie kommen mit Spießen und Kanonen in der Nacht über die Wiesen, herunter vom Hang. (*Zu* **Kattrin** *zurück.*) Beschirm unsre Mutter und mach, daß der Wächter nicht schläft, sondern aufwacht, sonst ist es zu spät. Unserm Schwager steh auch bei, er ist drin mit seine vier Kinder, laß die nicht umkommen, sie sind unschuldig und wissen von nix. (*Zu* **Kattrin**, *die stöhnt.*) Eins ist unter zwei, das älteste sieben. (**Kattrin** *steht verstört auf.*) Vater unser, hör uns, denn nur du kannst helfen, wir möchten zugrund gehn, warum, wir sind schwach und haben keine Spieß und nix und können uns nix traun und sind in deiner Hand mit unserm Vieh und dem ganzen Hof, und so auch die Stadt, sie ist auch in deiner Hand, und der Feind ist vor den Mauern mit großer Macht.

Kattrin *hat sich unbemerkt zum Wagen geschlichen, etwas herausgenommen, es unter ihre Schürze getan und ist die Leiter hoch aufs Dach des Hauses geklettert.*

Die Bäuerin   Gedenk der Kinder, wo bedroht sind, der allerkleinsten besonders, der Greise, wo sich nicht rühren können, und aller Kreatur.

Der Bauer   Und vergib uns unsre Schuld, wie auch wir vergeben unsern Schuldigern. Amen.

Kattrin *beginnt, auf dem Dach sitzend, die Trommel zu schlagen, die sie unter ihrer Schürze hervorgezogen hat.*

Die Bäuerin   Jesus, was macht die?

Der Bauer   Sie hat den Verstand verloren.

The Farmer's Wife (*to* **Kattrin**)   Pray, you poor dumb beast, pray. We can't stop the slaughter, but we can pray to God and maybe because you're a cripple He'll listen better.

They all kneel. **Kattrin** *kneels behind the farm couple.*

The Farmer's Wife   Our Father who art in heaven, don't let them murder the people in the city, who're asleep and don't know that death's come so near, at least wake them up, Father, so they can see the spears and rifles and the siege engines and fires, the enemy in the night. (*Nodding towards* **Kattrin**.) Remember her mother, Lord, who's gone there, and remember to keep the night watchman wakeful, maybe he'll sound the alarm, and remember and protect my brother-in-law and the four kids my late sister's* left him, may her soul rest, poor thing, save the four kids who never did nothing wrong.

Kattrin *groans.*

The Farmer's Wife   The little one isn't two yet, the eldest only seven.

Kattrin *stands, very upset. As the* **Farmer's Wife** *keeps praying,* **Kattrin** *moves quietly to the wagon, takes something from it, goes to the ladder and climbs to the roof.*

The Farmer's Wife   We have no defence but you, Lord. In your wisdom you saw fit to leave us helpless* and now we ask you to show us mercy, save us and save our son and save our animals and the crops and the sleeping people in the town, the little children and old people especially, death's come in the night, Heavenly Father, and all your children are in dreadful need.

The Farmer   And we hope to be forgiven our sins as we try to forgive them who sin against us. Amen.

On the roof, **Kattrin** *starts banging the drum she's taken from the wagon.*

The Farmer's Wife   Jesus, what is she doing?

The Farmer   Lost her wits!

Die Bäuerin   Hol sie runter, schnell!

Der **Bauer** *läuft auf die Leiter zu, aber* **Kattrin** *zieht sie aufs Dach.*

Die Bäuerin   Sie bringt uns ins Unglück.

Der Bauer   Hör auf der Stell auf mit Schlagen, du Krüppel!

Die Bäuerin   Die Kaiserlichen auf uns ziehn.

Der Bauer (*sucht Steine am Boden*)   Ich bewerf dich!*

Die Bäuerin   Hast denn kein Mitleid? Hast gar kein Herz? Hin sind wir, wenn sie auf uns kommen! Abstechen tuns uns.

Kattrin *starrt in die Weite, auf die Stadt, und trommelt weiter.*

Die Bäuerin (*zum Alten*)   Ich hab dir gleich gesagt, laß das Gesindel nicht auf den Hof. Was kümmerts die, wenn sie uns das letzte Vieh wegtreiben.

Der Fähnrich (*kommt mit seinen* **Soldaten** *und dem* **Jungen Bauern** *gelaufen*)   Euch zerhack ich!

Die Bäuerin   Herr Offizier, wir sind unschuldig, wir können nix dafür. Sie hat sich raufgeschlichen. Eine Fremde.

Der Fähnrich   Wo ist die Leiter?

Der Bauer   Oben.

The Farmer's Wife   Drag her down from there, quick!

The **Farmer** *moves towards the ladder, but* **Kattrin** *pulls it up on the roof and resumes her drumming.*

The Farmer's Wife   Oh, this is disastrous!

The Farmer   Stop that pounding, you cripple!

The Farmer's Wife   The Kaiser's whole army's going to come crashing down on us!

Kattrin *keeps drumming, looking towards the city.*

The Farmer's Wife (*to her husband*)   I warned you about letting gypsies put up here, think they care if the soldiers take our last cow?

The **Lieutenant** *and his* **Soldiers** *and the* **Farmer's Son** *run in.*

The Lieutenant   I'll fucking murder you!

The Farmer's Wife   Mr Officer sir, please, it's not us, she –

First Soldier   Jesus Christ.

Second Soldier   Fucking hell.

The Lieutenant   Where's the ladder? Where's the goddam –

The Farmer   It's on the roof, with her.

First Soldier   She – (*To the* **Second Soldier.**) Get the –* get the gun, do you –

Third Soldier   You told me not to, it's heavy, you – fuck, listen to her.

The Farmer's Wife   She got up there without our noticing.

First Soldier   Hey girl, get down or we're gonna come up and get you!

Second Soldier   Yeah, get down here and suck my –

The Lieutenant (*to* **Kattrin**)   All right, all right, stay calm, stay calm, this is –

The Farmer's Wife   She's a total stranger.

Der Fähnrich (*hinauf*) Ich befehl dir, schmeiß die Trommel runter!

Kattrin *trommelt weiter.*

Der Fähnrich Ihr seids alle verschworen. Das hier überlebt ihr nicht.

Der Bauer Drüben im Holz haben sie Fichten geschlagen. Wenn wir einen Stamm holn und stochern sie herunter …

Erster Soldat (*zum* **Fähnrich**) Ich bitt um Erlaubnis, daß ich einen Vorschlag mach. (*Er sagt dem* **Fähnrich** *etwas ins Ohr. Der nickt.*) Hörst du, wir machen dir einen Vorschlag zum Guten. Komm herunter und geh mit uns in die Stadt, stracks voran. Zeig uns deine Mutter, und sie soll verschont werden.

Kattrin *trommelt weiter.*

The Lieutenant   Shut up! This is an order! Throw the drum down.

Kattrin *keeps drumming.*

The Lieutenant (*to the* **Farmer**)   You planned this, you're responsible, if she –

The Farmer   There's some tall pine trees they cut down in the woods.

The Lieutenant   So what?

The Farmer   I dunno, maybe if somehow we could . . . you know, we could hoist one of the tall tree trunks somehow and use one end to sort of shove her off and –

First Soldier (*to the* **Lieutenant**)   Can I try something sir?

The **Lieutenant** *nods. The* **First Soldier** *calls to* **Kattrin***:*

First Soldier   Hey! Girl! We wanna make a deal with you, friends, right?

Second Soldier   They're gonna hear that, they're bound to – kill the bitch.

Third Soldier   Should I go back and get the –

First Soldier (*to the* **Third Soldier**)   QUIET, goddamn it! (*To* **Kattrin**.) You, you listening?

Second Soldier   Hey! Hey you, listen to him, he's trying to –

First Soldier   We're friends, we . . . Get down, right, if you get down we'll take you with us, we promise we won't touch you –

Second Soldier   Who'd want to touch an ugly fucking –

First Soldier   We'll take you into town with us and you point out your mother and she won't get hurt.

Kattrin *keeps drumming. The* **Lieutenant** *shoves the* **First Soldier** *aside.*

Der Fähnrich (*schiebt ihn roh weg*) Sie traut dir nicht, bei deiner Fresse kein Wunder. (*Er ruft hinauf.*) Wenn ich dir mein Wort gebe? Ich bin ein Offizier und hab ein Ehrenwort.

Kattrin *trommelt stärker.*

Der Fähnrich Der ist nix heilig.

Der Junge Bauer Herr Offizier, es is ihr nicht nur wegen ihrer Mutter!*

Erster Soldat Lang dürfts nicht mehr fortgehn. Das müssen sie hörn in der Stadt.

Der Fähnrich Wir müssen einen Lärm mit irgendwas machen, wo größer ist als ihr Trommeln. Mit was können wir einen Lärm machen?

Erster Soldat Wir dürfen doch keinen Lärm machen.

Der Fähnrich Einen unschuldigen, Dummkopf. Einen nicht kriegerischen.

Der Bauer Ich könnt mit der Axt Holz hacken.

Der Fähnrich Ja, hack. (*Der Bauer holt die Axt und haut in den Stamm.*) Hack mehr! Mehr! Du hackst um dein Leben!

Kattrin *hat zugehört, dabei leiser geschlagen. Unruhig herumspähend, trommelt sie jetzt weiter.*

Der Fähnrich (*zum Bauern*) Zu schwach. (*Zum ersten Soldaten.*) Hack du auch.

The Lieutenant (*calling up to* **Kattrin**)   You don't believe him, you aren't stupid, you know we're not friends and anyway, who'd trust someone with a face like his? But will you believe me if I give you my word as an officer of His Majesty the Emperor's army? My sacred word?

Kattrin *drums harder.*

Third Soldier (*muttering*)   Well that was effective. Jesus Christ.

First Soldier   You better do something, sir.

Second Soldier   They're gonna hear that in town.

The Lieutenant   We've gotta –

Third Soldier   Torch the house!

The Lieutenant   Make some sort of noise!

Second Soldier   You told us not to make any noise, we –

The Lieutenant   Drown out the –

First Soldier   I thought we weren't supposed to make any –

The Lieutenant   Drown out the drumming, a, a normal noise, you goddamned imbecile, a peacetime sound, like –

The Farmer   Wood chopping!

The Lieutenant   Good, do it, start chopping!

The **Farmer** *takes up his axe and starts chopping at a log lying on the ground.*

The Lieutenant   Can't you chop any harder than that?

Kattrin *drums a little softer, distracted by the chopping sound, but then she realises what's happening and starts drumming all the harder.*

The Lieutenant (*to the* **Farmer**)   Louder dammit! (*To the* **First Soldier.**) You too! Start chopping!

Der Bauer   Ich hab nur eine Axt. (*Hört auf mit dem Hakken.*)

Der Fähnrich   Wir müssen den Hof anzünden. Ausräuchern müssen wir sie.

Der Bauer   Das nützt nix, Herr Hauptmann. Wenn sie in der Stadt hier Feuer sehn, wissen sie alles.

Kattrin *hat während des Trommelns wieder zugehört. Jetzt lacht sie.*

Der Fähnrich   Sie lacht uns aus, schau. Ich halts nicht aus. Ich schieß sie herunter, und wenn alles hin ist. Holt die Kugelbüchs!

Zwei **Soldaten** *laufen weg.* **Kattrin** *trommelt weiter.*

Die Bäuerin   Ich habs, Herr Hauptmann. Da drüben steht ihr Wagen. Wenn wir den zusammenhaun, hört sie auf. Sie haben nix als den Wagen.

Der Fähnrich (*zum* **Jungen Bauern**)   Hau ihn zusammen. (*Hinauf.*) Wir haun deinen Wagen zusammen, wenn du nicht mit Schlagen aufhörst.

Der **junge Bauer** *führt einige schwache Schläge gegen den Planwagen.*

Die Bäuerin   Hör auf, du Vieh!

Kattrin *stößt, verzweifelt nach ihrem Wagen starrend, jämmerliche Laute aus. Sie trommelt aber weiter.*

Der Fähnrich   Wo bleiben die Dreckkerle mit der Kugelbüchs?

Erster Soldat   Sie können in der Stadt drin noch nix gehört haben, sonst möchten wir ihr Geschütz hörn.

Der Fähnrich (*hinauf*)   Sie hörn dich gar nicht. Und jetzt schießen wir dich ab. Ein letztes Mal. Wirf die Trommel herunter!

The Farmer   There's just the one axe.

The Lieutenant   Torch it, torch the house.

*The **Farmer** stops chopping.*

The Farmer   They'll see the fire in town, that's a bad idea.

Kattrin, *still drumming, laughs.*

The Lieutenant   That does it, she's laughing at us. Get the gun, shoot her down, I don't care, shoot her!

*Two of the **Soldiers** run out. **Kattrin** drums harder.*

The Farmer's Wife   That wagon over there's all they have. Take the axe to that and she'll have to stop.

*The **Lieutenant** hands the axe to the **Farmer's Son**.*

The Lieutenant   Do it, you heard your mother, chop that wagon to splinters. (To **Kattrin**.) You want him to take an axe to your wagon? Then stop!

*The **Lieutenant** signals to the **Farmer's Son**, who hits the wagon with the axe, a few tepid blows.*

The Farmer's Wife (*screaming up to **Kattrin***)   STOP IT YOU DUMB COW!

*As the boy hits the wagon, **Kattrin** watches with a stricken expression, making a few low groaning sounds. But she doesn't stop drumming.*

The Lieutenant   Where are those lazy cunts with the rifle?

First Soldier   LISTEN!

*Everyone, including **Kattrin**, stops and listens. Silence.**

First Soldier   They're not hearing her in town, there'd be alarm bells if they did.

The Lieutenant (*to **Kattrin***)   Nobody's hearing you, it's not working, and now you're going to get shot and killed for nothing. One last time: throw down that drum!

Der Junge Bauer (*wirft plötzlich die Planke weg*)   Schlag weiter! Sonst sind alle hin! Schlag weiter, schlag weiter …

Der **Soldat** *wirft ihn nieder und schlägt auf ihn mit dem Spieß ein.* **Kattrin** *beginnt zu weinen, sie trommelt aber weiter.*

Die Bäuerin   Schlagts ihn nicht in'n Rücken! Gottes willen, ihr schlagt ihn tot!

Die **Soldaten** *mit der Büchse kommen gelaufen.*

Zweiter Soldat   Der Obrist hat Schaum vorm Mund, Fähnrich. Wir kommen vors Kriegsgericht.

Der Fähnrich   Stell auf! Stell auf! (*Hinauf, während das Gewehr auf die Gabel gestellt wird.*) Zum allerletzten Mal: Hör auf mit Schlagen! (**Kattrin** *trommelt weinend so laut sie kann.*) Gebt Feuer!

Die **Soldaten** *feuern.* **Kattrin**, *getroffen, schlägt noch einige Schläge und sinkt dann langsam zusammen.*

Der Fähnrich   Schluß ist mitm Lärm!

Aber die letzten Schläge **Kattrins** *werden von den Kanonen der Stadt abgelöst. Man hört von weitem verwirrtes Sturmglockenläuten und Kanonendonner.*

Erster Soldat   Sie hats geschafft.

The **Farmer's Son** *throws the axe down and calls out abruptly:*

The Farmer's Son   Keep drumming! They'll kill them all! Drum! Drum! Drum!

Kattrin *resumes her drumming. The* **First Soldier** *knocks the* **Farmer's Son** *to the ground and clubs him brutally, with the butt end of his spear.* **Kattrin** *starts crying but keeps drumming.*

The Farmer's Wife   Oh God, please stop hitting him in the back, you're killing him!

The **Soldiers** *run in with a large musket on a tripod.*

Second Soldier   The Colonel's foaming at the mouth, Lieutenant. We're gonna get court-martialled.

The Lieutenant   Set it up! Hurry!

They set up the musket. The **Lieutenant** *calls up to* **Kattrin** *while this is being done:*

The Lieutenant   All right this is the final warning: Stop drumming!

Kattrin *is crying and drumming as hard as she can.*

The Lieutenant   STOP IT! STOP IT! STOP THE – (*He turns to his* **Soldiers**.) Fire!

The **Soldiers** *fire.* **Kattrin** *is hit. She strikes the drum weakly a few more times, then collapses, slowly.*

The Lieutenant   No more noise.

From the city, a cannon's shot answers **Kattrin***'s last drumbeat. Alarm bells and cannonfire sounding all together are heard in the distance.*

First Soldier   Listen. It worked. She did it.

Twelve

Nacht gegen Morgen. Man hört Trommeln und Pfeifen marschierender Truppen, die sich entfernen.

Vor dem Planwagen hockt **Mutter Courage** *bei ihrer Tochter. Die Bauersleute stehen daneben.*

Die Bauersleute Sie müssen fort, Frau. Nur mehr ein Regiment ist dahinter. Allein könnens nicht weg.

Mutter Courage Vielleicht schlaft sie mir ein.

Sie singt.

> Eia popeia
> Was raschelt im Stroh?
> Nachbars Bälg greinen
> Und meine sind froh.
> Nachbars gehn in Lumpen
> Und du gehst in Seid
> Ausn Rock von einem Engel
> Umgearbeit'.
>
> Nachbars han kein Brocken
> Und du kriegst eine Tort
> Ist sie dir zu trocken
> Dann sag nur ein Wort.
>
> Eia popeia
> Was raschelt im Stroh?
> Der eine liegt in Polen
> Der andre ist werweißwo.

Jetzt schlaft sie. Sie hätten ihr nix von die Kinder von Ihrem Schwager sagen sollen.

Die Bauersleute Wenns nicht in die Stadt gangen wärn, Ihren Schnitt machen, wärs vielleicht nicht passiert.

Mutter Courage Ich bin froh, daß sie schlaft.

Twelve

Night, nearly dawn. Trumpets and drums and fifes, an army departing.

Alongside the wagon, **Mother Courage** *sits, bent down over her daughter. The farm couple stand nearby.*

The Farmer (*angrily*)   You have to go now, lady. Only one last regiment left and then that's it. You wanna travel alone?

Mother Courage   Maybe she's sleeping.

Sings:

> Eia popeia,
> Who sleeps in the hay?
> The neighbour's brat's crying
> While my children play.
> The neighbour's kid's shabby
> But my kids look nice,
> With shirts like the angels wear
> In paradise.
>
> Neighbour can't feed 'em
> But mine shall have cake,
> The sweetest and choicest
> The baker can bake.
>
> Eia popeia,
> I see your eyes close.
> One kid lies in Poland.
> The other – well, who knows?

(*Speaking.*) You should never have told her about your brother-in-law's children.

The Farmer   You had to go to town to hunt for bargains, maybe if you'd been here none of this would have happened.

Mother Courage   Now she's sleeping.

Die Bauersleute   Sie schlaft nicht, Sie müssens einsehn, sie ist hinüber. Und Sie selber müssen los endlich. Da sind die Wölf, und was schlimmer ist, die Marodöre.

Mutter Courage (*steht auf*)   Ja.

Sie holt eine Blache aus dem Wagen, um die Tote zuzudecken.

Die Bauersleute   Habens denn niemand sonst? Wos hingehn könnten?

Mutter Courage   Doch, einen. Den Eilif.

Die Bauersleute   Den müssens finden. Für die da sorgen wir, daß sie ordentlich begraben wird. Sie können ganz beruhigt sein.

Mutter Courage (*bevor sie sich vor den Wagen spannt*)   Da haben Sie Geld für die Auslagen.

Sie zählt dem **Bauern** *Geld in die Hand. Die Bauersleute geben ihr die Hand, und der* **Bauer** *und sein* **Sohn** *tragen* **Kattrin** *weg.*

Die Bäuerin (*im Abgehen*)   Eilen Sie sich!

Mutter Courage   Hoffentlich zieh ich den Wagen allein. Es wird gehn, es ist nicht viel drinnen.

Ein weiteres Regiment zieht mit Pfeifen und Trommeln hinten vorbei.

Mutter Courage   Holla, nehmts mich mit!

Sie zieht an. Man hört Singen von hinten.

Gesang
Mit seinem Glück, seiner Gefahre
Der Krieg, er zieht sich etwas hin.
Der Krieg, er dauert hundert Jahre
Der g'meine Mann hat kein'n Gewinn.
Ein Dreck sein Fraß, sein Rock ein Plunder!
Sein halben Sold stiehlts Regiment.

The Farmer's Wife She isn't sleeping, stop saying that and look, she's gone.

The Farmer And you have to go too. There are wolves around here, and people who're worse than the wolves.

Mother Courage Yes.

She goes to the wagon and brings out a sheet.

The Farmer's Wife Do you have anyone left? Anyone you could go to?

Mother Courage One left. Eilif.

*She uses the sheet to wrap **Kattrin**'s body.*

The Farmer You've got to go find him then. We'll take care of her, she'll have a decent burial. Don't worry.

Mother Courage Here's money for what it costs.

*She gives the **Farmer** some money. The **Farmer** and his **Son** shake her hand and carry **Kattrin**'s body away. The **Farmer's Wife** follows them. She turns as she leaves and says to **Mother Courage**:*

The Farmer's Wife Hurry.

She leaves.

Mother Courage (*harnessing herself to the wagon*) Hopefully I'll manage to pull the wagon alone. I bet I can do it, not much in it any more. I have to get back in business.

*The fife and drums of another regiment marching by. **Soldiers** are singing in the distance. As they sing, **Mother Courage** begins to pull her wagon, pursuing them.*

Soldiers (*offstage, singing*)
Sometimes there's luck,* and always worry.
The war goes on, and perseveres!
For war is never in a hurry,
And it can last a thousand years.

The day of wrath will come like thunder
But who has time to make amends?

Jedoch vielleicht geschehn noch Wunder:
Der Feldzug ist noch nicht zu End!
    Das Frühjahr kommt! Wach auf, du Christ!
    Der Schnee schmilzt weg! Die Toten ruhn!
    Und was noch nicht gestorben ist
    Das macht sich auf die Socken nun.

You march in line, but never wonder
How it began and where it ends.

The spring has come, and winter's dead!

Mother Courage (*over the singing*)   Take me with you!

Soldiers (*singing over her, offstage*)
The snow has gone, so draw a breath!
Let Christian souls crawl out of bed,
Pull on their socks and conquer death!

The world will end, and time will cease!
And while we live we buy and sell!
And in our graves we shall find peace –
Unless the war goes on in hell!

Notes

21 *once you're in you're washed clean of sin*: this idea is not present in the original, which simply states that they only sing hymns on Sundays.

27 *It's not so terrible, a soldier's life*: in the original, this assurance is followed by the sergeant's claim that Courage wishes to live off the war but to keep her own family out of it.

27 *If off the war [...] also give*: in the original, these lines take an absurdly long-winded grammatical form that cannot be reproduced in English. Kushner finds an equivalent for that stylised oddness with this awkwardly phrased couplet.

29 *practically a turkey*: Kushner turns the original description of 'a huge chicken' into this more jocular exaggeration.

31 *Roast it, but hurry, [...] I'm telling you, it stinks*: this exchange is rendered more playful and witty than in the original, where Courage is more dead-pan and the Cook more defensive, and it also adds a religious tone to the repartee. Courage's 'It's from last year' becomes 'it's been dead three weeks and it stinks', while the religious mockery ('Praise Jesus ...') is invented by Kushner – in the original she states: 'Then it must already have stunk when it was alive.' Kushner also invents the joke on the dog/cow images and the alliterative coarseness of the Cook's simile: 'tender as a tit'. Courage's interjection 'After five hours, it'll be glue' is an addition, and her injunction to 'say a prayer' adds a further religious tone.

33 *what they learned from you, boy!*: Brecht is more specific here, with the General proclaiming that Eilif has taught the farmers 'morals'.

33 *like the suffering Christ he is*: in the original the Chaplain is simply described here as 'pious'.

33 *beast-who-barely-learned-to-cook*: this is Kushner's solution for the German compound 'Cook-beast'.

35 *Have another, son, [...] I hope*: the General's speech here is a fine example of Kushner's virtuoso adaptation, where the richness of Brecht's language is reflected in elaborate English. The original 'And the soul-shepherd just looks on' becomes 'this watery-eyed old simp of a soul-shepherd ...'. The latter part of the speech represents a change in mode, with the General's diction suddenly becoming exaggeratedly bureaucratic and formal, opening him up to further ridicule.

35 *beginning with 'M', like ... um ... 'meat'!*: it is impossible to reproduce the linguistic pun here, since the direct translation would be 'whenever they hear a word beginning with "Fl",

like "River"'. Kushner compensates for this with a different kind of joke, punning on the soldiers' obsession with meat such that Eilif can think of no other word.

37   *HUH! HUH! HUH!*: Eilif's dumb laughter is added by Kushner, accentuating his brutishness.

37   *You massacred the farmers*: this speech is shortened and the focus consequently shifts. Where the original states that soldiers used to have to fight religious battles on a meagre diet of bread and wine, the English version has them eating beef 'in the old days', too.

39   *No he's not, [. . .] properly managed*: Kushner compresses this dialogue, giving the Cook only one line and so focusing more on Courage's monologue.

39   *born a soldier*: Brecht's General makes the more explicit comment: 'I bet your father was a soldier'.

41   *My mother taught me a song*: in Brecht's play, Eilif says that his mother 'warned' him about becoming a soldier.

45   *You brazen sticky-fingered fork-tongued son of a Finn!*: a further example of Kushner's linguistic elaborations. The original reads: 'You Finnish devil!'

45   *what're they supposed to do? Throw rocks?*: the first of a series of questions that are phrased as statements in the original. Kushner has thus made the exchange more dynamic and far more sarcastic. The following question, 'What am I supposed to do when he wants his wine, serve rainwater?', is invented by Kushner.

47   *It's immoral*: Kushner adds Courage's reference to morality, making the contrast between her assumed protest (morality) and the actual problem (price) more patent.

49   *except when I'm wearing 'em*: Kushner adds this joke, emphasising Swiss Cheese's dumb honesty.

49   *Everybody lies*: the images in Yvette's speech are altered. In the German 'everyone' avoids her 'like a rotten fish', while Kushner makes her prostitution more obvious, mentioning customers. The joke about the sign over her 'cootch' is added by Kushner, while the coarseness of her language is increased through her cursing.

49   *what it's like to lose a man*: the reason for Yvette's unhappiness and her career choice is elaborated here by Kushner.

53   *Don't start up with soldiers*: following this, Kushner omits Courage's general warning to her daughter about love in

general. She notes that even with civilians it's no walk in the park.

55 *where he can have all the brandy he wants*: Brecht's Chaplain ties himself up in knots trying to make a religious point here, whereas Kushner's keeps it simple and speaks to the Cook in a language he understands: brandy.

55 *Point taken*: the Cook's words are altered by Kushner to refer more to his demands on Mother Courage's hospitality, but still the basic idea that wars of religion are just as vicious as other wars comes through. Kushner's Cook goes further by suggesting that the religious element 'exculpates' the shooting, looting and rape.

55 *nothing contemptible on my mind*: Kushner postpones the Cook's accusation that the Chaplain has been making lewd jokes all day ('you oughta hear his jokes! Revolting!'), to which Courage responds: 'Then I shall have to give you a drink, otherwise you'll make me an immoral offer out of sheer boredom.'

57 *I don't want clergy sniffing up my daughter*: Kushner adds this suggestion of salacious clergymen.

57 *What's the news from the front?*: this section (until p. 61) is significantly re-structured by Kushner, largely because the Cook's long speech in the original (pp. 56–8) is redeployed around banter between him, the Chaplain and Mother Courage. This initial exchange between Courage and the Cook, emphasising the characters' detachment from the war that so defines their lives, is invented, as are three further remarks: the Chaplain's mention of 'the tyranny of the Pope'; and the Cook's suggestions that liberty is being exported to other countries and that the rich get tax exemptions. These additions add a contemporary political flavour to the debate. The banter about liberty and the human body ('You shouldn't mock liberty [...] I'm sure you do', p. 59) is also added by Kushner, playing further with the notion of the Cook's profligacy and the Chaplain's immoral interest in the flesh.

60 *die Großkopfigen*: Brecht draws a clearer distinction between the leaders, who claim to have noble and religious reasons for going to war, and the 'little people', who realise that the leaders are only interested in material profit.

61 *If it's business, it makes sense*: Kushner adds this pithy phrase, underlining the capitalist orientation of Mother Courage's relationship to war.

63   *if they haven't shot him*: Kushner adds this morbid joke to the
     Cook's otherwise matter-of-fact tone.

63   *on the Bible*: in German, Mother Courage simply 'gives her
     oath'; Kushner makes it a religious one.

65   *Oh please God let it be the Catholics! [...] they're finnicky about
     costumes*: these two jokes at the Catholics' expense are added
     by Kushner.

65   *You're not the paymaster any more*: there is a linguistic oddness in
     the German here, literally: 'You're all paymastered-out'.

67   *When he's done raping her*: in the German, the connection
     between the soldiers' hunger and their raping is made more
     explicit, and there is less impression of wilful brutality: 'They
     go without food for weeks on end, and when they get it
     through looting, they fall on the women.'

69   *I don't know any Latin hymns*: this added quip by Kushner
     makes the Chaplain's opportunistic piety yet more vivid.

69   *an ecclesiastical sense of humour*: this is simply 'religious faith' in
     the German, making the comparison between faith and
     money more stark.

69   *Victory, defeat*: in the original version of this speech, Courage
     speaks more at length about the relationship between honour
     and material gain – saying that once she benefited from 'her'
     general's defeat, because in the ensuing chaos she managed
     to collar a horse that then pulled her cart for several months.

70   *Ein Händler wird nicht nach dem Glauben gefragt*: this phrase,
     'Nobody is interested in a merchant's faith, but only in the
     price', is cut by Kushner.

71   *Martin Luther met a priest*: Kushner changes the Chaplain's
     story from a general tale of the effects of the Lutheran faith
     (that it would 'turn everything in town and country on its
     head') to a parable featuring Luther himself.

71   *He was in the latrine?*: Kushner transforms the Chaplain's
     speech into a dialogue, rendering this section more dynamic
     and increasing the potential for comedy.

73   *Everyone's entitled to have hopes*: Brecht's wordplay cannot be
     reproduced in English. He puns on the noun 'Hoffart' and its
     adjective 'hoffärtig', which in modern German is negatively
     charged, suggesting vanity or arrogance, but which originally
     connoted the courtly and noble.

73   *Raising kids!*: Kushner shifts idioms here – from Brecht's
     'You'll be the death of me. I'd rather shepherd a sack of fleas'
     – to this more modern image.

85   *What's his name? Mouldy?*: this addition to the original ushers
      in a scene in which Kushner has made the most changes to
      the original wording and tone. At this point, the English
      offers a wordplay that the German does not – Yvette's
      colonel's name, Poldi, rhymes with 'mouldy'.

85   *And he thinks we should keep looking*: Brecht's Yvette tells
      Courage the opposite – that her colonel is advising her to
      take up her offer.

85   *Just pray Poldi holds up*: Kushner makes Mother Courage's
      attempt to scare Yvette into coughing up straight away more
      explicit than in the original.

87   *my knees go all stiff in this weather*: the Colonel's interjection is
      invented by Kushner, making him cut a more pathetic figure.

87   *that young blond lieutenant with the enormous feet*: Kushner adds
      the reference to feet, here. Brecht's version is much less
      suggestive – the lieutenant is merely always telling Yvette that
      'she reminds him of somebody'. In response, the Colonel
      warns her that the younger soldier will 'take advantage' of her
      indebtedness to him, which Kushner cuts. Instead, he adds
      the words 'taking money from someone you love when you
      aren't married to him' to Yvette's speech, driving home the
      dramatic irony of this exchange. Finally, the last, almost
      slapstick, words between Yvette and the Colonel are added by
      Kushner ('I'll find some way to pay you back. / I hate that
      lieutenant!'), replacing the more sober German: 'Do you
      advise me to go ahead? / I do'.

89   *I'll redeem the pawn*: Kushner adds this explicatory sentence. It
      replaces the Chaplain's concern that Yvette won't keep her
      side of the deal and Mother Courage's assurance that she will,
      since it's in her interest to get the money before the Colonel
      leaves her or dies. Kushner then significantly trims Courage's
      sardonic speech about the relationship between corruption
      and God's mercy.

91   *he keeps looking with that one eye*: Kushner takes advantage of the
      joke offered by the one-eyed soldier, while in the original the
      soldier just 'keeps on looking back'.

93   *he says it's nearly over*: the original reads literally, 'he says it's
      not worth it', reinforcing the idea of value and monetary
      worth in relation to human life.

99   *I'm not letting myself get fucked like this*: Brecht's Young Soldier's
      language is much less coarse than Kushner's.

99   *The Older Soldier restrains the Young Soldier*: Kushner adds this
      staging.

101   *How long?*: this speech is significantly elaborated by Kushner.
      Brecht's Mother Courage simply asks the soldier to imagine
      himself in the stocks, not that he might be flayed and
      blistered, raw and bleeding.

101   *just a lightning bolt that splits the air*: again, Kushner elaborates
      Mother Courage's figurative language, turning the original
      'cooled-off' anger into a lightning 'BANG!'.

109   *treacherous fuck*: Brecht's censure of the General is implicit,
      while Kushner makes it perfectly clear.

109   *tear up good officers' shirts to bandage farmers?*: in the original,
      Courage does not ask a rhetorical question but bluntly refuses
      to tear up shirts for bandages.

111   *They would have if anyone'd asked*: Mother Courage's words in
      the original are: 'They don't give a damn about religion.
      They've lost their farm.'

117   *rain rain go away*: the original reads: 'Rain or no rain'.

117   *On a memorable occasion such as this*: Kushner has added this
      quip from Mother Courage. In the original, she reports that
      the general of the Second Regiment has refused to pay his
      soldiers' wages, arguing that, since it is a war of religion, they
      should fight for free.

117   *They do what they're told*: Brecht's Chaplain is more
      magnanimous: 'They do what they can'.

119   *Food's scarce, not field marshals*: the original reads: 'There will
      always be heroes'.

119   *His fists are even faster!*: retaining the metre and rhyme in this
      song means that the sense is occasionally changed. The end of
      the original first verse name-checks the Emperor ('He must
      fight for his Emperor'), and a religious element is added to the
      end of the second verse: 'But please don't tell the pastor!'

119   *uncertainty's never bothered me before*: in the original, Courage
      simply bemoans, 'If only I could trust you …'.

121   *breeding like maggots in raw meat*: Kushner adds this simile.

125   *I'm not courageous. Only the poor people need courage*: Kushner sets
      Mother Courage apart from the 'poor people', while in
      Brecht's version it remains ambiguous, for she simply states:
      'Poor people need courage'.

125   *carrying the Emperor and his heavy throne and the Pope and his
      stone cathedral*: Kushner has elaborated on the original phrase
      that the poor people 'tolerate' the Emperor and the Pope.

127   *As if a rat had attacked it*: the original description of the Cook
      as 'a violent man' becomes much more derogatory in
      Kushner's version.

128 *Lassen Sie Ihr Herz sprechen*: Kushner cuts the Chaplain's plaintive appeal to Mother Courage's emotion ('Let your heart do the talking, don't harden yourself against it') but then adds 'I'm proposing! Respond to my proposal!' – driving the point home that Mother Courage does not respond to subtlety.

129 *fershtunkeneh*: Kushner is able to use the same word as in the German, a transliterated Yiddish word, giving his Chaplain a rather mixed cultural background.

129 *Maybe if we're quiet*: this added interjection by Mother Courage emphasises further her resistance to talking about emotions.

135 Kushner adds a verse to the end of Mother Courage's song (the last four lines). It is a reprise of the chorus from the play's very first song (pp. 7–9), so echoing the hope expressed in that first song and marking this point as the climax of the play in terms of Mother Courage's business career.

138 *Warum solln sie sonst die Glocken läuten?*: the Chaplain's question, 'Why else would they be ringing the bells?', is cut in the translation.

141 *What's this apparition I see before me?*: Kushner adds yet more sarcasm to the Cook's exclamation, which in the original reads simply: 'Who's this? The Chaplain!'.

143 *I like a woman who knows how to handle a harmonica*: the wording of this exchange is changed completely by Kushner, bringing the latent sexual innuendo in the original to the fore.

145 *I didn't know you owed him perusal of your accounts*: Kushner adds this jealous interjection from the Chaplain.

149 *Washing bottles is better work than saving souls*: in English, the Chaplain elaborates on why he prefers this work to the business of saving souls.

149 *Is, was, and always will be*: Kushner turns the original 'Quite right' into this liturgical phrasing.

151 *No, his father!*: in the original, Yvette has taken up with the Colonel's elder brother.

153 *Touch and go*: Kushner inserts an extra pun here – 'I touch them for their money and then I go'.

153 *God how I loved this man!*: in the original, Yvette goes on to state that the Cook was two-timing her with a 'little black woman with a crippled leg'. Kushner replaces this with her disclosure on the following page that she 'found four other girls in town in a similar condition'.

156 *Die Menschheit muß hingehn durch Feuer und Schwert*: Kushner
    cuts this claim that man's original sin means he must pass
    through fire and violence.

163 *I've always admired vitality*: Kushner elaborates on the original,
    which reads: 'Where there's smoke, there's fire'.

165 *from Metz to Mähren!*: Kushner turns Mother Courage's song
    into a shared piece.

167 *so ravenous they've eaten little children*: and, Brecht's Courage
    adds, 'nuns have been caught looting'.

183 Throughout this scene, where Brecht has given dialogue to
    'The Farmers' (Die Bauersleute), Kushner divides the
    speeches up between the Farmer and the Farmer's Wife.

185 *Doesn't know where his dick is*: Kushner adds this innuendo and
    the 'Fucking peasants'.

185 *Before the army I was a butcher's apprentice*: Brecht's First Soldier
    is much more candid: 'If you don't see reason, I'll hack your
    cattle up.'

189 *my late sister*: the Farmer's Wife does not mention that her
    sister is dead in the original version.

189 *you saw fit to leave us helpless*: Kushner adds this pointed
    remark about the plight of the poor.

190 *Ich bewerf dich!*: in this exchange, cut by Kushner, the Farmer
    threatens to pelt Katrin with stones, and his wife pleads with
    her: 'Have you no pity?'.

191 *She – (To the Second Soldier.) Get the –* : from here until the
    bottom of the page is all new material by Kushner. Similarly,
    the majority of the dialogue on the following page is added.

194 *Herr Offizier, es is ihr nicht nur wegen ihrer Mutter!*: Kushner cuts
    the Farmer's Son making the point that Kattrin's concern is
    not only for her mother but also for the nieces and nephews
    of the Farmer's Wife, at risk from the storming of the city.

197 *LISTEN! [...] Silence*: this pause in the chaos is added by
    Kushner, introducing a moment of suspense that is absent in
    the original.

203 *Sometimes there's luck*: the song that closes the play has been
    extended by Kushner. In the original, it finishes with the
    chorus from the very first song ('The spring has come ...'),
    which in Kushner's version is also reprised in Scene Seven.
    Here, four further lines follow this otherwise uplifting call-to-
    arms, which make for a more sombre tone, pointing towards
    a final peace only in death and closing the play with the
    ominous evocation of 'hell'.